The
Hitchhiker's
Guide
to
Japan

D1219955

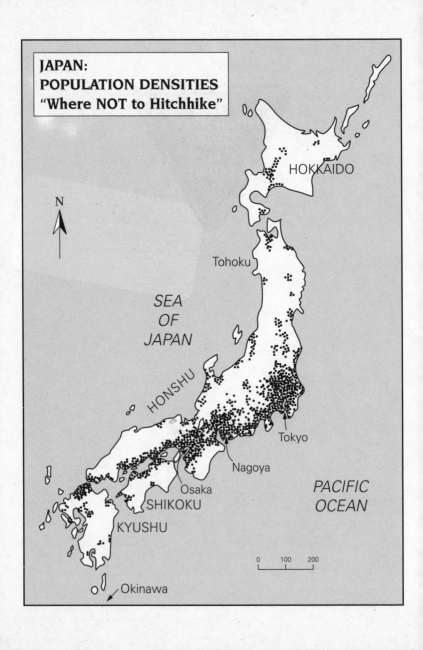

JAPAN:
POPULATION DENSITIES
"Where NOT to Hitchhike"

N

HOKKAIDO

Tohoku

SEA
OF
JAPAN

HONSHU

Tokyo

Nagoya

Osaka

SHIKOKU

KYUSHU

PACIFIC
OCEAN

Okinawa

0   100   200

Will Ferguson

with supplementary research and translation assistance from
Terumi Matsumoto

Charles E. Tuttle Company
Rutland, Vermont & Tokyo, Japan

Published by Charles E. Tuttle Publishing,
an imprint of Periplus Editions (HK) Ltd.

©1998 by William Stener Ferguson

All rights reserved

LCC Card No. 97-60051
ISBN 0-8048-2068-6

First edition, 1998

Printed in Singapore

Distributed by:
USA **Charles E. Tuttle Co., Inc.**
Airport Industrial Park
RR1 Box 231-5
North Clarendon, VT 05759
Tel: (802) 773-8930
Fax: (802) 773-6993

Japan **Tuttle Shokai Ltd.**
1-21-13 Seki
Tama-ku, Kawasaki-shi
Kanagawa-ken 214, Japan
Tel: (81) (44) 833-0225
Fax: (81) (44) 822-0413

Southeast Asia
Berkeley Books Pte Ltd.
5 Little Road #08-01
Singapore 536983
Tel: (65) 280 3320
Fax: (65) 280 6290

Tokyo Editorial Office:
2-6, Suido 1-chome,
Bunkyo-ku, Tokyo 112, Japan

Boston Editorial Office: .
153 Milk Street, 5th Floor
Boston, MA 02109, USA

Singapore Editorial Office:
5 Little Road #08-01
Singapore 536983

Contents

Acknowledgments

This guidebook would not have been possible without the assistance of Terumi Matsumoto. Terumi is a graduate of the English Department of Seinan Jogakuin in Kita Kyushu. She has been involved in international exchange programs between Japan and Australia, and has done translations for various government organizations, including the Minamata Disease Museum. Terumi recently graduated from the Travel and Tourism Program at NBCC in St. Andrews, Canada.

I would also like to thank Kiyomi and Tatsuhiro Hiramatsu for their many years of friendship and support, and a special thank you to Tatsuhiro for driving me all over the place to gather photographs for this book.

I also thank Kazue Hizen, who made over a dozen phone calls for me to tie up loose ends and check last-minute facts; Mayumi Hirose for the tip about the Two-Headed Snake Shrine; and Kerry Bingham for rescuing us with her Macintosh software.

I have lost track of many of the hundreds of people I have hitched rides with in Japan over the years, but some deserving special recognition for their help and good cheer are:

In *Hokkaido*: Makoto Inoue, Tomoyuki Sugawara, Takayuki

Ideta, Mr. Tawaraya, Isohichi Sato, Tetsuya Mori, Hiroshi Ota, Mitsuru Sekinei, Tomio Honda, Junko Iida (who was more than generous with her samples of Sapporo beer) and Toshiyuki Kitajima, Toko Tanaka, and Takeyuki Yamamoto.

In *Tohoku*: Masatoshi Kimura (who gave me a wonderful wooden snake), Yumiko and Satoru Nara (who tracked me down to return a lost camera), Yoshinori Hirano, Kenji Fujimura, Genzou Yamaguchi, Tokiwa and Yoshio Takahashi, Daisuke Ito, Norio Ito, and a special big thanks to Mami Onotora and Yuko Onodera for their kindness and good company on the Iwate coast.

In *Central and Western Honshu*: Ryo Wakabayashi, Yoshiyuki Takeda, Teruko and Masaru Ito, Tomoyuki Toda, Shigeki Oishi, Shoichi Nakamura, Hitoshi Kusunoki, Kikumi Otsuji, Hisao Hasegawa, Shintaro Kobayashi, and Atsushi "Hot Sushi" Yamada and friends.

In *Shikoku*: Akihira Kawahara, who gave me a tour of Sado Island; Shuho Jishi and family for inviting me into their home; and Yoshio Nakasawa, Saburo Nakamura, Yoshiaki Kato, and Yukio Yanagida.

In *Kyushu and the Southern Islands*: Kaori Yamaguchi, Masayuki Migita and family, Mayumi Tamura, and Akemi Fujisaki, Kenichi Inada, Kiminori Maruyama, Hirotake Hyakutake, and Hamasho "George" Sunagawa at Yonaguni's best sushi bar.

Thanks also to my friends on the Amakusa islands: Chiemi and Yoshihiro Nakamura, and their daughter Ayane; the Wakata and Miyamoto families; and Mitsuo Aizu—whom I first met while hitching rides—his wife Yoriko, and their children: Saori, Kenji, and Yukina.

Introduction
The Joys of Hitchhiking

When most of us imagine Japan, we imagine the crowded subways of Tokyo, the five-dollar cups of coffee, the congested city streets, and the high-tech electronics. But there is more to Japan than its overpriced, crowded cities. An entire world exists beyond the modern urban sprawl, just as another Japan exists beneath the formalized manners and public smiles.

Japan can be an aloof place to visit. Contact with the Japanese is often limited to fleeting public encounters: the maid in the inn, the crowds of curious schoolchildren, the businessmen in sing-along bars, the ambivalent laughter in a late-night noodle shop.

How, then, to save money *and* see the real Japan, beyond the standard, tired tourist routes? The answer is as close as your own thumb.

Hitchhiking in Japan is fast, easy, and inexpensive. More than just a way to save money, hitchhiking is a way *inside*. In Japan, the car is an extension of the home, but without the formalities and protocol of a home visit.

Hitchhiking is so unusual in Japan that no prescribed forms

of behavior have developed to deal with it. You will be treated as a guest (certainly) and as a friend (hopefully), but above all you will be treated as a travel companion, and that is what you are. Not a visitor, but a fellow traveler.

The hitchhiker travels *with* the Japanese, not among them. Call it Zen and the Art of Hitchhiking, Japan from the Roadside, The Way of the Freeloader. All it takes is a sense of adventure, an open mind, and a steady thumb.

I have been hitchhiking in Japan for more than five years. I have thumbed rides from one end of the nation to the other, and I have hitched through every region, from the semitropical islands of Okinawa to the snow country of the Japan Alps. I have hitched along coastal roads, through volcanic calderas, and in and out of urban tracts. I have hitched in groups, alone, and with a friend. I have hitched rides with monks and fishermen, carpenters and college students.

In my most ambitious journey, I hitchhiked the length of mainland Japan, end to end, in one go—a route that covered 3,000 kilometers. It took 18 days of thumbing and 48 rides (although the trip itself was longer because of detours and extended sightseeing). Along the way, I was welcomed into homes and shown forgotten corners of Japan. I traveled through small villages and secluded hot-spring resorts, and I met more people and made more friends than I ever would have had I followed the usual tourist beat—and I traveled for a *third* of the cost.

What I learned over the last five years is this: Japan is a hitchhiker's paradise. It is a safe country. The rides are consistently good. The people are kind to visitors, and the back roads can be breathtakingly beautiful. Japan just may be the best place on earth for hitchhiking.

Don't just dabble with hitchhiking. Make it the central part of your Japanese travel plans. Instead of thinking of hitchhiking as a strictly pragmatic way to get from Point A to Point B, make hitchhiking *an aim in itself*. Make the journey its own destination.

Explore Japan. Meet people. Take your time. Avoid the urge to treat your travels as if you were crossing off items on a shopping list of sites. You will appreciate Japan much more after you have hitchhiked through it—and you'll save a lot of money as well.

Hitchhiking makes Japan affordable. It also makes your time in Japan unforgettable. In these days of global tourism it is becoming harder to have authentic travel experiences. Hitchhiking, however, is a completely singular activity. It is unrepeatable, unpredictable. No two hitchhiking journeys, or rides, are ever the same.

The Hitchhiker's Guide to Japan gives you all the inside information and strategies you need to make the most of your hitchhiking journey. Which roads are the best in Japan? Which ones should be avoided? When should you *not* use a destination sign? What are the laws dealing with hitchhiking in Japan? Is hitchhiking even covered by Japanese laws? How can you stay for less than five dollars a night—or even better, for free? What do you do when a small inn doesn't want to rent a room to you because they are nervous around foreigners? All the answers are here.

Japan may be the best country in the world for hitchhiking, but it is not without problems. This guidebook includes tips and tricks, solutions to common mistakes, advice on hitchhiking etiquette, and in-depth sample itineraries. After that, it's up to you. Expect to get lost once or twice, but expect to get rescued as well. In fact, the best advice I can give any traveler in Japan is, simply, "Get lost."

And send me a postcard when you get there.

The Hitchhiker
in
Japan

The Highways
and Back Roads of Japan

Japan is an archipelago that stretches in an arc from the Russian coast to within sight of Taiwan. Although there are over 4,000 islands in the Japanese archipelago, most of the land mass is made up of four large islands—sometimes referred to as the "mainland" of Japan: Hokkaido, Honshu, Shikoku, and Kyushu. South of Kyushu is the smaller island chain of Okinawa.

The mainland of Japan straddles the same latitudes as Miami in the south and Montreal in the north. The northeast of Japan has some of the heaviest snowfalls in the world; the far south is dotted with coral reefs and subtropical forests. Japan is a land of marked extremes.

Japan also straddles several tectonic plates, which makes it one of the most volcanic and earthquake-prone areas on earth. The Japanese islands are in fact the "seam" between tectonic plates; for all the hardships and natural disasters this entails, it also gives Japan a stunning landscape: crumpled mountains, towering volcanoes, rocky fjords, terraced rice fields.

Size and Population

Japan is not a small country, no matter what the Japanese themselves may think. The island of Honshu—just Honshu—is bigger than Great Britain.

Japan's population has the same rate of urbanization as Australia or Canada: around 78 percent. But Japanese cities are much more compact. Consider this—50 percent of Japan's 123,000,000 people live in three crowded, central urban sprawls: Tokyo–Yokohama, Osaka–Kobe, and Nagoya. In comparison, the entire island of Kyushu contains only 12 percent of Japan's population.

Beyond the city centers lies rural Japan, still steeped in traditions and older rhythms. The contrast between the two is stark. As a hitchhiker, your goal is to see as little of the urban critical mass and as much of the back roads as possible.

Below is an overview of Japan's four main islands and the southern chain of Okinawa, from the perspective of an independent traveler.

HOKKAIDO: The northern frontier—the Texas and Alaska of Japan, all rolled into one. Sapporo, the largest city, is a lively, northern metropolis with wide avenues and good access to the national parks of the interior. Hakodate is a European-like harbor town built on the neck of a peninsula. The hitchhiking in Hokkaido is the best in Japan, but the landscape and sights strike many as being somehow "un-Japanese."

HONSHU: The main island, it is also the most varied. The northern area, Tohoku, is a remote, relatively undeveloped place. The Kanto Plain contains Japan's greatest concentration of industry and people, including the Tokyo–Yokohama megalopolis. Not far behind is the Kansai district, which includes the Osaka–Kobe urban corridor. Just north of Osaka are Japan's culturally rich, historical cities: Kyoto and Nara, old capitals renowned for their gardens, ancient temples, and moments of pure Japanese beauty. Further down is the heartland of the Inland Sea, including Hiroshima. The western coast of Honshu is known, with slightly negative connotations, as The Back of Japan. This area has open countryside and cities well spaced along the way, which makes for good hitchhiking.

SHIKOKU: Japan's least-explored, most-underrated island. Shikoku has several extant castles, rugged coastlines, quiet villages and an ancient 88 Temple pilgrimage route. The Inland Sea coast of Shikoku has been disfigured by overdevelopment, but central and southern Shikoku is still a beautiful, unspoiled area, and the hitchhiking is excellent.

KYUSHU: The cradle of Japanese civilization, a land of volcanoes and hot springs and some of Japan's most traditional, picturesque villages. Nagasaki on the western peninsula is a city of depth and character, and a viable hitchhiking destination. The hitchhiking in Kyushu rivals that of Hokkaido, and the southern half of the island is particularly good.

OKINAWA was once a separate country and is still a distinct culture. Okinawa is a land of white sand beaches, jungle islands, and coral reefs. Because of its distance from the mainland, I have not included this area among the recommended hitchhiking itineraries.

These are the main divisions of Japan that I will be referring to in this guidebook. For hitchhikers, the four main areas of travel will be Hokkaido, Tohoku (Northern Honshu), Shikoku, and Kyushu.

Japanese cities (*shi*) and towns (*machi*) are actually more like counties. They often cover a considerable area, and usually contain open countryside and the occasional village (*mura*) within their boundaries. Don't be fooled by maps that represent towns as a single dot—this only designates the city or town center. If you look carefully, you will see larger borders drawn around the town, showing the real town boundaries. Towns often encompass an entire peninsula or island, and the smaller villages contained within these city or town classifications are not always shown on maps.

Beyond these official designations, Japan is further divided between *inaka* and *tokai*: the countryside and the city. This is a division that runs right down the center of the Japanese psyche, and as the cities become more and more congested and the villages die, the division between rural and urban has deepened. The objective of the hitchhiker in Japan is to spend as much time as possible in the countryside and to avoid the larger metropolises. When in doubt, head for *inaka*.

Highway Classifications

Do not be misled by the word "highway." Many of Japan's national and prefectural highways are little more than two-lane roads winding through the mountains. Japan's system of highways is *not* hard to use: it is modern, and easy to understand. Don't let the confusion of Japanese city streets frighten you; once you get out onto the open road, hitchhiking is a breeze.

The classification of highways in Japan is as follows:

Expressways (*kōsoku kokudō or kōsoku dōro*)   These are the main arteries; many of them are toll roads. It is illegal to walk, ride a bicycle, or ride a motorcycle smaller than 150cc on Japanese expressways. Expressways are identified by name, not number (i.e., Tohoku Expressway). Expressway signs are green and rectangular, and are labeled in English and Japanese. On road maps, expressways are usually shown as parallel blue lines. Because expressways are central to long-distance hitchhiking, they are dealt with separately in the following chapter.

National Highways (*ippan kokudō or simply kokudō*) These connect cities; they are the highways you will spend most of your time on as a hitchhiker. They vary wildly, from spacious modern highways to crumbling old roads that have fallen into disuse. National highways are identified by number. National highway signs are blue and diamond-shaped, with the triangle pointing downward. Destinations and directions are usually labeled in English and Japanese. On road maps, they are shown in red or pink.

Prefectural Highways (*kendō*) These connect smaller cities and outlying areas with national highways. As you become a more experienced hitchhiker, you will use prefectural highways more often. Although prefectural highways are numbered, local residents will not always know the number of the prefectural highway in their area but will refer to it by some descriptive name, such as "the coastal road." Prefectural highway signs are blue and hexagonal (reminiscent of North American stop signs). Prefectural highways are shown in green, though smaller ones may be shown in yellow. Sightseeing areas will almost always have English signs, no matter how remote or obscure the attraction.

Most road atlases do not always print the number of a prefectural highway, since they change as they cross borders. The numbering of many prefectural highways was revamped recently, and though I have tried to be as accurate as possible, some numbers may have changed. For this reason I have described the routes of prefectural highways in detail so that they are easily recognizable on road maps.

Note: Hokkaido is not a prefecture. In Hokkaido, nonnational highways are called *dōdō*. In this guidebook, however, I have translated both *kendō* and *dōdō* as "prefectural highways" since they serve the same function.

Secondary Roads (*within a city, shidō; within a town, chōdō; and within a village, sondō*) These are shown in yellow on most road maps.

City streets, when shown, are usually shown in white. Unlike highways, city streets in Japan are not numbered and are rarely named.

Skyline roads (*sukai rain rōdo*) These are often referred to simply as a "line." In Japan a "line" refers to roads as well as to rail and ferry lines, and the naming of skyline roads is not standardized. For example, both the Cobalt Line and the Yamanami Highway are skyline roads. These roads are shown as a solid blue line on most road maps, and the toll is usually listed on maps as well. Like expressways, the toll charges on skyline roads are outrageous, but because the drivers are planning to pay it anyway, hitchhikers will not be expected to help. In many cases, skylines are simply pretty stretches of prefectural or national highway specifically built with tourism in mind, which is why they often sport such fancy names. These roads run along mountaintops and above seacoast bays and provide Japanese Sunday drivers with a view. The designated viewpoints along the way provide toilets and shelter and are good for unofficial camping. Skyline roads make excellent scenic hitchhiking routes since much of the traffic is sightseers who are more inclined to pick up hitchhikers.

Coastal Scenic Routes (*kaigan dōro*) These are another strong hitchhiking option. Japan is an island nation and the traveler in Japan is never far from the sea. If you are new at hitchhiking, or just nervous about getting rides, stick with the coastline; even the quietest coastal road will get some traffic.

Forestry Roads (*rindō*) These look similar to skylines, though they should not be confused. Forestry roads usually begin as well-paved routes that look scenic and inviting—but they soon deteriorate into potholes and gravel. Although they offer views as splendid as skylines, there are no sightseers along forestry roads, and rides are nonexistent. If you ever find yourself on a forestry road, the best thing you can do is beat a hasty retreat. Do not venture further into the mountains. If you are not sure, check at the start: *Kono michi wa rindō desu ka*? (Is this a forestry road?)

The Urban Plain Blues

Avoid wide, flat, farming areas and urban plains. These areas are usually crisscrossed with roads and choked with towns that never seem to end but just blend into each other. And the scenery is boring—unless you like rice fields. It is also more difficult to get long-distance rides when you hitch on the plains. In mountain valleys and along the coast, traffic is funneled into a few roads and it is easier to catch a long-distance ride with someone going in your direction. In the plains, however, there are any number of roads to take, and drivers can follow an almost limitless number of routes. What this means to you as a hitchhiker is that no one seems to be going very far in any one direction and many of the rides will be just a short hop down to yet another intersection. I have always found escaping well-populated flat areas to be a tough haul.

The Best Highways in Japan

In Japan, the shortest way between two points is not always the preferred route, and the busiest road is not always the best one. On a lonely stretch of highway the sole car that approaches almost always stops, out of concern or curiosity if nothing else. But on busy, multilaned thoroughfares cars can clip by for hours before someone pulls over.

I evaluate any road or route based on three criteria: *First*, is the road worth the trip? Does it offer traditional Japanese villages, old temples, hidden hot springs, unusual attractions, things sundry and distinctly Japanese? *Second*, are the rides good? Is there enough traffic to make hitching viable? Is the road wide or straight enough to find a good roadside spot? This is a real concern; roads in Japan are often narrow and twisty, especially for someone coming from Australia or North America.

Third, are there enough towns along the way to find lodgings and food? My preference is for smaller, livelier cities (e.g., Miyazaki, Uwajima, Hakodate) over the vast expanses of uninspired ferro-concrete that only long-term residents are enamored with (e.g., Kita Kyushu, Osaka, Nagoya).

Using the above criteria, I would list the five best roads for hitchhiking in Japan as follows:

1. The Nichinan Kaigan between Toi-Misaki and Miyazaki (Southeast Kyushu)
2. The Miyagi–Iwate coastal highway (Eastern Tohoku)
3. National Highway 32 and Prefectural Highway 32 along the Ōboke Gorge and Iyadani Gorge (Central Shikoku)
4. The Yamanami Highway from the Aso volcanic caldera to the hot-spring town of Yufuin (Central Kyushu)
5. Any rural highway in Hokkaido

I would also include the Oirase Valley in central Aomori, Tohoku. This is one of the prettiest roads in Japan and the hitching here is easy. But the Oirase is so beautiful that it deserves a slower pace, and I prefer to walk it rather than hitch. I have hitched through the Oirase twice and walked once; walking is better.

Note: The Oirase Valley, like the Nichinan Coast and the Yamanami Highway, is a popular sightseeing getaway for urbanites who flock to the area in peak holiday seasons. During New Year's and national holidays, these routes become one long, scenic traffic jam. Avoid the peak seasons at all costs. Check the peak seasons listed in Chapter 6 before you plan your trip.

Timing Your Journey

Unless you take a wrong turn and end up in the middle of nowhere, you shouldn't have to wait more than half an hour for a ride. Usually a car will stop within ten minutes. Times vary greatly, however, which is another reason for picking a pleasant road to hitch along. An hour spent choking on exhaust fumes at an expressway off-ramp will feel much longer than an hour spent high in the mountains or on a palm-tree-lined coast.

I expect a car to stop within 20 minutes, and I am not usually disappointed. In Hokkaido, on an empty stretch of highway south of Rumoi, I once waited over an hour before a single vehicle appeared, but when it did, I simply held out my thumb and the car stopped. It was easier than hailing a taxi. When rides are slow, relax, and remember the mantra of hitchhiking: eventually someone *will* stop.

Except on the expressways, speed limits in Japan are around 50 kph even on national highways, so reduce all mileage expectations. Using national and prefectural highways, you should be able to cover 90 km a day with ease. I expect to hitchhike around 120 km a day on average. You can cover much more if you want to, but try to keep a flexible schedule.

As a visual gauge, here are some examples to use when looking at a map of Japan:

- Niigata city to Akita city on the northwest coast would be a full day of hitchhiking.
- Matsuyama to Takamatsu on the northern coast of Shikoku is a full day of hitchhiking as well, with short stops along the way.

If you want to cover longer distances at a higher speed, you need to use the faster expressways.

The Atlas

Shobunsha's *Road Atlas Japan: English Edition* ought to be called the "Orange Bible" by hitchhikers. The itineraries provided in Part II of this guidebook are designed to be used with this atlas.

It contains 271 pages of detailed road maps, city plans, and mileage counters—all in English. (City names are given in both English and Japanese.) It has complete expressway maps, including the names of the interchanges and even the rest areas along the way. It also lists toll charges and points of interest. It is well worth the investment of ¥2,890 (approx. US$30). This is the only atlas that I cross-reference, and as such, it really is the only one I recommend.

However, it does have a few flaws. It shows prefectural highways but doesn't number them. The index of place names is ridiculously limited. No campsites are shown. Private rail lines are often missing. Not all train stations are named. Another problem is that the atlas lists very few villages. This is because, technically, villages are contained within a larger city or town boundary. By not listing most villages, Shobunsha has given the impression of emptiness in places that are in fact dotted with small communities.

None of these flaws are fatal, of course, but you should be aware of them. The atlas still contains by far the best English maps available on Japan. In my itineraries I have used the atlas as the reference point and I make note if any information is missing in the atlas.

Finding a copy of the atlas should be easy. Most large Japanese cities will have at least one bookstore—usually Kinokuniya or Maruzen—that has an English section, and the atlas is generally in stock. Look for the orange cover.

Other Road Maps

The best road maps for Japan, of course, are in Japanese. If you can read hiragana or have a working knowledge of kanji I advise buying both the atlas and a Japanese-language map of the area you will be hitchhiking through. Japanese maps are easy to find; any bookstore will stock a large array of Japanese pocket guides and maps. Even if you can't read any Japanese it is still a good idea to get a Japanese road map or guidebook of the immediate area. Once you figure out how to cross-reference the English maps with the Japanese one—not difficult because both will be visually the same—you can simply point out the train stations, campsites, or destinations you are trying to get to. To find a Japanese map, go to any large or mid-size bookstore and ask the clerk: (Ho*kkaido*) *no chizu wa arimasu ka*? (Do you have maps of [Hokkaido]?). To ask for maps of "this area," use *kono chiku* instead of a proper place name.

There are also many inexpensive, glossy magazine-style guidebooks which include detailed road maps. I prefer to use these because they have photos of points of interest, listings of hotels, and ferry schedules. To ask for them say *gaido bukku* instead of *chizu* in the above sentence. A good Japanese road map will also show campsites, marked with red tent symbols, which are a big help in finding a place to stay.

Free Maps

The Japan National Tourist Organization (JNTO) distributes glossy tourist pamphlets in English and they include basic road maps. These maps show the main national highways and are a convenient, compact, and free alternative to using the bulkier atlas. For the itineraries in this guidebook, however, you will need the atlas. The information in the JNTO pamphlets is useful as well. I always make a point of contacting JNTO prior to any trip. JNTO also provides a *Tourist Map of Japan*, for free. This map is handy as a general overview—flipping through the pages of the atlas can get frustrating—but the JNTO map is not detailed enough for any extensive hitchhiking trips. It does not number any highways, nor does it give the names of the expressways. But it does contain downtown maps of the following cities: Hiroshima, Fukuoka, Kagoshima, Kyoto, Nara, Kobe, Yokohama, Nagoya, Osaka, Sapporo, and Tokyo. For JNTO offices overseas and in Japan see Appendix 2.

Free Expressway Maps

The atlas labels interchange and service areas across Japan, both in English and in Japanese. But if you are planning to stick with expressways only, there is no need to buy the atlas. A free English expressway map of Japan, listing every service area and almost all interchanges, is available upon request at the larger service areas or from the Japan Highway Services Association.

The all-Japan English expressway map is named the *Japan Expressway Rest Station Information*, but few people in the information desks will recognize the English. Instead, ask for *Eigo no Nihon zendo no sābisu eria no chizu*.

Japanese-language maps of specific regions are also available. These maps are known as *sābisu eria no chizu*, meaning "service-area maps." For a map of a certain region (Kyushu, for example) ask for the (*Kyushu*) *kōsoku dōro no sābisu eria no chizu*. The abbreviation SAPA (Service And Parking Area) appears on the maps, but isn't commonly used in conversation.

If you want to order the maps ahead of time, send your address and a note saying "Please send me (type of map)." For two maps include ¥270 in *yūbin-kitte* (postal stamps). For one map, send ¥190. For international mail, include three International Reply Coupons to cover postage.

Send the stamps, your address, and your request to:

> Dōro Shisetsu Kyōkai
> Kōhō-shitsu
> Shin Aoyama Bldg. East, 1-1-1 Minami Aoyama
> Minato-ku, Tokyo 107 Japan
> Tel.: 03-3403-9111

As noted, these maps can also be picked up for free at most large service areas, but the English map is not always available at the smaller ones. If possible, it is best to obtain a copy before you set out.

Important Changes in Expressways

Japanese expressways are being expanded constantly. Some of the key changes that you should know about are listed below.

In Tohoku The Banetsu Expressway has been extended from Kōriyama to Iwaki. It will soon be extended all the way to Niigata City.

In Shikoku The Takamatsu Expressway has been extended farther west toward Matsuyama. It now runs to the town of Kawauchi, just 20 km from Matsuyama. This expressway will eventually be extended south, through Ōzu, to the town of Uwa.

The Kōchi Expressway, in turn, will be extended west past Kōchi city and all the way to Susaki.

In Central Honshu The Sanyō Expressway was being extended from Himeji to Nishinomiya-kita, but the Kobe earthquake of 1995 has caused undetermined delays in expressway construction schedules.

In Kyushu The Kyushu Expressway is now complete between Hitoyoshi and Ebino. This expressway will eventually be extended to Usuki and Tsukumi.

The Ōita Expressway is near completion between Hita and Yufuin, and should be open by the time you read this.

Tokyo Metropolitan Expressway Map

An English map of Tokyo's convoluted expressways can be obtained in Japan by sending ¥190 in *yūbin-kitte* stamps and a note saying "Please send the Metropolitan Expressway Map," to the following address:

> Shutokōsoku Sābisu Suishin Kyōkai
> 1-1-3 Isomura Biru 5-kai
> Toranomon, Minato-ku
> Tokyo105
> Tel. 03-3502-7311

Expressway Hitching

Despite the high tolls, expressways are ideal for long-distance hitchhiking and are especially useful when you are in a hurry. If you want to go directly from point A to point B—say, Hiroshima to Kyoto—then expressways are the way to go. In fact, in the more densely populated areas, hitchhiking on expressways is often faster than taking a local train. The appeal of expressways is understandable, but you inevitably bypass the smaller nooks and crannies of Japan. Take highways when possible.

Expressway Rules

You cannot walk through an expressway entrance and you cannot walk or stand beside an expressway except at designated service areas or at a bus stop.

This means that even if you hitch a ride *through* the entrance, you should never ask to be dropped off on the side of the expressway—even if you are way up in the mountains and far from any city. If a patrol car happens to pass by, you *will* be picked up.

Alibis

Long-distance buses use expressways, so if you do end up on the side of an expressway and the highway patrol pulls over, your best strategy is to play stupid and tell them that you are looking for a bus stop. B*asu teiryūjo wa doko desu ka?* (Where is the bus stop?) The patrolman will know that you are lying, of course, but he won't be able to do anything about it, a case of "plausible deniability."

Expressway Interchange Entrances

I have surveyed many Japanese drivers over the years, and they generally give three reasons why they hesitate to stop at expressway entrances:

1. They are in a hurry (that's why they call them expressways) and have other things on their mind. Often they don't see a hitchhiker until they have already passed. Many times I have caught a surprised look from a rear-view mirror in a car that has just gone by.

2. At busier expressway interchanges, it is difficult to stop because of the traffic flow.

3. But the main reason they hesitate is because they are not sure if it is *legal* to pick up hitchhikers at expressway interchanges. Interchange entrances are a legal "gray zone" in the eyes of the highway patrol. It is not illegal to stand in front of them, but if an overzealous police officer decides that your actions are creating a traffic hazard, he is fully within his rights to order you to leave the area. For this reason, make sure you stand far back from the tollbooths.

Busy expressway entrances are tough to negotiate; as cars and trucks zoom up, the last thing they expect to see is someone standing by the roadside with their thumb out. If you have nerves of steel you can pick a spot right in front of a tollbooth entrance; otherwise begin hitchhiking much further back, at the offramp leading to the expressway interchange. Hold up a sign that says "IC" and everyone will understand that you are going to the interchange. (The English lettering of "IC" is used on Japanese street signs as well.) When a car stops make sure that they are in fact going *through* the interchange. To do this, ask to be dropped off at an expressway service area. The beauty of expressway hitching is that once you do get a ride it is long one. So be patient. Smile. You will get a ride eventually. Expect to spend at least 40 minutes to an hour outside a moderately busy expressway entrance.

Note: At the smaller interchange entrances the tollbooths are completely automated. Don't be tempted to sneak through them. They have cameras and you will be caught. This is what happened to me outside of Kanazawa city.

The Japanese pronunciation of interchange is *in-tā-chen-ji*. Entrance is *iri-guchi*, exit is *de-guchi*. Most interchanges contain both an onramp and an offramp, though the exit and entrance may be separated by the expressway itself, so make sure it is understood that you are going to an interchange *entrance*.

Hitchhiking Destination Signs for Expressways

Generally, destination signs are actually counterproductive; however, expressway entrances are an exception since traffic separates into two or more directions at interchange entrances. A sign will save you the delay of helpful cars offering rides in the wrong directions. Write your destination in Japanese characters if you can, but otherwise neat capital English letters will work just as well.

Below your destination write "Thank You!" or "Hello!" which are easy English phrases recognizable to almost all Japanese people. Don't laugh. I know of an American who uses this phrase all the time in his signs, and apparently it works. Personally, I almost never use signs and when I do I try to keep them as simple as possible.

There is one exception I should note. People of Asian descent or anyone who may be mistaken for Japanese should use a sign but in *English only*. The reason? Japanese drivers will rarely if ever stop for other Japanese, so you want to make sure they understand that you are in fact a foreigner.

In that case, you don't even have to write your actual destination on it. Instead, just make a generic "Hello! from USA! Please Stop" sign and use it wherever you go. You may even want to draw your national flag on it. Make it neat and cheerful so you can use it wherever you are headed.

Junctions

Avoid major interchanges ("junctions" on road maps) where two or more expressways meet in a web of cloverleaf overpasses. It can take you the better part of an afternoon to sort it out. Instead, get on the expressway earlier, at a secondary entrance point. This way you will arrive and pass through the junction with a Japanese driver who can help you get on the right route. He or she may even drive out of the way and partly down the expressway to the next service area before dropping you off.

Again, do not let anyone drop you off at the side of the expressway. So where should you get dropped off, then?

Parking Areas and Service Areas

For hitchhikers, both parking and service areas are excellent locations for getting rides. Parking areas, complete with washrooms, noodle shops, and vending machines, are roughly every 15 km along expressways. Similarly, larger service areas with restaurants, gas stations, and travel information desks are located about every 50 km. Only at larger service areas will you be able to pick up maps.

Many Japanese drivers are not aware of the distinction between the two, and in this guidebook I have used the term "service area" to refer to both since the Japanese typically make no distinction.

When hitchhiking from a service area, don't walk out onto the expressway. Instead, stand by the exit road that leads from the service area back to the main expressway, near enough to the parking lot and visitor center that people can see you. A sign is useful if you are heading a long way and want to hop a ride the whole way. But if it is just a short hop to the next major city, you don't need to bother with a sign at service areas, because at service areas—unlike interchange entrances—all traffic will be flowing in the same direction.

At service areas, you can even hitch at night. Parking lots are well lit and the sight of a stranded hitchhiker at night will get a sympathetic reaction. If you are hitchhiking as a couple you will probably be picked up quickly at rest areas, usually by other concerned Japanese couples or families. In the middle of a stifling Japanese summer, hitching via rest areas in the evening is a cooler alternative to the midday swelter.

Occasionally, your Japanese drivers will approach other drivers and ask them if they are going your way, and you can jump from one car directly into another.

If you want to begin your expressway hitching at a service area (a strategy I recommend) you can avoid expressway entrances altogether by taking buses through the interchange and then getting off at the first rest area on the way.

Hitchhiking Strategies

The most persistent mistake hitchhikers make in Japan is to assume that what works in Western countries will work in Japan. This is simply not true. The rules of hitchhiking in Japan are not similar to anywhere else in the world. Hitchhiking in Japan has its own unique logic, problems, and pitfalls.

Appearances Are Everything

This is no time for faded, patched-up jeans and old T-shirts. Men should be clean-shaven or at least neatly trimmed, women should look tidy. In Japan, how you present yourself to the outside world, the care you take with appearance, is indicative of the type of person you are. A man with a ponytail hitchhiking in cutoffs and a frayed jacket may seem the epitome of freedom in the West, but the Japanese will leave him standing by the road for a very long time. In Japan, you should strive to look like a Boy or Girl Scout who happens to be waiting cheerfully for some kind person to offer them a ride. While hitchhiking, neither men nor women should show a lot of skin. And so, even though they are socially acceptable in Japan, you should avoid hitching rides while wearing tank tops, halter tops, or short shorts. You won't offend anyone, you will just have to wait longer for a ride.

Hitchhiking in Japan is not well known, so avoid the usual, relaxed hitchhiking body posture of the West. Instead, put your arm straight out to your side with your thumb erect, as though you were a Roman emperor presenting a verdict. This will feel awkward and stiff at first. Good. You shouldn't look too comfortable. You also shouldn't try to look too hip; no hand in your pocket or mirrored sunglasses or thumb leisurely held down by your side. Look very earnest, and smile, smile, smile. Try your best to look a little embarrassed, as if you are thinking, "Gosh, I rarely hitchhike and I hope someone will save from this embarrassment."

If you have a huge or very battered pack you might want to put it discreetly to one side. I always try to look like I went out for a stroll, walked a little too far, and am now trying to get back. No matter how haggard you may feel, never show it.

Note: Don't grin like a maniac. Smile shyly. It works.

Eye Contact

Smile hopefully at every single vehicle that passes and if possible, try to catch the driver's eye. Never be tempted to dismiss a car that didn't stop with a gesture or a look of disgust, even when they slow right down, take a good look at you, get your hopes up, and then drive off.

If the cars behind see you looking angry at the cars ahead, they will never stop no matter how much you smile when it's their turn. As a foreigner you are highly visible, and people will be watching you from a long way away. People may be watching from nearby gas stations or parking lots as well, trying to decide whether or not to pick you up, and if you display any hint of aggression, you can forget it. Often, the cars that slow down to look at you will circle back around and pass you again before they decide to stop. This happens countless times, especially if there are several people in the car and they are hurriedly discussing what to do.

Although the Japanese understand what "thumb out" means, Japan has no tradition of hitchhiking, and stopping for a hitchhiker *takes a lot of courage and consideration*. It is rarely done spontaneously. The only time people *will* stop spontaneously is when they think you are lost or are in trouble; the rest of the time they mull it over first. Many Japanese hesitate to stop simply because they really don't know what is involved. One woman in rural Shikoku drove by me four times before she finally decided to stop. Each time she passed, I smiled sweetly, and eventually I won her over.

Bowing

Always give a slight nod when a car does stop. You may want to bow as each car passes as well, but this can get hard on the back. Bowing does work, though. Whenever people are slow to stop I begin bowing to the traffic and someone soon pulls over. Don't make theatrical, deep bows. In Japan, bowing is closer to nodding, except that you nod "from the waist." A slight bobbing action is all that you need.

Hitchhiking by the Numbers

It is never a good idea for a woman to hitchhike alone, even though Japan is one of the safest countries in the world. Muggings and assaults are rare and the streets are not dangerous, but none of that changes the fact women should never hitchhike solo.

Below, I have listed the combinations for hitchhiking in Japan from "best" to simply "good."

Mixed couples (man and woman)   By far the easiest and best way to hitchhike. A female friend and I were virtually chauffeured across Okinawa one winter and across Kyushu the next. There is no need to lie about your relationship if you are not married, since there are no taboos about unmarried couples traveling together. Drivers will inevitably ask you if you are married but this is only out of curiosity. Take turns "thumbing," and don't forget to smile shyly and bow.

Two women As a male I am not in a position to comment, but I do not advise women to hitchhike—except in pairs. Certainly, two women will have as easy a time as a mixed couple. In fact cars will stop sooner, but often because they are worried. A pair of Australian Exchange Teachers routinely used to hitchhike from southern Japan to Tokyo, but all along the way people fretted and warned them about "gangsters," "bad men," and general unspecified "dangers." More than one driver insisted on taking them to a train station. One woman was so worried for them that she tried to buy them bus tickets.

Single man Solo hitchhiking is rewarding, and regrettably, something women should not do. Traveling alone plunges you right in, head first.

A man alone will not travel at quite the clip that a couple will, but other than that, there will be few problems. Some of my most successful trips—and certainly my most challenging— have been while hitchhiking alone. It forces you to communicate with your driver and hosts, thus making the journey richer for both of you.

Mixed groups The only drawback to traveling in a group is that you will have to wait for a vehicle large enough to hold everyone. However, if you are hiking or camping you may be picked up by a group of Japanese campers and it can lead to riotously good times. Two friends and I hitchhiked across the mountains of central Shikoku with ease, even though we were loaded down with heavy packs and tents, as several families in vans stopped. Unfortunately, the more people you travel with, the more of a clique your group becomes and the harder it is to get to know your Japanese hosts. Your groups should make a concentrated effort to converse with your hosts since they have gone out of their way to pick all of you up.

Two men   I don't recommend this. Since 1991 I've been asking the people who stopped for me a standard list of ten questions: *Would you stop for two men? A mixed couple? Two women?* etc. Almost everyone has said they would hesitate before picking up more than one man. I would recommend that two men traveling together split up and meet later to compare notes and travel anecdotes. This will make hitching quicker and more of a personal adventure. In fairness, I should also point out that when the Japan Exchange Teachers of Nagasaki sponsored a cross-Kyushu hitchhiking rally, the winners were a Canadian and an American, two men who traveled with ease the whole way, beating several male/female couples.

Destination Signs, and Why You Should Not Use Them

As I have stated, expressway entrances are the only place where you should use a sign. In nearly all other situations, using destination signs is a waste of time and effort. When I asked Japanese drivers "What does a sign signify to you?" almost without exception, the drivers said that someone holding a sign wanted to go to that location. And would they stop for a hitchhiker if they were only going part-way to the location named on the sign? "Oh, no," they answered, "That wouldn't be right." I saw this in action when I was driving to Kumamoto city with a Japanese friend of mine. She has lived in the United States and speaks English fluently, so when we saw a hitchhiker by the side of the highway, I expected her to stop. But to my surprise, she drove right past. When I asked her why, she said, "Didn't you see the sign? He's going to Fukuoka city, we're only going to Kumamoto." When the cars stop just ask them to take you farther down the road. When I traveled Japan from end to end I did not use any destination signs whatsoever, and I made the trip in record time.

When to Hitchhike

All Japanese cities, even the smaller ones, have rush hours, usually from 7:00 A.M. to 9:00 A.M. in the morning and from 5:00 P.M. to 7:00 P.M. at night. Although there are more cars on the road at rush hour, your chances of catching a ride then are almost nil. Japanese roads are narrow and hard to stop on in heavy traffic. Circling around, a favorite technique for the uncertain driver, is too difficult to do in rush hour. Everyone is either off to work or heading home and they have other things on their minds. The worst times I have had hitchhiking were on the outskirts of cities at rush hour. Except at expressway rest areas, never hitchhike after dark. By the time drivers see you, they have already whipped past, and turning around on a narrow street at night is worse than trying to circle back during rush hour. Hitchhikers must end their days at dusk and start as early as possible. Some of the farthest rides occur just after sunrise, when long-distance travelers, salesmen, and fishermen are out on the road.

Who Stops

At least one guidebook has suggested that in Japan truck drivers are "particularly good bets for long-distance hitchhiking." That may be true in Australia or the United States, but it is not true in Japan. I contacted four large national Japanese trucking companies: Nihon Tsu-Un, Yamato Unyu, Kyushu Sanko, and Seibu. Every one of them told me that regulations forbid their drivers from carrying passengers. You may, as I have, run into the occasional free-spirited trucker who simply doesn't care or know about the restrictions, but otherwise I wouldn't bet on Japanese truck drivers as a reliable source. Most of your rides will be with Japanese people who are taking trips themselves, either families on an outing or men on a business trip driving to an adjoining city. But generalizing is almost impossible. For example, I have traveled with Buddhist priests, retired couples, duck hunters, social activists, housewives, university students, musicians, artists, lots of English teachers, a man who artifi-cially insemi-nates cattle, a sushi chef, a writer, a woman who teaches tea cer-emony, a traditional carpenter, several druggists, a maid, a translator, a judo master, and a man who I suspect was a gang-ster. I have never had any trouble with any of the people who stopped for me. Never.

Finding the Right Spot—A Simple Trick

The quickest, cheapest way to get out of the clutter of any Japanese city and onto an open stretch of highway is to take a local train (*kakueki-teisha*). In Japan, the train system is extensive and most lines run right beside, or very near, the main highways. Take a local train out of downtown, getting off at the first rural station which puts you beside the highway. You can check with Japanese maps or the atlas first and make sure that the station you choose *is* beside the highway. Or, you can simply take a train out of town and get off when you see open rice fields, shoreline, or forest. Don't be too picky. When you see a break in the cityscape, jump off. Keep up with which side of the tracks the highway is on, because that is where you'll be hitchhiking. In Japan train tracks are often dividing lines, with farmland to one side and town centers on the other. Make sure you don't wait too long, because before you know it, you'll be into another city. *Warning*: Make sure you get on a slow-moving local train. It should look like an old junker, and the other passengers should be elderly people, farmers, students. It should not be a sleek silver or white bullet filled with businessmen. Do not take an express or limited express which zips from city center to city cen-ter. You want to be able to get out at a moment's notice in the country. No matter what the man at the counter or anyone else advises, take the local *kakueki-teisha*.

Many rural stations are little more than shelters beside the tracks. Some don't even have a man to check the tickets.

Passengers put their tickets into the box at the exit on the honor system. If you do not have an exact station in mind and are planning to get off the train as soon as you see a good spot, be quick! They stop for less than a minute at most stations. If you go this route, you won't know your final fare ahead of time. Instead, before you board the train, put about ¥150 worth of coins into the ticket-vending machine and get a ticket for that amount. In Japan you can adjust your fare either on the train or when you get off. Simply show the ticket to the man at the counter and he will tell you how much you owe. In stations in larger cities, there is a separate booth or machines for this, usually labeled in English as well as Japanese. So if you end up staying on the train beyond the worth of your ticket you can pay the difference when you leave. Likewise, if you get off sooner, you can get a partial refund—if there is a stationmaster at that station.

Occasionally, a conductor will come through while the train is in motion and ask to examine your ticket. If you have passed your ticket destination, he will be very worried and assume you missed your stop. Just smile and say *tsugino* (the next one), meaning, "I'm all right, I'll get off at the next station." If he comes back again, repeat the phrase.

Now what? You are out of the city, in a rural or at least semi-rural area. If you have checked the maps you will know which national or prefectural highway runs parallel to the tracks, but even if you don't, you can simply ask for directions to the nearest highway. The sentence is long: "Excuse me, is there a main road or national highway near by?" I have added pauses to make it sound more natural. *Sumimasen/ chikaku ni/ōkii michi ka/kōsoku dōro ga/arimasu ka?*

Try to memorize this phrase. You will be using it a lot. Most highways will be a short walk from the station, many will run right beside the station.

If there is no stationmaster on duty, drop your ticket in the box and leave. Find someone and ask for directions. When you need directions or help and there is no stationmaster or police box nearby, ask junior high or high school girls; you'll know them by their school uniforms. They are usually nervous but ultimately polite when approached by a lost Westerner, and they have all studied English for several years, so they will eventually patch together a sentence or two. Many times the people you ask directions from will accompany you all the way to the road to make sure you get there. High school boys are too unpredictable or too "cool" to be bothered.

Once you get onto a highway, the rest is common sense. You want room for a car to pull over safely. Avoid sharp corners and steep hills. When I am desperate, such as in an area that is too crowded, I sometimes stand just beyond the five-meter limit near a traffic signal and try to look wistful. Drivers stopped at red lights will eventually start to feel sorry for me and will wave me over.

Schoolyards

Hitchhiking in front of Japanese schools is a good strategy. Almost every major Japanese high school and junior high school has a foreign English assistant teacher on staff, and with a little luck you may be mistaken for that person or one of their friends or relatives. Teachers are very good for picking up hitchhikers, because they have become used to being around non-Japanese people. If you luck out, a Japanese English teacher will stop, which makes things that much easier.

If you do hitchhike in front of a school, make sure you do so after school hours. Between 4:00 P.M. and 6:00 P.M. is ideal. Many of the teachers will be heading home, and most of the students will already have gone. Saturdays and Sundays are good also, because many club activities and sporting events center around Japanese schoolyards. The down side is that you may have to put up with being an object of interest among the students, which can get tiresome after awhile.

When the Car Stops

First say *sumimasen* (excuse me) and *dōmo* (thanks) and give a quick bow. The driver may say nothing at first and may even look at you with a puzzled expression. Some people may even think you are in trouble, but most will ask you something along the line of "*Doko made?*" (Where to?) There are three ways to answer:

1. Tell them exactly where you are going by giving the place name followed by *made*. For example, "*Miyako made.*" (Pronounced not like the English word "made" but like "mah-day.") If you are near your destination, this strategy works well. But if it is far away, the Japanese driver may panic because they think that you are expecting a ride all the way to that exact location.

2. Tell them that you are going "in the direction of" your destination. "*Miyako no hō.*" Even then, if you are heading for a destination far away, pick an interim destination to aim for at first. I usually pick the next major city down the road, and then—once I am safely ensconced inside the vehicle—I tell them where my *ultimate* destination is that day. This saves you from scaring away a lot of rides who are worried that they will be expected to take you all the way—*even though* you carefully said "in the direction of." Why? Because many Japanese feel guilty about not taking you all the way to your final destination. Again, this is because they are not familiar with the principles of hitchhiking: Namely, that drivers take you down the road only as far as they were originally planning to go.

3. Tell them "Anywhere down this road is fine." This may make some drivers wary. In Japan only drifters and ne'er-do-wells have no final destination. So I recommend a fourth, compromise approach: Say "I am going in the direction of (place name), but anywhere down this road is fine."

The Ace up the Sleeve

The biggest single advantage that hitchhikers have over other travelers is this: As a hitchhiker you have an ally—the driver. The Japanese are remarkably dependable once they have taken ad hoc responsibility for you. You can ask them to help you find the nearest campsite, or a cheap inn, or even ask them to phone hostels for you. Once you catch your first ride of the day, it becomes easier and easier. Learn to rely on the kindness of others. Ask for help. Ask for directions. Ask for advice. This is what makes hitchhiking in Japan such a unique experience: Western individualism meets Japanese kindness, and together they travel down the road.

The Hitchhiker and the Law

Hitchhiking is so rare in Japan that it is not covered by any highway regulations. Since there are no laws on the books, there are also no rules regarding hitching after dark, no restrictions on hitching within city limits, no codes of conduct.

Don't fret over any of the items listed in this chapter. The Japanese police are a help, not a hindrance, and if you are ever in any kind of a bind do not hesitate to approach them. If you are lost, you can go to the nearest neighborhood *kōban* and get directions and sometimes even maps.

Small police boxes, called *kōban*, are manned around the clock by a small staff, often just one or two officers. In Japan, red lights mark police stations and police boxes, not brothels. There are over 15,000 *kōban* across Japan, and the system is being studied and adopted by Western countries.

The First Rule of Hitchhiking

Never hitchhike in front of or near a police box or station, even if you are perfectly within your rights to do so. You will only perturb the officers inside, who feel that they have to do *something* about this odd foreigner standing out there with his thumb in the air. Section 5-2-A of the Japanese Highway Code states that "It is illegal to change lanes such that it will cause the car behind you to suddenly brake or swerve." What this means for a hitchhiker is that the Japanese police frown on hitchhiking beside four-lane roads because of potential accidents that may be caused by people suddenly shifting lanes to pull over. The police will almost never approach you, regardless. But if they ever do ask you to move on, be polite. Where possible stick with two-lane highways. I have been asked to leave an area only once in five years of hitching, and I deserved it. I was standing outside a busy four-lane highway that ran in front of a police station. Legal, perhaps, but not wise.

Rules Prohibiting Pedestrians

There is no gray zone here. It is illegal to walk on any Japanese expressway or major motorway. Unless for mechanical reasons, it is also illegal for a car to stop along them, as well. Thus, a hitchhiker on an expressway is doubly at fault—first, for walking along a pedestrian-prohibited road, and second, for causing vehicles to stop illegally.

The restriction on walking along expressways and major motorways is the one regulation that *will* be enforced. Don't assume that just because a major six-lane thoroughfare is—technically—not an expressway it is OK to hitchhike on it.

If you do get picked up by the highway patrol, don't panic. The only punishment prescribed by Japanese law is a stern warning and a record made. A patrolman could conceivably decide you were "obstructing traffic," which is a more serious offense, but the chances of this are rare.

The Japanese police, for all their stern stereotypes, are unfailingly patient with Western hitchhikers. Apologize and you will be treated well. Become confrontational and you will be responded to in kind. Charging a foreigner with an offense is something that the Japanese police want to avoid as much as possible, but if you really annoy them they might make an exception.

Stopping and Parking—An Important Difference

In Japan, the following distinction is made between parking and stopping:

Section 5-8-1: When one stops to let people in and out of the car or if bags and goods are unloaded for five minutes or less, it is a stop and not a park.

As we will see, this is a very important distinction as far as hitchhikers are concerned.

The X and the Slash

You *can* hitchhike in a No Parking zone, because the cars will be *stopping* to pick you up—not parking. No Parking zones are marked by a blue sign with a red diagonal stripe, or "slash," across it. You will see No Parking signs everywhere. As a hitchhiker, feel free to ignore them. Areas where both parking *and* stopping are not allowed are designated by a blue sign with a red X. Do *not* hitchhike in these areas. Most cars won't stop and those that do will have committed a traffic violation.

If do you attempt to hitchhike in a No Stopping area, the police may come and move you along. *Remember*: If there is only a slash you can hitchhike; when there's an X you can't.

Fire Hydrants and Construction Sites

It is legal to stop—but not park—in front of a fire hydrant, so don't worry about hitchhiking in front of one. As well, you *can* hitch in front of or just after road construction sites, as long as you are at least five meters beyond the area of the road under construction. I like areas just *after* road construction because the drivers are going slow and are very aware of what is in front of them, making hitchhiking a little easier. If a policeman ever does decide that you are creating a traffic hazard by hitchhiking near a construction site, you will be asked to move along.

Note: If a policeman approaches you and makes an X with his forearms he is telling you to beat it. In Japan, crossing your arms or index fingers is a gesture meaning "no," "closed," or "forbidden." The key word to listen for is *dame* (pronounced "dah may"), which in this context means "forget it."

Obstructing Traffic

As a hitchhiker you will naturally spend some time standing or walking along the roadside. In Japan, roads are often narrow and lack sidewalks. Look for a white line beside the roadside which designates the pedestrian area. If a patrol car passes when you are hitchhiking make sure your feet are behind the line. Standing too near to traffic or thrusting your hand out in a way that you cause cars to swerve is a serious offense. If you hitchhike at night, such as at an expressway rest area, wear reflective materials. For around ¥500 at most bicycle shops, you can buy a safety band called *hansha anzen tasuki* or, simply, *tasuki* to wear over your shoulder. If you are hitchhiking at night without a safety band, a passing patrol car may decide that you present a road hazard, though more than anything he will be worried about your safety.

Intersections and Other Restrictions

As a hitchhiker, please be aware of the following restrictions. If you ignore them drivers will rarely stop and those who do stop will have broken the law. Do you really want it on your conscience if someone gets a traffic ticket because they stopped to give you a ride?

Stopping Is Prohibited

- At an intersection or within five meters of the edge of an intersection. This is a shame because intersections are a good place to hitch.
- Within five meters of the corner of a road or a pedestrian crossing, and within ten meters of a bus stop or a tram stop. If there is little traffic on the road, don't worry too much about these restrictions. I have often hitched in front of bus stops and was surprised when I later learned that I had been enticing drivers to break the law.
- Stop signs are written in Japanese characters on a red triangular sign, with the tip pointing downward. Do not hitchhike within five meters of them.
- No stopping is permitted at the top of a hill or on a very steep slope, or within ten meters of a railway crossing. Japan is a very mountainous country and often you will have no choice in the matter. Don't worry; this regulation is flexible and refers mainly to situations that are clearly dangerous.

Drinking and Driving

Japan has zero-tolerance drinking and driving, and currently enforces one of the toughest laws in the developed world. Someone who has had just one drink will be arrested if he or she operates a motorized vehicle. Licenses are revoked and public employees are fired for minor infractions. As a hitchhiker/passenger, you should be aware of the following sections of the Japanese Highway Code.

1.4.D: It is a violation of the law to ask a nonlicensed individual or a person who has had even a single drink to operate a motor vehicle or give you a ride.

1.4.E: The law also prohibits the offering of alcohol to any individual who will have to drive. It is illegal for another party to encourage one who will be driving to drink alcohol.

Outside of this, Japanese society is surprisingly tolerant of alcohol consumption. Passengers may drink open liquor in a car as long as the driver doesn't join them. So don't worry if your driver offers you a cold beer while you're on the road. North Americans in particular will find this hard to get used to.

Seat Belts

In Japan, passengers in the front seat must have the seat belt fastened. If you don't, your driver can be penalized and points put on his record, so be sure to buckle up.

Other than seat belts and avoiding police boxes, you do not need to worry about most of these traffic restrictions once you get beyond the city limits. Hitchhikers do not get harassed in Japan. Enjoy the ride and don't worry about the police.

Motorcycles

It has long been a dream of mine to hitch a ride on a motor-cycle, but so far I have had no luck. If you manage it, you should know that it is illegal for learners (i.e., drivers who have had their license for less than a year) to carry passengers. It is also illegal to carry motorcycle passengers when driving on an expressway.

The Long and Winding Road

A sign that depicts a bus and a truck with a red slash through them indicates that the road is off-limits to buses or large vehi-cles. Hitchhiking is allowed, but the road will soon narrow into a one-lane residential street, which is not a good choice for hitching rides.

Hitchhiking Etiquette

Don't open the car door too soon after the car stops. Westerners, men in particular, are perceived as being aggressive and vaguely threatening. I always stand back when I first approach the car, and the first thing I always do is apologize. Even if the driver waves me in, I always ask first, *ii desu ka*? (Is it all right?), before I open the door.

Check for passenger slippers. I never knew these existed until I started hitchhiking. When getting into newer cars and especially in the back of vans, you will occasionally spot a pair of these slippers. If you make a small inquiring gesture to the driver, he will usually wave his hand and say you don't need to put them on. But if it is muddy out or your shoes are dirty, it might be a nice gesture to take them off and wear the slippers, even if the driver protests. Leave your shoes on the rubber mat at your feet.

When the driver pulls over to a row of vending machines, you can *try* to do the buying, but the odds aren't good. Rather than wrestle with the driver over who will get to pay, a better strategy is to buy some snacks for the driver and any other passengers. Again, always make a show of trying to pay for gasoline, but expect to have the driver wave your money away. Apologize profusely, and be glad you aren't paying; gasoline prices in Japan are incredibly high—over ¥550 a gallon.

Making Conversation

The rudest thing that hitchhikers can do is to ignore the people giving them the ride and talk among themselves in English or remain silent the entire way. Hitchhiking is rare in Japan, and for most of the people who stop for you it will be their first time. In the West it may be just a matter of catching a lift, but for the Japanese, giving someone a ride is a very big deal. To be blasé about the whole thing somehow diminishes what was an adventurous decision for them. Unless the driver can speak the language, hitchhikers have to avoid having extended conversations among themselves in English. It makes the Japanese driver feel excluded in his own car. This is the time to practice any Japanese you have learned.

Predictable Annoyances

Many Westerners find it disconcerting how often they are asked blunt questions such as "How old are you?", "Why aren't you married yet?", "How much money do you make?", and even "How much do you weigh?" If someone asks you a question that you don't want to answer, just smile in a strained way and say *himitsu desu* (It's a secret).

Beyond the blunter questions, Japanese people inevitably ask two standard, rather silly questions to foreigners. These questions have become a standing joke among long-term Western residents of Japan: *Nihon shoku wa taberare masu ka*? (Can you eat Japanese food?) *Hashi wa tsukae masu ka*? (Can you use chopsticks?). Apparently the wielding of chopsticks is something requiring great hand-eye coordination, because whenever you use chopsticks people will remark—in the same tone you might congratulate a child for getting his underwear on the right way round—*Hashi o jōzu ni tsukae masu ne!* (Boy, you sure are good at using chopsticks!)

The Hitchhiker as Guest

If you approach hitchhiking with a sense of humor and a genuine interest in your hosts, the odds are very good that at some point you will be invited into their homes and even offered a room for the night. These are the moments that you will remember best about your journey into Japan.

Planning Your Trip
as a Hitchhiker

The number one *commandment* for the independent, budget-minded traveler in Japan, and especially the hitchhiker, is this: Do *not* arrive in Tokyo. Hitchhiking into Tokyo is very easy; hitching *out* of Tokyo is almost impossible. You may get a great discount air ticket into Narita Airport, but the time and money you will then have to spend trying to get out of the urban sprawl around Tokyo is just not worth it. A direct bus from Narita airport to Tokyo station costs ¥3,000. It takes an hour and a half, and it puts you in the middle of one of the largest cities on earth, not a good place to begin a hitchhiking journey. The best way to enter Japan is at one of its smaller international airports. Many flights connect to the West via other Asian countries, and this is often as cheap as flying directly into Narita.

If you absolutely must arrive in Tokyo, for English assistance, advice, and materials go to the **Narita Tourist Information Office** (Tel. 0476-34-6251). It is in the arrival lobby of Passenger Terminal 2, and is open daily 9:00 A.M. to 8:00 P.M.

Tokyo is the most expensive city in the world, followed by Osaka; this suggests that neither Tokyo or Osaka is a very good choice for budget travelers. Japan as a whole is expensive, but costs vary widely depending on the size of the city. In Japanese cities with populations over 1 million, the daily cost of living is 10.6 percent higher than in cities of under 50,000.

Expenses by Region and Airport

The Kanto (Tokyo) area is the most expensive region in Japan, followed by the Kinki (Osaka–Kyoto) area, and then—surprisingly—Hokkaido, which has frontier-style prices. The cheapest area in Japan is Okinawa, followed by Shikoku, Kyushu, and Tohoku, all of which are well below the national average in daily living expenses. Because of their attraction for the budget-minded traveler, I concentrate on Shikoku, Kyushu, and Tohoku. Hokkaido, while slightly more expensive, is also covered, because the open beauty of its landscape makes hitchhiking extremely attractive.

Osaka, Kansai Kokusai-kūkō

Osaka is a large, expensive city. But its less crowded international airport is easy to escape via ferries which connect it to Shikoku and the Inland Sea. The newly built Kansai Kokusai-kūkō (airport) is south of Osaka, situated on an artificial island connected the mainland by a private rail line. For English assistance and information, stop in at the **Kansai Tourist Information Center** on the first-floor arrival lobby (Tel. 0724-56-6025). It is open daily 9:00 A.M. to 9:00 P.M.

Like Tokyo, Osaka charges a fee to all international passengers flying out of the city. The Kansai Kokusai-kūkō Passenger Service Facility extortion charge is ¥2,600 per person, slightly higher than Narita's. This fee notwithstanding, Osaka is still a less expensive port of entry. From Kansai Kokusai-kūkō to downtown Osaka takes between 30 and 40 minutes and costs ¥800–¥1,250 depending on whether you take a regular train or a "super limited express."

Escaping

You can bypass Osaka entirely. If you want to visit Kyoto and Nara, it is cheaper to go to Nara first and then later take a local train into Kyoto. A **limousine bus** from Kansai Airport to the JR Nara Station runs every hour, takes one hour 35 minutes, and costs ¥1,800. A **JR train** to Nara costs ¥1,630 and takes one hour 25 minutes. To go directly to Kyoto first, take a super-express **Haruka** train from Kansai-kūkō; trains run every 30 minutes, cost ¥3,430, and take one hour 15 minutes.

From Kansai Kokusai-kūkō to Shikoku

Ferries run directly from the airport to Shikoku. To travel to Takamatsu is a ¥6,000, two-hour trip; going to Tokushima costs ¥4,000 and takes one hour 22 minutes. A cheaper ferry runs to Sumoto on Awaji Island (between Honshu and Shikoku) for ¥1,750 and takes 40 minutes. Although I have never tried hitchhiking across Awaji Island, frequent traffic, open roads, and beautiful scenery make Awaji a promising option.

Sapporo (Shin-Chitose-kūkō)

Sapporo is the largest city in Hokkaido, but it is still a good entry point for hitchhikers and independent travelers. The new airport in Sapporo is actually located in Chitose, south of Sapporo. The airport is called Shin-Chitose-kūkō, and is connected with the JR Shin-Chitose-kūkō-eki (station).

Note: The atlas lists the old Chitose-kūkō, which is just north of the present one. Remember, when taking the train out or hitchhiking in, that it is Shin-Chitose-kūkō that you want.

Shin-Chitose-kūkō (airport) has international flights from Honolulu, Seoul, Hong Kong, Guam, and Sydney. Shin-Chitose itself is practically in the countryside, so once you arrive, instead of heading into Sapporo, you may want to head southeast on the train a couple of stops and begin your hitchhiking immediately.

Niigata-kūkō

Arriving in Niigata is like entering Japan from the back door. From Niigata, take a train north past Murakami and you can hitchhike along the rugged Sasagawa-nagare coast. Turn inland and you can hitchhike to the Three Sacred Mountains of Dewa Sanzan. Niigata is also the gateway to Sado Island.

Niigata-kūkō has flights to Seoul, as well as Khabarovsk, Irkutsk, and Vladivostock, so travelers coming to Japan via the Trans-Siberian can enter Japan at Niigata.

Fukuoka-kūkō

Fukuoka-kūkō serves as an international gateway to and from southeast Asia. Flights arrive daily from Honolulu, Korea (Seoul, Pusan, and Cheju Island), Malaysia, Indonesia (Denpaser/Bali, Jakarta), Sri Lanka, China (Beijing, Shanghai), Singapore, Taiwan, Vietnam, Hong Kong, the Philippines, Guam, Saipan, Sydney, and Bangkok.

Fukuoka-kūkō is one of the easiest, most conveniently located airports in Japan. A subway runs from the airport to the city center and becomes the local train headed west, so you can go from the international airport to open road in less than an hour and for around around ¥500. For a hitchhiking journey that includes Nagasaki, you should enter Japan at Fukuoka. (See the Northern Kyushu Loop itinerary in Chapter 14 for additional details.)

Sendai-kūkō

If you are planning to hitchhike through Tohoku, enter Japan via Sendai. The airport connects with flights from the following: Honolulu, Singapore, Korea (Seoul, Pusan), Beijing, Hong Kong, Guam, Saipan. A bus runs downtown for under ¥1,000, and from Sendai you can take a short ride on a local train to the famous pine tree islands of Matsushima Bay. (See the Tohoku itinerary in Chapter 12 for more details.)

Nagoya-kūkō

Nagoya is not a good entry point; its international airport puts you in the middle of one of Japan's most densely populated areas, with Tokyo to the northeast and Osaka to the southwest. Nagoya has direct flights to Portland, Vancouver, Los Angeles, Sao Paulo, Paris, Moscow, and all major Asian travel points. Despite its conveniences, you should try to enter elsewhere.

Other Airports

There are other smaller, regional airports that have international flights which connect with South Korea, Hong Kong, and other major international airports. A good strategy for independent budget travelers is to enter Japan via Korea and fly into one of Japan's smaller airports. Check with a travel agent for details about flying into Aomori, Hiroshima, Kagoshima, Kumamoto, Nagasaki, Okayama, and Toyama.

From South Korea

Arriving in Japan via ship or international ferry is another option, especially if you are coming to Japan as part of a general Asian tour.

Overnight ferries between Pusan, South Korea, and Shimonoseki on the southern tip of Honshu are operated by the **Kampu Ferry Company.** In Japan, call 0832-24-3000 for information. Tickets can also be arranged through a travel agent. Ferries leave at 6:00 P.M. and arrive the following day at 8:30 A.M. The cheapest ticket is a second-class B ticket, which is just a space on a carpeted floor for ¥8,500. There is a 20 percent discount for students. Passenger boats between Pusan and Hakata port in Fukuoka are operated by the **Camellia Line Company.** In Japan, call 092-262-2323, or contact a travel agent. Ferries leave Pusan in the evening every Tuesday, Thursday, and Sunday. The cheapest-grade ticket costs ¥8,500.

The fast hydrofoil Beetle II runs daily between Pusan and Hakata as well. It is operated by the **JR Kyushu Company**. In Japan, call 092-281-2315. A one-way ticket on this state-of-the-art high-speed service costs ¥12,400. Keep in mind that an economy-class plane ticket from Pusan to Fukuoka costs only ¥15,400.

From Taiwan

For travelers wishing to enter Japan via Okinawa, international ferries operate between Taiwan (Keelung, Kaoshung) and Ishigaki, Miyako, and Naha in Okinawa. Ferries are operated by the **Arimura Sangyo Shipping Company** Naha office; phone 098-868-2191 for schedules. (Tokyo office: Tel. 03-3562-2091/ Osaka office: Tel. 06-531-9267.) These long, slow ferries require reservations well in advance—the company advises three months. Schedules vary, and you can expect to pay around ¥18,000 for an economy-class ticket, and ¥14,000 for a student ticket.

Note: Citizens from the U.S., Canada, Australia, New Zealand, the U.K., Germany, France, and Japan can enter Taiwan without visas and stay for 14 days, making Taiwan a viable connecting point. Fly into Taiwan and take a ferry to the Okinawan islands.

Ferries also operate between Naha and Osaka, for ¥20,600 for a second-class ticket. So you could take a ferry all the way from Taiwan to Okinawa and then to mainland Japan, if you don't mind spending a couple of days on a stretch of ocean known as "Typhoon Alley."

Climate

Japan contains five distinct climate zones, from the jungles of Okinawa to the seven-foot snowdrifts of the far north, and the climate varies considerably from one region to another at any given time. The rainy season in central Honshu does not occur at anywhere near the same time as that of Okinawa. Kagoshima has *two* rainy seasons. Hokkaido has none.

As a hitchhiker, avoid the shimmering heat and unbearable humidity of July and August if at all possible, but more critically you do not want to hitchhike during any area's rainy season. Japan is within the Temperate Monsoon Zone; with twice the average rainfall of the United States, and more rain per annum than England, *tsuyu*, a two-month rainy season, is not the time to travel. Unfortunately, standing alone in the rain does not increase your chances of getting a sympathy ride. In Japan, a foreigner hunched over in a downpour with his thumb out does not look sad and forlorn—he looks insane.

Altitude affects temperature more than latitude. The mountains of Japan can be windy, chilly, and potentially dangerous places even in spring. On the plus side, during the summer the mountains are usually several degrees cooler than the coast, so if you are stuck with visiting Japan during its hot, sticky summer months, try to spend as much time in the interior as you possibly can.

Regional weather and rainy seasons

Japan has several regional differences when it comes to weather—for example, the rainy season doesn't affect the entire country at the same time.

Hokkaido   Unless you are a skier, hitchhiking should be done from mid-May to mid-September to avoid the harsh winter. Summers in Hokkaido are cooler than in the rest of Japan, with less humidity and no rainy season. Hokkaido has no rainy season officially, but September is its rainiest month. October is wet and cold as well.

The western side of Tohoku and Niigata   Part of Japan's famous Snow Country, this is where towns and highways are buried under some of the highest snowfalls in the world. The Pacific coast of Tohoku is far more temperate and can get quite hot in the summer. Tohoku's rainy season is mild compared with the rest of Japan. September is the rainiest month.

The mid-western side of Honshu   Winter lasts a long time in the so-called Back of Japan. The mountains and coastline between Niigata and Fukui are cold and miserable from November to the end of March.

Tokyo   The capital swelters in the summer heat and is quite chilly but clear in winter. The Kanto (around Tokyo) area is rainiest during June and again in September and October.

Kyoto   The old capital is best visited in September and October, when the autumn colors are at their best, or in April, when the cherry blossoms are in bloom. Expect crowds.

The coast of Shikoku   This region has a warmer winter than much of Japan, though the interior is naturally much colder. Like Tohoku, Shikoku's Pacific side is a different climate zone: warmer, wetter, and more humid in summer. The southwestern side of Shikoku has a long rainy season, lasting from between the middle of June to the beginning of July. The Pacific coast of Shikoku is hit by typhoons in August and September, and Kōchi is usually right in the middle of it.

Kyushu   Hot and humid in the summer, this island should be avoided completely between July and August, unless you are a sun worshiper, a scuba diver, or a masochist. The best times to visit southern Kyushu are between mid-September and early November, or between the beginning of April and early June—before the rains set in. The rains in this semi-tropical area begin in the middle of June and last well into July. Kagoshima is practically under water during June. Southern Kyushu also has a smaller second rainy season in April. Heavy rainfalls accompany the typhoons of August and September as well.

Below are the official rainy seasons for some cities across Japan; dates represent a 30-year average, and are fairly accurate. The last column tells what percent of the year's total rainfall during the rainy season.

	Rainy Season	Precipitation	Percentage
Aomori	June 15–July26	162 mm	12
Fukuoka	June 6–July 18	507 mm	30
Hiroshima	June 7–July 18	493 mm	31
Kagoshima	June 1–July 15	755 mm	32
Nagoya	June 9–July 17	355 mm	23
Niigata	June 9–July20	273 mm	15
Osaka	June 8–July 17	377 mm	27
Sendai	June 11–July21	246 mm	20
Takamatsu	June 5–July 16	306 mm	26
Tokyo	June 9–July18	255 mm	18

Temperatures

Rather than give average annual temperatures, which tend to dull the extremes, I have listed the average temperatures on four specific days—corresponding to each of the seasons. The average highs and lows for each day are listed. Because you will not be hitchhiking very much in winter, I have concentrated mainly on days between early spring and late autumn. Temperatures are given in Celsius. A chart like this can be overwhelming at first, but if you use it as a reference in planning your trips it will give you an idea what range of temperatures to expect in any given area. Note, for example, that although Mount Aso and Kagoshima are in the same area, Aso is twice as cold in spring. Always remember: *Altitude affects temperature more than latitude*.

Keep in mind that in Japan it is the humidity that will kill you. If you are coming between July and early September, try to avoid the coast and large cities, where the lack of wind and the islands of concrete only intensify the discomfort.

		April 1	July 1	October 1	December 1
Aomori	H:	9.0	22.8	20.6	7.0
	L:	0.1	14.7	10.1	−0.1
Akita	H:	10.0	24.2	21.0	8.2
	L:	1.7	16.9	11.8	1.5
Kagoshima	H:	18.5	29.1	27.5	16.8
	L:	8.7	22.5	18.7	6.2
Kanazawa	H:	14.0	26.7	23.6	12.2
	L:	4.3	19.4	15.4	4.5
Kyoto	H:	16.1	28.5	25.2	13.6
	L:	5.5	20.5	16.1	4.1
Morioka	H:	10.1	24.0	20.2	7.0
	L:	−0.2	15.5	9.8	−1.1
Mount Aso	H:	9.4	20.3	17.7	6.1
	L:	1.6	15.8	11.7	−0.2
Nagano	H:	12.7	26.1	21.4	9.0
	L:	1.3	17.7	12.6	−0.2
Nagasaki	H:	16.5	27.2	25.9	14.7
	L:	8.5	21.8	18.4	7.2
Nagoya	H:	15.9	27.8	24.9	13.5
	L:	5.8	20.4	16.3	4.0
Niigata	H:	12.0	25.2	22.4	10.6
	L:	3.8	19.1	15.0	3.9
Osaka	H:	16.0	28.6	25.5	13.9
	L:	7.2	21.5	17.7	6.1
Sapporo	H:	6.7	22.8	19.3	4.8
	L:	−0.9	14.2	9.1	−2.2
Sendai	H:	11.7	23.1	21.5	10.5
	L:	2.5	16.9	13.5	2.1
Takamatsu	H:	15.4	27.9	24.4	13.6
	L:	5.5	21.0	16.1	4.4
Tokyo	H:	15.3	26.3	23.6	14.1
	L:	7.0	20.1	17.1	5.9

When Not to Go

New Year's   December 27–January 4 (and any connecting weekend).

Golden Week   This is a time when several national holidays fall together, creating an extended vacation, usually from

April 29 to May 5, plus any weekends that connect on either end.

Mid-Summer O*bon* The mid-summer Festival of the Dead is a time of homecoming in Japan that lasts for a week in mid-August. In central Japan, Obon is also observed in mid-July, but the holiday mainly centers around mid-August. August is also the summer vacation for Japanese students.

During these three peak seasons—New Year's, Golden Week, and Obon—the roads and airports of Japan are clogged with visitors and booking accommodations becomes a headache. There is more traffic of course, so the hitching is better, but the traffic is slow and congested and accommodations are hard to come by. In the more tourist-heavy regions, hotels jack up their prices during these seasons.

When to Travel

Although Golden Week is a nightmare for getting around in Japan, the weeks *just after* Golden Week (May 8–24) are a good time to travel. In most areas of Japan the weeks just *before* rainy season are also a good time to travel. (The temperature begins to climb dramatically after the rainy season ends).

Mid-September through mid-November is also a good time, though typhoons frequently blow through southern Japan well into October. Most typhoons last only a few days, and can be waited out in a hot spring or hotel.

Visa and Passport Requirements

Everyone entering Japan needs a valid passport, a ticket out, and sufficient funds (roughly ¥10,000 a day until your departure). If you don't have the necessary funds on hand, make sure you are neatly dressed and have a tidy haircut to avoid being hassled at Immigration. A necktie for men is a good idea. The chances of being turned away for not having either the funds or a ticket out are slim, but they rise quickly if you are slovenly or wild-looking.

Visitors from Australia and South Africa cannot enter Japan without a valid visa arranged prior to arrival. Other countries' agreements with Japan have different allowances: U.K. and Ireland: six months without a visa. The United States, Canada, and New Zealand: 90 days without a visa.

Visas should be obtained from the Japanese consulate or embassy nearest you, prior to departure. Standard tourist visas are good for 90 days once they have been stamped at the point of entry.

Shopping Hours

Sunday is a full shopping day in Japan. Department stores, shops, and restaurants usually close down for one day during the week, often Monday or Wednesday, but this is not standardized. Drugstores are often open late—look for the green cross. Banks are open until 3:00 P.M., though they are rarely open on Saturday and never on Sunday. Many post offices are open for a half-day on Saturday. (See Chapter 7 for more details.) It is always a good idea to make an early start when sightseeing in Japan. Attractions, museums, temples, and gardens close at 4:00 P.M. or 5:00 P.M.; last admittance is usually 30 minutes before closing time.

Drugs and Other Hazards

Japan requires no inoculations. The water is safe. Drinking and smoking abound, but illegal drugs are strictly outlawed. No distinction is made between hard drugs and soft, or between small amounts and large. Bringing marijuana into Japan is like trying to smuggle heroin into the United States.

What to Bring

Spend more time than usual on selecting the apparel you

bring. Hitchhiking in Japan is all about projecting a crisp, clean-cut, and somewhat nerdy appearance. Bring only spotlessly clean clothes. Smart, light cotton pants are best for summer—leave the jeans at home. During cooler months, bring some long underwear to supplement. Washing and drying jeans takes too long, and hitchhiking in grubby ones is a terrible strategy. A nice new baseball cap is a very wise accessory; baseball is very popular in Japan and the sport has positive Western connotations. Pick a well-known American team like the Yankees, Cubs, or the Mets. The cap presents you as a fun-loving, baseball-playing, nice Western-type person (even if you hate baseball). I had one man stop specifically because he likes American baseball. The real advantage of a cap, of course, is to keep the sun off, and a cap is better than tying a handkerchief around your head, as I have seen some Westerners do. When hitchhiking it is better to look like a baseball fan than a pirate.

Birth control pills are next to impossible to renew quickly in Japan, and the pills that are available are not the same as those in the West, so bring enough to last. Feminine hygiene products are readily available, as are other personal items; you don't need to arrive with extra stocks of toothpaste or razor blades. Bring some strong sun block as well. It can be a little hard to find in the smaller towns and you don't want to be caught in the UV-rich sunlight of Japan. Cloth-style bandages can be hard to find—and expensive—so if you are prone to blisters you should bring your own supply of cloth Band-Aids, plasters, cornpads, etc. If you are susceptible to car sickness, bring a supply of motion-sickness suppressants, such as Gravol or Dramamine.

You do need a good pair of walking shoes or, even better, lightweight hiking boots that are easy to remove; you will be taking your shoes on and off constantly in Japan as you enter homes and inns, and even cars on occasion.

Japanese floors are not insulated and can get cold at night, so bring at least one pair of thick socks. You do not need to bring slippers unless you have large feet—in that case a simple pair of plastic thongs will do. You should also bring a mid-size bath towel. Most hotels and hostels supply only tiny hand towels, often at a price.

Travel lightly, with a small, half-empty backpack, ideally one with an aluminum frame. You will spend a certain amount of time standing straight-backed beside the road; shapeless, unsupported backpacks might cause shoulder and back pain after extended roadside waits. Your backpack should fit comfortably on your lap or in the back of a small vehicle's trunk. Bring a tent if you're planning on camping. A small, reliable compass is also a good idea.

Laundromats can be hard to find, and might have only a couple of very slow, very expensive machines. Dryers are expensive and not very useful; I usually wash my clothes and string them up overnight in front of the air-conditioning vent in my room. Anytime you are invited to spend the night in someone's home, don't be shy; ask if you can wash your clothes in their machine.

Photographs

Don't forget to bring family photos! Bring a stack of your brothers, cousins, pets, neighbors, school, house, car. Your Japanese hosts will be fascinated—especially if your car is Japanese. If you visit someone's home or spend a lot of time with them, it is expected that you will send copies of the photos you took of them and with them. This is not a strict social rule, but it is a custom.

Toilet Talk

Japanese toilets are squat-style; when using them, face the hood. Skirts give women a distinct advantage. Tight pants are hard to maneuver around, so when you are packing your clothes keep in mind that you will have to be squatting in them. To avoid Japanese-style toilets, look for the international handicap toilet symbol (a stick figure in a wheelchair). In Japan, handicap toilets are always Western-style. Larger hotels, department stores, and major train stations should all have handicap stalls.

Restrooms usually have toilet paper (except train stations and public facilities), but rarely paper towels, so most people carry their own handkerchiefs to dry their hands. *Do not use your personal handkerchief to blow your nose.* Blowing your nose on a handkerchief is shocking to the Japanese, akin to blowing your nose on a towel in the West. So, when blowing your nose, use tissues only, turn away or leave the room if you can, and be as quiet as possible.

You may see Japanese men urinating by the side of the road or in alleyways. Unless you are caught in an emergency, I do not recommend that Western men follow suit; this is not acceptable—especially not for foreign visitors. In a pinch, you can always use the toilets in a pachinko parlor.

One last tip: A popular promotion for businesses in Japan is to hand out small packets of tissues as advertising. Whenever you pass someone handing these out in the city make sure to stock up. You never know when a restroom won't have paper.

Gifts and Other Bribes

Although you will likely be treated as a guest, and any offer to pay for gasoline will most likely be refused, tollbooths are another matter. If you offer to pay them the Japanese drivers may accept. This sounds reasonable, except that Japanese toll charges are ridiculously high. They often cost more than taking a train the entire way. If you are hitching at the entrance of a toll road the driver will not ask you to pay because he or she was already expecting to pay the toll anyway. If the driver decides to take the expressway for your benefit, quickly and emphatically ask him not to. If he pays the toll you will feel rotten, and if you pay you will feel even worse.

If your driver takes you onto an expressway despite your best protests, ask to be dropped off at the next rest area. In Japan, you pay long-distance tolls when you exit, so if you can escape before that, you won't have to squirm in your seat as your driver forks out a bunch of money.

A good way to repay kindness is with lunch or dinner. Don't make this offer if you don't mean it, because unlike gas money, dinner will probably be graciously accepted. The best way to show your appreciation to Japanese drivers is with small gifts. In Japan, it really is the thought that counts, so you don't have to spend a lot of money. Bring more than you think you will ever need. Stickers for children, coins, stamps, baseball cards, pins, postcards of Mounties, kangaroos, koala bears, men in kilts, pictures of your national cliché—anything will do, as long as it's light and portable. Bringing as many small gifts as you can is cheaper than paying tolls. Small tokens of appreciation go a long way to establishing harmony and rapport, especially with any children in the vehicle.

Addresses

Many Japanese will present you with name cards. *Treat these with respect*. Don't sit on them, fold them, write on them, or use them to pick your teeth. Accept a name card with two hands if possible, look at it carefully even if you can't read it, nod thoughtfully, and then put it in a jacket or shirt pocket. Name cards are usually exchanged at the *beginning* of a conversation, not near the end. Automobiles are a more relaxed environment, however, and many times drivers won't think to introduce themselves formally at all. If you have business cards, bring a couple of dozen. If you don't have any, just *print* down your home address in English, and present it to your driver. Always, always have a note pad handy. For drivers and Japanese passengers who do not have name cards on them, or whose name cards are in Japanese only, ask them to write their names and addresses in the notebook in *rōmaji* (the Western alphabet).

At the end of your trip you will have the names of all the people who helped you during your travels. Sending them a card from your homeland is probably the best gift you can give.

International Reply Coupons (IRCs)

When asking for tourist or travel information from outside of Japan, you will need to include IRCs for return postage. Regardless of what these coupons cost you in your home country, they are worth only ¥130 when converted into Japanese stamps. Make sure you include enough IRCs to cover return postage when requesting information such as the Youth Hostel Guide, travel pamphlets, and expressway maps.

Pocket Dictionaries and Language Guides

You will need a good pocket English-Japanese dictionary. There are many available. I use the Taiseido Romanized English-Japanese/Japanese-English Pocket Size Dictionary. Before you choose, make sure that your dictionary is English-Japanese and Japanese-English. It should also include kanji characters and phonetic spellings of Japanese words. Kanji is useful because you can just point to make yourself more understood.

Free Handbook of Japanese Phrases for Travelers

Many regional tourist pamphlets contain a short list of Japanese phrases, but the city of Sendai in Miyagi Prefecture has outdone itself. The Tourist Handbook: Sendai–Matsushima contains 54 pages of vocabulary and conversation forms. Sections include transportation, hotels, restaurants, and emergencies. It also offers advice on such things as how to hail a cab, take a bus, or check into a hotel. It even has complete menus written in Japanese and English. Best of all, this amazing booklet is free. Just send the following to the address listed below.

1. Your return address
2. Return postage—use International Reply Coupons if you

are writing from overseas. International postage for the Handbook comes to ¥240, so you will have to include two IRCs.

3. A note saying: "Please send me *The Tourist's Handbook: Sendai–Matsushima* with Japanese language phrases for travelers."

> Tourist Information Center
> JR Sendai Station
> Aoba-ku Chuo 1-1-1
> Sendai-shi, Miyagi-ken, Japan 980
> Tel. 022-222-4069

If you call from within Japan, they will mail you a copy without waiting for postage. If you are traveling as a couple, request two.

Telephone Cards

Handy, pre-paid, ¥500 and ¥1,000 telephone cards are readily available from vending machines near phone booths or from convenience stores. Every time you use them, the amount of your call is deducted. Toll-free numbers in Japan usually begin with 0120. To make a toll-free call in Japan, insert either a pre-paid telephone card or a ¥10 coin and dial. The dial tone comes on after the coin or card has been inserted. (The coin will be returned when the call is finished. The card will have no charges deducted from it.)

English Helplines

The Japan National Tourist Organization (JNTO) operates two toll-free **Travel Phone** services for foreign travelers in Japan, seven days a week, 9:00 A.M.–5:00 P.M. English staff members can assist you in travel plans, but they do not make reservations.

> Eastern Japan 0088-22-2800 (or 0120-22-2800)
> Western Japan 0088-22-4800 (or 0120-44-4800)

Within Tokyo or Kyoto the number is *not* toll-free. When calling from within Tokyo, dial 3503-4400. From within Kyoto, dial 371-5649.

For emergency assistance in English, toll-free, 24 hours a day, seven days a week, call the **Japan Helpline** at 0120-461-997. In Tokyo, call the **Tokyo English Life Line** at 03-3968-4099.

This is for real emergencies. If you are ill or in an accident or stranded in a town at midnight and can't find accommodations, or if you have lost all your money, or if you have been brought into a police station and don't understand what is happening, call. But don't use this service for non-emergencies.

The Japan Helpline Card lists telephone numbers for emergency and other services that will answer in English. It also has a list of emergency Japanese phrases. Having a card that you can show people is much quicker than flipping through a guidebook. The card also comes with a short medical/address form that you can fill out if you want The Japan Helpline to keep your name and data on record. If there is an emergency, they will contact your family. And if your family needs to contact you while you are on the road, they can call the Helpline.

Note: This is not a telephone message service. Use it for emergencies only. Don't abuse this service.

The Japan Helpline Card is free; to request one, send a fax with your name and address and request to The Japan Helpline: 03-3435-8127, or 03-3435-7742; or send a letter or postcard to: The Japan Helpline, P.O. Box 833, Tokyo 100-91, Japan

If you are writing from outside Japan, include an International Reply Coupon to cover return postage. It may take up to two months before you get the card.

Money Matters

Japan is a very safe country, and the chances of being robbed, assaulted, or otherwise bothered are very slim. The real danger, sadly, is other independent travelers. Airports and tourist areas are never completely safe anywhere you go in the world, and you should be on guard in youth hostels as well.

Take the usual precautions you would at home. Be careful but not obsessive about your belongings. When hitchhiking do not insult your hosts by acting nervous when they put your bags in the trunk, or by getting suspicious if you get separated from your pack, such as when the driver drops you off at a restaurant entrance and then goes to park the car. Keep your passport and money on you at all times and then you won't have to worry about your backpack.

Carry cash. Lots of it. I would say keep at least ¥20,000 handy at all times. Japan runs on cash. Small family inns and love hotels (see Chapter 9) expect cash, not credit cards, and even major purchases such as cars are often paid for with a big satchel full of money. Traveler's checks are hard to convert off the beaten track, and few establishments accept credit cards.

Take your credit card for emergencies, but once you get out of the larger urban centers, don't expect to be able to use it. Some youth hostels do accept VISA cards, MasterCard, or American Express—as do many of the lodgings associated with the Japanese Inn Group, but these are exceptions.

Changing Money

Other than at the airport, in Japan you can exchange your money in four ways:

1. At larger, central banks. Most banks offer fair rates, but of course they keep bankers' hours, meaning generally 9:00 A.M.– 3:00 P.M. Also, some banks cannot exchange money before they receive the day's exchange rate, which often is not until after 11:00 A.M.

2. Post offices. Designated post offices can exchange money. In the morning they use the previous day's rate, and are usually open a little longer than regular banks—usually until 4:00 P.M., and in some branches until 6:00 P.M.

3. Larger tourist hotels, though most only change money for registered guests.

4. Department stores in larger cities are good only in a pinch. Their hours are longer, they are open on weekends and often until 8:00 P.M., but the rates are higher than at the airport.

Japan does not have the infestation of late-night, overpriced money-changers that you see in other countries. My advice would be to change some money—at least ¥30,000—at the airport. Then go to the central post office of the city you are in and change the rest of your money. Trying to change small amounts constantly is not a good strategy; once you get out of the cities, it becomes harder and harder to change foreign currency. Especially as the weekend approaches, make sure you have enough cash on hand to last several days.

Buy American (or British)

When arriving in Japan with checks or cash, make sure it is in a major currency—American dollars or pounds sterling if possible. Better yet, try to convert your money into yen traveler's checks *before* you leave home. Changing traveler's checks is never easy in Japan, but having them in yen makes them much less of a problem.

Postal Banking Services

Japanese post offices are very different from those in the West; they include full banking services, money machines, and check-cashing services. The symbol for the post office is a red capital T with an extra crossbar on top T̄. Japanese post offices buy and sell traveler's checks in U.S. dollars, French francs, pounds sterling, German marks, Canadian dollars, and Japanese yen—but only at *larger* post offices. When making financial transactions in Japan, I prefer the post office; they seem well informed and professional. The hours are listed below:

Mail Service
Monday to Friday	9:00 A.M.–5:00 P.M. (6:00 P.M. at larger branches)

Postal Banking Service
Monday to Friday	9:00 A.M.–4:00 P.M.
Saturdays	Closed
Sundays/Holidays	Closed

Make sure to pick up a copy of the free English guide to postal services and banking procedures, available at any branch.

Budgets

Traveling in Japan is comparable to traveling in Scandinavia—expensive, but not impossible. If you take the Bullet

Train and stay at average, mid-range hotels, Japan will be an expensive place. But by camping in municipal campsites and hitchhiking long distances, you can cut U.S.$100 off your budget.

For a budget traveler in Japan, a typical daily breakdown in yen would range as follows:

Transportation:	0–¥700
Breakfast:	¥600
Lunch:	¥700
Supper:	¥1,000
Incidentals:	¥1,000–¥2,000
Accommodations:	¥500–¥7,000
Range:	¥3,800–¥11,300
Average:	¥7,550

To be safe, I usually count on spending around ¥8,000 a day, though usually I am well under this amount. However, when you find yourself stuck in a dreary city center with only overpriced business hotels to choose from, you will need the extra cash.

Accommodation Costs

From least to most expensive, costs roughly break down as follows:

- Many campgrounds are free. Most have only a small charge, usually about ¥500 per person. Tent rentals are extra.
- Youth hostels typically cost around ¥3,000 a night.
- Capsule hotels are usually around ¥3,000–¥4,000 a night.
- Love hotels are between ¥5,000 and ¥7,000 a night. But that's per couple, making them the key to budget accommodations for couples.
- The Japanese Inn Group, noted in Chapter 9, runs a network of clean, lower-priced Japanese inns, most of which are in the ¥4,000 range.

- Cheaper, seedier business hotels will run around ¥4,000 a night without meals, but most business hotels charge ¥6,000–¥7,000.
- Japanese-style bed-and-breakfasts, *minshuku*, are usually comparable in price to lower-range business hotels in the ¥6,000–¥8,000 range—less, if you don't have meals.
- Traditional Japanese ryokan (inns) run from ¥8,000–¥15,000 per night, including two meals.

Practically every castle, temple, garden, and giant Kannon statue in Japan charges admission. And ropeways (the Japanese word for gondola-style cable cars) usually cost around ¥1,500. What are you going to do, skip the view? You can't go all the way to Hakodate without seeing the night view from the mountain. The same goes for the view of Nagasaki or the mountains of interior Hokkaido. Resign yourself to spending at least ¥1,500 per day on entrance fees and other incidentals and you will enjoy your trip more.

Eating Cheap

For information about Japanese food, the free JNTO pamphlet *Your Travel Companion: Japan* has color photos and brief explanations of popular Japanese dishes. The free *Tourist's Handbook: Sendai–Miyagi*, mentioned in Chapter 12, also has sample menus in English and Japanese.

Food will *not* be your major expense. You can eat cheaply as long as you stick to blue-collar places, noodle shops, and take-away box-lunch shops. The key is *caution*. Make sure you know exactly how much an item is before you order. One solution is to decide on how much you want to spend and simply ask the shop master to give you "¥1,000 worth of *yakitori* please." As for coffee (pronounced "ko-he"), bring a small thermos for the road. In restaurants, ask them to fill it with hot water and you can make instant coffee for later. You can buy small packets of instant coffee in most little corner stores in Japan. If you are really desperate for a caffeine fix you can buy thick syrupy canned coffee—hot or cold—from most vending machines. If you find Japanese coffee too bitter at first, ask for *amerikan kōhī*, which is weaker.

Cutting Costs

The cheapest way to eat is to buy snacks at convenience stores and then eat chocolate all day to kill your appetite and keep your energy up. When I am on a very tight budget, I try not to go to restaurants when I'm hungry. I eat something sweet and filling just before dinnertime to spoil my ravenous appetite. It isn't much fun, but it is cost-efficient.

Because the Japanese government monitors and even distributes rice, produce, and other foodstuffs, buying groceries and cooking yourself is almost as expensive as eating out. Finding cooking facilities is difficult as well, except when you are camping. Many campsites have kitchens with coin-operated propane stoves, so you can boil noodles, make spaghetti, heat up instant curry, etc. This is yet another benefit of planning your trip around campsites.

Most food stores, and especially the food sections in department stores, will put their prepared foods on sale between a half hour and an hour before the shop closes, usually around 7:00 P.M. If you wait until near closing time, you can stock up on salads, fried rice, tempura, Chinese food, even sushi, prepackaged and ready to eat—and at significant discounts. Look for a bright sticker attached to the packages of prepared food, which indicates the amount of yen reduced from the list price.

Bakeries and the bakery sections of food shops do have throwaway crusts for sale—often free—because crusts in Japan are trimmed before bread is put on the shelf. With these tail ends of bread-loaves, all you need is a jar of peanut butter and you have some power-snack sandwiches. (They have peanut butter in Japan. Just ask for *pīnatsu batā*.).

In restaurants, Western food generally costs more than Japanese food. Japanese curry rice, however, is very Western in taste and heartiness—it is even served with a spoon—so if you want to fill up, order *karē raisu* (curry rice). If you want a breaded pork cutlet on top, ask for *katsu karē*. Many restaurants in Japan have plastic models of the food in a display window; you can ask the waitress to step outside and then point to the dish you want.

Breakfast and Lunch

Japanese inns (*minshuku* and ryokan) include breakfast with the package, but Westerners are not always enthusiastic about the raw egg and grilled fish that is generally offered. You can ask them to cook the egg and provide coffee, but the coffee will cost extra. If this doesn't appeal, seek out the nearest coffee shop (*kissaten*) or Western-style hotel, and order *mōningu setto* (morning set), which is usually a fried egg, a small salad, some thick toast, and a small cup of coffee, for around ¥700. When you ask for a morning set, you may have a choice of Japanese-style (*washoku*) or Western (*yōshoku*).

Lunch sets are a better deal, and usually between 12:00 and 2:00 P.M. you can often find excellent meals. Ask for the *ichi-ban yasui teishoku* (cheapest complete meal) and you will get a full meal for around ¥800 or ¥900. The term *teishoku* (set meal) can also be used for complete supper meals as well, but they are not as cheap as the lunch menus. A typical *teishoku* includes the main dish, plus *gohan* (rice), *miso-shiru* (Japanese soup), *tsukemono* (pickles), and *ocha* (green tea) or occasionally coffee.

Supper

The real fun comes at supper time. Japan must have more small restaurants than any other industrialized nation. Somehow Japan has managed to modernize without succumbing entirely to the chain restaurant malaise of the West. There are all kinds of small, independent eateries in every nook and cranny of Japan, and the following is a brief overview of some of the choices you will have.

Noodle Shops and Red Lanterns

The general term for noodles is *menrui*, but most Japanese will refer to a specific type of noodle. One of the most popular is *rāmen*, a Chinese-style noodle. *Rāmen* shops, sometimes little more than food stalls huddled near train stations, serve big bowls of delicious noodles for under ¥500. Other noodles include *soba* (flat buckwheat noodles) and *udon* (thick white noodles) meant, like all Japanese noodles, to be slurped with gusto. Chicken *udon* is similar to chicken-noodle soup, only with jumbo noodles. *Yaki-soba* is grilled noodles, with seafood and chopped cabbage mixed in.

The summer specialty is *sōmen*, a light, cold noodle served in seasonal shops in scenic spots in the mountains. Some *sōmen* shops have bamboo "waterfalls" with noodles cascading down them; reach in with your chopsticks, pull out some noodles and slurp away. If you are hitchhiking in the summer months you will often come across these wonderful places.

A red lantern, *aka-chōchin*, outside a door indicates a working-class neighborhood establishment known more as a place to have a drink than a full-service restaurant. You can eat here, but generally the food is not substantial enough for a meal. The more tattered and ragged the lantern, the cheaper the price.

Bentō

Japanese *bentō* (box lunches) are inexpensive, well balanced, and portable. *Bentō* shops are popular at lunch time and display their menus with photographs and prices of their various box lunches. Just point. Meals range from ¥500 to ¥700 and are remarkably tasty. One of the biggest chains is called Hoka-Hoka Bentō, and any town of more than 25,000 should have one. Ask for directions. *Bentō* shops usually open around 11:00 A.M. and close around 9:00 P.M. (though some are late-night or all-night). They usually shut down for a few hours after lunch to prepare for the supper rush.

Yakitori and Robatayaki

Between convenience-store snacks, noodle shops, and *bentō*, you can eat almost as cheaply and as well as in the United States—and cheaper than in Britain. The term *yaki* means grilled. *Yaki-niku* is Korean-style grilled beef. Try *yaki-onigiri*, a delicious grilled rice ball. (If you don't want your rice balls grilled, just ask for plain *onigiri*.) *Yaki-tori* is grilled chicken, a popular Japanese shish kebab. However, it's easy to overindulge and be presented with a bill for ¥3,000. Prices range from ¥100 to ¥200 per stick, so keep track.

Robatayaki are similar to *yakitori* restaurants, since both feature grilled food. *Yakitori-ya* only sell shish kebab, while the variety of cuisine at a *robatayaki* restaurant is cooked on a large grill. If you subscribe to the stereotype that the Japanese are a reserved people, a night at a rowdy *robatayaki* restaurant will change your point of view forever.

At night, look for food stands called *yatai*, which offer anything from *rāmen* to *yakitori* to *tako-yaki* (octopus chunks in steamed dough). Some places in Japan, such as Fukuoka's Nakasu area, are renowned for the quality and selection of their *yatai*.

Sushi

Sushi is too expensive to make a meal out of if you are on a budget, but you can usually order a few pieces as a snack. *Sashimi*, sliced raw fish, is more expensive. Some fast-food sushi shops near stations are quite affordable.

Sukiyaki and Shabu-Shabu

These are expensive meat dishes. The first is cooked in front of you and the second is boiled in soup in a big pot. Tasty, but usually beyond the daily price range of most hitchhikers. Save up and spend one night at a good *shabu-shabu* restaurant. It's well worth it. Expect to pay ¥4,000 for two.

Snack Pubs

Occasionally you will see signs with the word "snack" above the door. Never, never go into these places. First-time travelers in Japan, and I was one, often assume that an establishment called a "snack" will serve snacks. Only later, with wallets much lighter, do they realize that in Japan "snack" means "small hostess bar charging more for a glass of beer and a plate of peanuts than you would spend for an entire keg of beer back home." Avoid any establishment that boasts the word "snack"—unless, of course, someone else is paying.

Accommodations

The room you sleep in at night will be your biggest single expense as a hitchhiker. In this chapter I will review the different types of accommodations available and the general price range of each. I will also give you a couple of devious tricks to help you sleep for cheap and even (occasionally) for free.

As a hitchhiker, you have an advantage. The people who stop to give you a ride will also help you find accommodations if you ask them politely. I have had people search out inns and small bed-and-breakfasts, and even comparison-shop for me.

The first thing to know is that Japanese hotels and inns generally charge *per person*, not by the room. If one person pays ¥5,000 for a room, two people will be charged ¥10,000 for the same room. Business hotels do offer slight discounts. A single might be ¥6,000 and a double ¥8,000, but the savings are still minimal. The exception to this is love hotels, which charge both by the room and by the hour; love hotels are the best bargain for couples traveling together.

In most Japanese-style inns, at most youth hostels, and even the cheaper business hotels, you will be expected to bathe or shower at night (just before supper is the usual pattern). In the morning you may not have access to hot water. In love hotels and in hotel rooms with private baths, however, you can take your shower or bath anytime you like.

Camping

This is the best-kept secret in Japan and the key to successful budget travel. There are more than 900 public and private campsites throughout Japan, and the number continues to grow. Unfortunately, very few Western travelers are aware of this. Camping is the most overlooked form of Japanese lodging available. We don't think of Japan as a "camping country." Yet there is a whole network of well-kept, inexpensive, conveniently located campsites just waiting to be discovered.

Almost every popular beach area, wind-swept cape, or national park has a campsite; most towns or cities have at least one located within its boundaries. Many Japanese campsites are deep in the back country, though still near enough to a national highway to make them ideal for hitchhikers. By hitchhiking and camping, you can travel for *half* of what other travelers pay. Even better, most public campsites are free, and the private ones are inexpensive. Most are in the ¥500–¥1,000-per-night range. Most campsites between mid-July and mid-August are very crowded, and finding space might be difficult.

The general term for campsites is Camp-jō, pronounced *kyampu-jō*. More and more campsites in Japan are upgrading to attract families in camper-vans, and they add the term "auto" in front of the name to promote this fact. In all but a few, rare cases you don't need a vehicle to stay at an auto camp. Campsites are also called "travel villages," or *ryokō mura*. In Japan, municipally run public campsites are very basic—just quiet, well-kept lawns in the country with a couple of toilets (and sometimes not even that). In most private campsites—and in well-run public ones—you pay two separate fees: a per-person "entrance fee" and another one for a place to put up your tent. Typical charges would be ¥200 per person to enter and another ¥600 for a space, which would mean that two people with their own tent would pay ¥1,000 for a night's lodging. It doesn't get much cheaper.

Fee-charging campsites usually have everything you need, including showers, rain shelters, kitchens with coin-fed propane stoves, and sometimes small shops. Some campsites rent tents for ¥800–¥1500; these tents are usually already standing, saving you time and effort. Comfortable cabin-style bungalows, capable of sleeping five or six people, may be available as well for ¥1,000–¥2,000. In some upscale campsites, deluxe bungalows may cost as much as ¥10,000 a night. Having your own tent, though, provides greater flexibility and security; you can camp for free along secluded beaches or mountain trails. I *strongly* advise a small, self-standing dome-style tent. If you do pitch a tent on the beach, make sure it's above the high-tide mark. Unfortunately, most beaches in Japan not used for swimming are rarely cleaned and can be filthy, especially if they face open ocean.

Many of the most scenic areas are full of tourists during the day. However, bring your tent, wait for the busloads to leave, and you will have the place to yourself—sinks and toilets included. When evening falls, pitch your tent, or simply unroll your sleeping bags under one of the conveniently provided shelters and enjoy the fresh air. I have slept under ferry-port shelters as well, but the early morning ferry arrivals can leave you groggy all day.

Unfortunately, the JNTO information sheet *Camping in Japan* lists only 32 campsites out of the hundreds available. However, the various itineraries in Part II of this guide list over a hundred campsites in Japan. I have included directions, fees, telephone numbers, and information such as whether the campsites have tent rentals and/or bungalows available.

Many campsites have very short seasons, sometimes only from July to August. But if you show up in the off-season and are quiet about it, you can stay for free. Of course, no tent rentals or other services will be available during the off-season, so bring your own water, flashlight, and—if you are planning to head deep into the countryside—a portable stove and cooking utensils. Be aware that camping in national parks outside of designated areas is prohibited.

Youth Hostels

Youth hostels are some of the cheapest lodgings available. Many of Japan's 350+ hostels are located in remote, beautiful locations—temples, shrines, or in cottages high amid mountain passes, where they are often the only lodgings available. Hostels are good sources for travel information; many arrange transportation and organize outings for guests. Hostels have no maximum age limit, but they do have a minimum age of four. Most are in the ¥3,000-per-night price range.

Note: All lodging prices given in this guidebook are for *members*. If you do not have a Youth Hostel Membership—either Japanese or international—you will have to pay the extra ¥600. Six stamps entitle you to a Japan Youth Hostel Card. If you are certain that you will spend at least six nights in Japanese hostels, skip the welcome stamps and purchase a card outright for ¥2,800. The best strategy is to arrange an International Youth Hostel Membership Card in your own country before you head out.

When asking for directions, remember to use the Japanese pronunciation: *yū-su ho-su-te-ru*. Many people in Japan are not familiar with youth hostels, so you may get some puzzled looks—especially from older people. The hostel movement is still fairly new in Japan. The word "youth" (*yū-su*) is sometimes used to describe hostels. The English letters "YH" usually appear on signs.

The Japanese Youth Hostel Association publishes an annual handbook that lists every youth hostel in Japan, with helpful photographs of each hostel and some rudimentary English to help explain the entries. They also have a free English *Youth Hostels Map of Japan*, a good, compact map that can be used for charting your basic travel course. It lists 268 of the more than 350 hostels across Japan, and it gives addresses, phone numbers, and key information. Make sure you get a copy, even if you don't get the Japanese handbook. To get the *Youth Hostel Handbook* (and free map), send ¥580 and your request to:

> Japan Youth Hostels Hoken Kaikan
> 1-2 Sadohara-chō, Ichigaya
> Shinjuku-ku, Tokyo 162
> Tel. 03-3288-1417

To order internationally, you will have to include at least nine IRCs to cover the postage and the cost of the handbook. (Don't send international money orders or traveler's checks for ¥580 because it will cost more than that to cash them.) This can be very expensive, depending on the charge for an IRC in your country, so you may want to wait and pick one up when you get to Japan. If you call ahead, they may be able to send one to the first hostel you are planning to visit.

Hostel Meals, Hours, and Regulations   Breakfast at Japanese youth hostels is served between 7:00 A.M. and 8:00 A.M. and costs ¥450–¥650. It is usually a good idea to order a hostel breakfast if you are in a small town or outlying region, because few restaurants will offer any alternative. Supper at youth hostels is served between 6:00 P.M. and 7:00 P.M. and costs ¥650–¥1,250.

Japanese hostels expect travelers to adhere to hostel schedules. If you are planning on having supper at the hostel you are expected to check in before 6:30 P.M. If you do not plan on having supper, you are still expected to check in before 8:00 P.M. Any later and you really should apologize profusely, and after 10:00 P.M. you will probably find yourself locked out. Even if you are not going to be late, avoid showing up unannounced at a hostel. You should always give some advance warning, even if it's only ten minutes before you arrive.

Quiet hours at hostels are 10:00 P.M.–6:30 A.M. Generally speaking, hostels are dormitories, with all that implies. Many Japanese youth hostels have large communal tatami rooms, and you may find it hard to sleep, especially when all the eager hikers and assorted health nuts start packing and moving out in the wee hours of the morning. Thus, the single most important survival item needed for staying in hostels in Japan is a set of foam earplugs (*mimi-sen*); any Japanese drugstore (*kusuri-ya*) will carry them. Checkout time is usually before 10:00 A.M. and most are closed between 10:00 A.M. and 3:00 P.M. for cleaning and maintenance.

Sound regimented? It is. If you don't show up after having made a reservation, or fail to cancel more than 26 (yes, 26) hours ahead of time, you will be charged a ¥1,000 penalty in absentia, which will catch up to you later when you try to check in at another hostel. As a hitchhiker, you may only be able to give a day's notice at most; only call when you are certain you will be staying.

Peak seasons for Japanese youth hostels occur during Japanese school holidays: New Year's, mid-March, late April to mid-May, and from mid-July through August. Autumn and early spring are reasonably good times to stay at hostels if you want to avoid the noisy crowds of schoolchildren. Many hostels close during winter, especially in Hokkaido.

Capsule Hotels

With rooms the size of coffins and baths the size of gymnasiums, vending machines that dispense toothpaste, socks, and fresh underwear, a capsule hotel is a unique travel opportunity which you should try. Most capsule hotels are for men only, though in the Tohoku and Kyushu itineraries of this guidebook I have listed two capsules that have a floor reserved for women.

Many capsules are on the second or third floor of a building, often right downtown near the night-life district. Most capsules cost between ¥3,000 and ¥4,000 for a berth per night. Drunk businessmen and dodgy characters seem to make up a good deal of the clientele. When asking for directions, always pronounce it the Japanese way: *kapu-se-ru ho-te-ru*.

I have included phone numbers, but I do not advise calling ahead. First of all, you don't need reservations for a capsule hotel, and second, they may not welcome foreign guests at first. Hearing a foreign accent on the phone will just put them off and you may get a brusque, "Sorry, all full," even though capsules are almost *never* full. Instead, just show up and smile and ask for a capsule. The phone numbers I have given for capsule hotels are only if you have trouble finding them and need a Japanese person to call to get directions for you.

The check-in procedure can be confusing. Upon entering, take off your shoes and put on a pair of plastic slippers. Some owners are dubious about letting foreigners stay, and showing that you at least understand enough to take your shoes off in the entranceway will improve your chances. You will get a key to a locker; place your valuables here since the capsules do not lock. You will also get a pair of pajamas. You may have to ask for the *eru-eru* (LL, or extra large) size. After you check in, you can go right back outside, but while in the capsule you are expected to wear the pajamas and leave your clothes in the locker.

Most capsule hotels have a large sauna and Roman-style bath, usually on a separate floor. You will have to change again into a light cotton bathrobe (*yukata*) which you should tie left over right. (The other way is how corpses are dressed.) Take off all your clothes before entering the final bath area. There will be baskets for your *yukata*, and remember, wash and soap and rinse yourself off before climbing into the communal tub.

Having soaked and steamed and cleaned yourself you can now retire for the night in your space-age capsule sleeping unit. Each capsule is about the size of a train berth and comes equipped with a television, light dimmer, alarm clock, and a small, red emergency button. (Try not to hit that last item.)

Love Hotels

For couples traveling in Japan, love hotels are the *real* money savers since they charge by the room, not by the person. They require no reservations and you can check in late at night. Two people at a seedy business hotel may spend ¥9,000 between them. Had they spent the night at a love hotel they could have spent as little as ¥6,000—roughly the same as staying at a youth hostel.

Love hotels are usually are lit in purple and pink with signs in that sexy romantic language we call English. (In Japan, English has the same allure that French does in North America.) Most love hotels are concentrated either in downtown night-life districts or out of town on the highway. If you are hitching rides out in the middle of nowhere and you come across a bizarre purple castle called Hotel Elegance, with a discreet, hidden entrance—voilà. You have just discovered a love hotel.

Outside of every love hotel will be a red "X" or a green "OK," to indicate if all rooms are full. Almost every love hotel operates on a 10:00 P.M.–10:00 A.M. time schedule for overnight stays. If you enter *before* 10:00 P.M. you will have to pay extra. Occasionally, love hotels do use other time limits; always check the sign outside for a posted time.

You will usually have to leave before 10:00 A.M. the next morning. Be careful, because coming in too early or leaving too late can almost double the room charge.

Love hotels are meant for discreet rendezvous. After you enter through a side door, maybe some flaps, you will see a display panel with pictures of the rooms available. Below each room you will see two prices. The cheaper price is the "rest" rate of two or three hours, the other is the "stay" rate for overnight.

If a room's picture is lit up, it is available. Pick the cheapest one and press the button. Sometimes a key will drop out of a slot, but usually all that will happen is that the light illuminating the picture will go off. Remember the room number and then go up the stairs or in the elevator. A light above the doorway to your room will be blinking. A few minutes after you enter, a phone will ring. Answer it with a mumbled *moshi, moshi* (hello) and say *tomarimasu* (overnight). A few minutes after the phone call there will be a knock on the side door. Find the small opening in the door and lower it. A pair of hands will slide a tray in. Put your money in it, collect your change, and you're set for the night. Occasionally you will pay by pneumatic tube instead, which is a lot of fun. Put your money inside, close the gate, press the green button and *whoosh*, your money will be sucked away. A few moments later, the canister will return with your change inside.

The next morning, the phone will usually ring ten minutes or so before checkout time. A woman will say good morning and ask if you used any of the food from the refrigerator. (If it is a computer-locked refrigerator she will already know, so don't lie.) If you haven't taken anything from the refrigerator and your account is settled, you will hear the door click as it is unlocked and you can go. In some love hotels you don't pay anything until morning, by the same procedure. You will soon get the hang of it.

Two other variations of love hotels exist. One has a standard lobby just like a regular hotel, except that the front desk is blocked with frosted glass and you deal only with a pair of hands. These places are harder to get into because they may screen out undesirables (which sometimes include foreigners). A third kind of love hotel—and a blessing for hitchhikers—is the drive-in, usually encountered on highways in the countryside or on the edge of town. These places are two stories high, with each room located above a parking space. There are no photos to choose from and often no lobby of any kind. Hitchhikers can just walk in and go up the stairs.

Outside, near the stairs on the ground floor, you will find a small light that will show either green (available) or red (occupied). Make sure you switch this light to red before you go up, otherwise a Japanese couple, seeing no car in the spot and the light still green, will try to enter your room.

Love hotels are fun, clean, kitschy, spacious, and affordable. You can squeeze three or four people in and *really* save money, but if the management notices they will charge extra. Two men or two women can stay at a love hotel; there is no social taboo against this sort of thing. The only problem is that there is only one bed and the baths always have large windows, so unless you are *very* good friends, you may find it awkward to split a room. Once you become used to love hotels you won't want to go anywhere else. You will come across Mickey Mouse rooms (Hotel France, Kagoshima), Undersea Bubble rooms (Beppu Love Hotel), and rooms that are best left to the imagination. After a hard day of eating exhaust and hitching rides, why not enjoy a little hilarious luxury?

The Japan Inn Group
Make sure you ask your JNTO office to provide an English booklet of *Japanese Inn Group* addresses, directions, and maps. This association of around 70 inns across Japan welcomes foreign guests. The rates average ¥4,000 a night without meals. These inns are not a chain; they vary in size and decor, and many are traditionally Japanese in style. Most of them accept American Express or VISA as well.

Business Hotels
Business hotels are usually clustered around train stations.

They provide a room, a bed, a unit bath, a *yukata* (don't forget—left over right), and a coin-operated pornographic television. Toothbrushes and shampoo are available through vending machines. Most business hotels are clean, but some are surprisingly dilapidated.

Business hotels range from large chains to station-side, threadbare family operations. Room rates can run anywhere from ¥4,000 to ¥7,000 for a single, with most in the ¥6,000 range. Check-in is between 5:00 P.M. and 7:00 P.M. Ask the last lift of the day to help you arrange a room. The Green Hotel, Washington, Tokyū, and Sun Route business-hotel chains offer Western-style rooms.

Business hotels are convenient—every town will have them, all you have to do is find the main station—but they are not the bargain they are made out to be. A couple will stay at a love hotel for less, and a single traveler will stay at a capsule hotel for almost half the charge. Camping, of course, is cheaper still. Instead of spending ¥5,000 every night for a boring little box of a room, camp out or stay in youth hostels instead and use the money you save for one night at a top-notch, traditional Japanese ryokan.

Kokumin-shukusha

Anytime you arrive at a destination before 4:00 P.M. ask for directions to the town office (*yakuba*) or city hall (*shiyakusho*). Walk in, present yourself, smile, and ask if there are any *kokumin-shukusha* (public lodges) available. Since many of these lodges are located in beautiful natural surroundings, town officials are very proud of them; you should be able to arrange a lift out to the nearest spot.

Kokumin-shukusha are hyped as the secret to budget travel in Japan. This isn't exactly true. Although the ¥6,000–¥7,000 per night is more than a hostel or lower-level business hotel, the rustic location and the meals of seasonally prepared delicacies make these a good option every once in a while. Please note, meals can cost an additional ¥1,000–¥3,000. You must call well ahead to make reservations, unless accompanied by someone from the town hall. In peak season, you will find it difficult to find space.

Note: In Japanese the name is not broken up, but *kokumin-shukusha* is a mouthful, so I have added a hyphen in the middle, where the pause is most natural: *kokumin-shukusha*. Don't pronounce it "koku-minshuku-sha," because people will think that you are talking about a specific *minshuku* and not a people's lodge.

Minshuku

Minshuku are family-run inns, less grand then traditional ryokan. You will be expected to lay out your own futons in a *minshuku* and put them away again before you leave. *Minshuku* range from dilapidated station-side dives to small traditional places in quiet rural locations. Where business hotels are strictly functional—and usually Western in style—*minshuku* are more enjoyable, and they cost roughly the same. Most *minshuku* prices include an evening meal and breakfast. Prices usually range from ¥6,000 to ¥8,000 per night but in the countryside you can find smaller *minshuku* for ¥4,000 a night, less if you don't want meals.

Ryokan

Ryokan are Japanese traditional inns, and they can get very expensive. Many are in the ¥10,000 price range, and some run much, much higher.

If you get to the end of your hitchhiking journey with extra money in your pocket and an urge to squander it, you could do worse than to check into an expensive ryokan. Ryokan usually serve delicious seasonal meals, and many are associated with a hot spring (*onsen*).

Ryokan have fewer and larger rooms than do hotels. Typically, a ryokan will have 20 large tatami rooms capable of sleeping groups as well as couples. Unfortunately, ryokan in hot-spring or resort areas are geared more for groups and do not like to rent to single travelers (or even couples during holidays or on the weekend). If you get turned down, it may not be because you are a foreigner, but because they want to save their rooms for larger parties—or for people who have made reservations far in advance.

Maid service provides green tea and lays out and puts away your futon for you. Your maid may even bring your meal to your room. *Yukata* are provided and can be worn around the ryokan, to dinner, and out on the street. If it is cold, a heavier outer jacket, called a *tanzen*, will be provided to wear over the *yukata*. Don't wear the *tanzen* by itself, but only over the *yukata*.

As in most establishments, take off your shoes and put on slippers when you enter, and remember to step up out of your shoes onto the raised floor without touching your sock feet to the area where shoes are worn. When inside the ryokan, take off your slippers when you come to tatami mats, and walk on them only in bare feet or socks.

Schedules are fairly rigid in ryokan. Check in between 5:00 P.M. and 7:00 P.M. if you want supper. You will eat at a set time—usually between 6:00 P.M. and 7:00 P.M.—either in your room or in a dining hall, where your place and meal will be assigned ahead of time. Checkout is usually very early. Expect to be chased out of your room by the maid at 8:00 A.M. just in time for breakfast.

Onsen and Sentō

Many ryokan are connected with hot-spring spas, called *onsen*. Outdoor hot springs are called *rotenburo*. Do not confuse either with public baths, called *sentō*. A night in a traditional hot-spring ryokan is just about as good as life gets. Many *onsen* areas are their own ramshackle towns filled with steam vents and visitors wandering about at night in *yukata* and wooden clogs. The symbol for *onsen* is a stylized round tub with three wisps of steam rising from it. The atlas labels *onsen* areas in red, with the *onsen* symbol ♨ beside the name.

Shukubō

Shukubō (temple lodgings) were once offered throughout Japan for pilgrims, mendicant monks, and solo travelers. Some youth hostels are beside or inside Buddhist temples, but except for the tourist-intense Kyoto area, temple lodging is becoming scarce. Approaching temple priests requires tact and respect. If you are lucky you may run into a very friendly temple family who will welcome you in. If not, be gracious about it and move on. For every ten temples I have approached, nine have said no. The key is to state that you are interested in Japanese culture. Say "I am on a pilgrimage. May I stay at your temple tonight." If you feel uncomfortable about making such a claim, think of it this way: Life is a pilgrimage, and we are all travelers on the same road.

The key expression whenever you are trying to convince someone in Japan to do you a favor is *onegai shimasu* (please take care of me). Whenever I talk to a temple priest I use this phrase liberally.

Temple charges range from free (rare indeed) to ¥9,000 a night. Throughout the itineraries in this guidebook, I have tried to include as many Buddhist temples and Shinto shrines as possible that offer lodgings to travelers. One I highly recommend is Konegayama Jinja shrine on Kinkasan island in Tohoku. (See Chapter 12 for details.)

Many Japanese youth hostels are inside Buddhist temples and Shinto shrines. Temples are marked on maps and guidebooks with a reversed swastika 卍. Shrines are marked with a torii 开, a gateway arch that looks like a side view of a picnic table.

Accommodations—Problems and Solutions

It is difficult to make hotel reservations when you are hitch-hiking. You never know how far you will get in any one day, or whether you will come across a place you want to stay in and explore, or when someone will invite you in to stay at their home. So although Japanese hotels can get irate if you don't call ahead first, I really don't advise making any reservations more than a few hours ahead of time. Japanese inns and hotels don't like unexpected drop-in guests. Love hotels and capsules expect them. You can ask the last ride of the day to help, but sometimes you will be on your own.

If you have just appeared blindly off the street, you may find yourself politely rejected. Owners of small, family-run inns will often tell a foreigner that they have no rooms for the night simply because they are uncomfortable with having a foreign guest. This is not exactly racism, though it can feel like it.

One reason *minshuku* owners are reluctant to let foreigners stay is because they are worried that the foreigners will not want to sleep on a futon or eat Japanese food. It helps if you take your shoes off and step into guest slippers when you first come in to reassure them that you understand the mysterious Japanese ways that we foreigners are assumed to be ignorant of. If you still get turned down, look for the number of shoes in the entrance-way and shoe-racks. If they really don't have any rooms available, they should have stacks of shoes crammed in. If not, then the innkeeper is just nervous. The key is make him or her stop being nervous. Failing that, make them feel guilty. Do not get angry and start demanding your rights. This kind of behavior will get you nowhere.

Back-up Plan

Sigh. Smile sadly. (Being able to smile in a wistful yet sadly disappointed manner is an indispensable skill in Japan. It will get you much further than anger or indignation.) Turn to leave, hesitate, sigh again. Say *dōmo* . . . *go-shinsetsu ni. Sumimasen, dōmo.* (Thank you . . . You are kind. Sorry to bother you. Thanks.) And then, with great sincerity, give them a pin from your country and turn to leave again. The guilt should be so overbearing, they will give in and rent you a room.

Common
Hitchhiking Problems

Aside from the language challenges, here are seven common problems you are likely to face during your trip.

1. Lost and Found

The Problem: Drivers, especially older, paternal types, will often assume that you are lost, and instead of driving you farther down the road, they will take you to the nearest train station instead. Or even worse, they will take you to the nearest police station.

The Solution: Stop it before it happens. Never assume that when a Japanese person smiles and nods that they have really understood you. If you have a definite goal you are aiming for, a town or an intersection, you should point it out on a map. If not, keep repeating "Just down this road, please," until you are sure they understand. Keep your eyes peeled, and if they turn off the road, immediately sit up, look concerned, and say once again, "I want to stay on this road." Don't panic, though, because usually they are taking a shortcut instead.

2. Adopted!

The Problem: In Japan it is quite common to decide things for others, especially those below you (such as freshmen, lower-ranked employees, younger people) or those for whom you are responsible, without consulting them first. If they do tell you, it is often to inform you *after* the fact, when all the arrangements have been made. Thus, the driver and the other Japanese passengers may decide that another destination is "better" for you. This has only happened to me a few times, but it can be very annoying.

The Solution: No matter how persistent and bothersome they are being, keep in mind that they truly are concerned for you and that they sincerely think that they are keeping your best interest at heart. Second, although the stubbornly independent Western mind rankles at allowing outside pressure—hear them out. They *may have* a better idea. Sometimes they are planning on taking you on a short sightseeing tour. While hitching on the coast of Yamagata, I was shown an entire mountainside carved with Buddhist imagery, not listed in any guidebook. However, if they are planning to take you off your path or into an urban zone, you had better act fast. As soon as they leave the road you are on check exactly what is going on. If you don't like it, simply tell them thank you, but you have to meet a friend in the direction you were going.

3. Center Blues

The Problem: Drivers do not take you off your route or to a police station, and they sincerely want to drop you off at a good hitchhiking spot. Unfortunately, they think the best place to drop you off is in the nearest city center. This has happened to me so often that I have almost come to expect it. They really are trying their best to look out for you. It's just that they assume that there are more cars in the city center and if you get stranded there is shelter and public transportation available.

The Solution: You must always keep in mind that most Japanese people don't really understand how hitchhiking works. Be specific when it comes time to be dropped off: You want an open stretch of road outside the city limits. In the West, hitchhikers really have to take what they can get and ride only as far as the driver is heading; in Japan if you don't like the location where they want to drop you off, just ask them politely and they will take you to a better spot. No one will resent your request.

4. Shady Characters and ESP

The Problem: Occasionally, you may feel uneasy about the person who has pulled over, though I have only turned down two rides in five years. One was with a Western woman outside of Sapporo who was so snippy and rude in the few seconds it took me to put my backpack in the back seat ("Hurry up!") that I promptly pulled my pack out and waved her on.

The Solution: If you ever have any uneasy feeling, follow your instincts. Step back from the car, bow, say, "Thank you, I'm sorry," and then act as if they don't exist, a technique common in much of Asia. You simply make undesirable people invisible. In Japan, if a shady person is trying to cajole you into accepting a ride or is simply annoying you in some manner, do not make eye contact or acknowledge their existence. They will eventually go away.

5. Secondhand Cancer

The Problem: More than 60 percent of Japanese men smoke, and they do so at the dinner table, in the office, and in the car. As a hitchhiker you will spend a lot of time cooped up in smoke-filled vehicles, and you cannot afford to accept rides only with nonsmokers, because you will have eliminated more than half your rides. Even if the driver doesn't smoke, the odds are that one of the passengers does. If you are a nonsmoker, the secondhand smoke will become a major problem. In fact, I would say that this is the only really negative aspect about hitchhiking in Japan.

The Solution: The notion of "nonsmokers' rights" is only now catching on in Japan, and most Japanese genuinely do not realize that their smoke is bothering you. True, if you ask him to, the driver will put out his cigarette—but only to be polite. He will probably resent not being allowed to smoke in his own car. Instead, take an indirect approach. If he does ask you if it is all right if he smokes, say, "Yes, yes, please go ahead." Then discreetly cough. Then, ask him if it is all right if you roll down the window a crack. Cough again. Roll the window a little farther down. When he begins to get concerned, tell him you have an allergy to smoke. He will of course stop smoking, but the key here is never to ask him directly.

6. Breaking Up Is Hard to Do

The Problem: As a hitchhiker you put your Japanese driver in a potentially difficult position. He or she might feel obligated to help you or stay with you long past what is necessary. This won't happen if you are being dropped off along the road, although it will sometimes manifest itself in drivers who feel obligated to stop other vehicles and try to arrange your next ride. The real problem comes when you are taken to some specific place. For example, if your ride takes you to a famous shrine or scenic point, he or she may feel they have to wait until you have finished viewing it and then chauffeur you somewhere else after.

The Solution: If your driver is an outgoing sort who insists on taking you out or showing you around, by all means enjoy the hospitality. But if you feel an awkward or prolonged silence—and it will be obvious, trust me—take it upon yourself to let them get on with their life. Take a big breath, smile, pause, and say *ja* . . . (Well. . .) and shake your driver's hand as you bow. Thank them sincerely several times—in English is fine. Don't quickly spring a "Thanks, bye!" on them without a proper pause.

In Japan, it is crucial to be polite and to thank your hosts for their kindness; this is only done properly when it is not rushed.

7. The Hitchhiking Blues

The Problem: "I am tired of waiting!" At least with a train or a bus you know exactly when your next ride will be.

The Solution: If you are starting to feel impatient, I urge you to start timing your rides. You don't mind waiting 20 minutes for a bus, because you know when the bus will be coming. But waiting 20 minutes for a ride feels longer simply because you never really know when a car will stop. In the remoter areas, where buses run only a few times a day, or where train lines don't even exist, hitchhiking is actually the most efficient way to travel. If you ever do get hopelessly stranded, simply flag down the next car that passes and tell them that you are lost and need to get to the nearest train station or bus stop. But make sure you really are stranded before you panic. It almost never happens. Hang in there and remember the mantra: Eventually, someone *will* stop.

Hitchhiking Itineraries

These itineraries are designed to be used with the Shobunsha atlas recommended earlier. Maps in this guidebook provide only a general overview of the routes described; for detailed highway numbers and routes, the itineraries should be cross-referenced with the atlas. Most of your hitchhiking will take place along national highways (*kokudō*), so I have not bothered labeling them as such—they are simply "highways." Highway 7 would mean National Highway 7. I have, however, identified prefectural highways (*kendō*), as in Prefectural Highway 241. Remember that the numbering of prefectural highways is inconsistent. To avoid confusion, I have described prefectural highways as well as given their numbers, and where possible I have also given the local name for the road, which is how people living in the area would refer to it.

Signs

The signs in Japanese train stations, when written in English, do not include hyphens or the suffix *-eki* (station). Kitakumamoto-eki appears as Kitakumamoto. As a hitchhiker, you will be *speaking* station names, so it is essential that you be familiar with the suffixes listed in Appendix 1. The train stations and bus stops that I have given are primarily as reference points for your drivers. If a campsite is a five-minute ride north of Ōnuma-eki, the station will help you locate the campsite.

MAP SYMBOLS

▬▬▬▬▬	national highways	◎ city
════════	prefectural highways	◉ town
▬▬▬▷	expressways	○ village

Hokkaido

With its open vistas, grassy fields, rolling mountains, cattle ranches, and ghost towns, Hokkaido even looks like the American Midwest. Hokkaido was developed along an American model and under American influences, such as that of the agriculturist Dr. William Smith, the first president of Hokkaido University. Hokkaido, the second largest island in Japan, was not formally colonized until after the Meiji Restoration of 1868, and not completely opened by settlers until the 1880s—at about the same time that the American West was booming and Dodge City was at its peak.

Make sure you bring a tent. Hokkaido is the best place in Japan for camping, whether bedding down at designated campsites or simply bivouacked on a trail or at a scenic lookout after dark. By hitchhiking and camping, you will be able to cover more ground at less cost in Hokkaido than in anywhere else in Japan. Hokkaido also has the most youth hostels in Japan, many in stunning natural locations. However, more remote hostels close down between the end of October and the beginning of June.

Hokkaido's climate is similar Scandinavia's; the brutal winter arrives early and stays late. Summer is the best time to hitch-hike in Hokkaido; autumn weather is wildly unpredictable, and early spring can be drab and drizzly. The good news is that Hokkaido has no rainy season.

Hokkaido is also one of the few places in Japan where Japanese hitchhikers can sometimes be seen, usually college students or mountain hikers. The area's wide, open, lonely rides make for terrific hitchhiking.

The mountains of Hokkaido are home to a variety of bear species, and you should take any warnings seriously. Buy a small bell to attach to your pack or walking stick and never approach a bear. If you meet a bear, do not run away because this may elicit a chase response in the bear. If the bear is not aware of your presence, back away slowly. If the bear is aware, walk away while speaking in a clear voice and slowly waving your arms. The word for bear is *kuma*. So, if someone comes charging out of a mountain path screaming "*Kuma! Kuma!*" you should consider changing course.

KEY TO MAP

1. Hakodate	18. Wakkanai	36. Iwaobetsu-mura
2. Ōnuma	19. Rishiri-tō	37A. Shiretoko-hantō
3. Oshamanbe	20. Rebun-tō	37. Kamuiwakka-yunotaki
4. Usu-zan	21. Sōya-misaki	
5. Shōwa-shinzan	22. Monbetsu	38. Rausu
6. Tōyako	23. Yūbetsu	39. Bihoro
7. Yōtei-zan	24. Saromako	40A. Abashiri Kawayu-sen Highway
8. Shikotsuko	25. Engaru	
9. Eniwa-dake	26. Rubeshibe	40. Kussharoko
10. Shin-Chitose-kūkō	27. Kamikawa	41. Teshikaga
11. Sapporo	28. Sōunkyō	42. Akanko
12. Ishikari	29. Kuro-dake	43. Shihoro
13. Rumoi	30. Asahi-dake	44. Shikaoi
14. Haboro	31. Asahikawa	45. Shimizu
15. Yagishiri-tō and Teuri-tō	32. Notoroko	46. Obihiro
	33. Abashiri	47. Hiroo
16. Toyotomi	34. Shari	48. Erimo-misaki
17. Sarobetsu	35. Utoro	49. Erimo

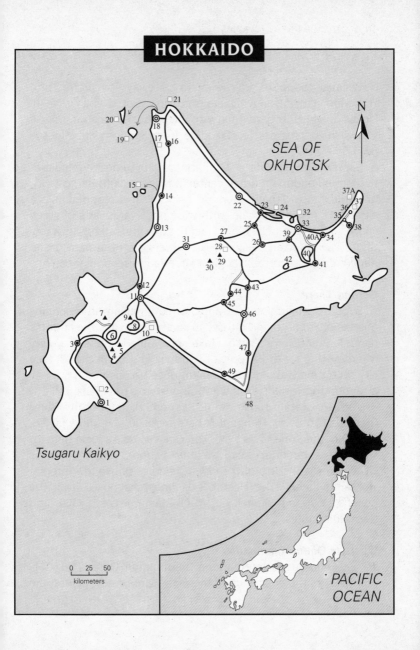

HOKKAIDO

SEA OF OKHOTSK

N

Tsugaru Kaikyo

PACIFIC OCEAN

0   25   50
kilometers

SAPPORO

Because Sapporo is the main gateway for flights into Hokkaido, I'm introducing Sapporo first. But if you arrive in Hokkaido via Hakodate, then skip ahead to that section now. If you wish to progress to Hakodate from Sapporo directly, see p. 117.

Sapporo (population 1.7 million) is Hokkaido's administrative capital and main urban center. It is Japan's fifth largest city, but unlike most Japanese cities, it doesn't feel crowded. It is a city built on a grand scale, with wide boulevards, lots of green space, and straight city blocks laid out in a grid, all of which testify to its American designer. The streets are even named and numbered consecutively. Logical street addresses? In Japan?

Getting There

Sapporo's main domestic and international airport is actually outside of Sapporo, in Chitose, 40 km to the south. The airport's name is Shin-Chitose-kūkō. Make sure you add the suffix -*kūkō* when looking for the airport or you may end up in the Chitose city center instead. I missed a flight once because I did not pay attention to the suffixes and got off one stop too soon.

The *kaisoku* train runs from JR Sapporo-eki (station) to Shin-Chitose-kūkō every 15 minutes between 8:00 A.M. and 7:00 P.M. The 40-minute ride costs ¥940. You can also take a local train for slightly less, but it takes over an hour. Sapporo's other airport is Okadama-kūkō, north of the city; it handles only a few internal Hokkaido flights. The Hokuto bus line runs buses from the Zennikkū Sapporo Branch out to Okadama. It costs ¥300 and takes 30 minutes.

Where to Obtain Information

The **Lilac Paseo International Information Office** (Tel. 011-213-5062) in the north side of the main Sapporo-eki behind the cafeteria/coffee shop has English materials and maps, and is open daily until 5:00 P.M. Alternatively, the information offices in the MN Building are better stocked and equipped for English visitors. Short-term travelers should head to the **Plaza "i" Information Center** (Tel. 011-211-3678) on the first floor of the MN Building, open Monday–Friday, 9:00 A.M.–5:00 P.M. They can arrange youth hostel memberships and provide hiking information and maps. To get to the MN building, first go to the clocktower (*tokeidai*), south of the station, about halfway to the Susukino district, on your left. The clocktower is small and easy to miss, but ask anybody for directions and they will be able to show you. The clocktower is a city landmark—it is the city's only surviving example of Russian architecture. The MN Building is across the street.

The **Sapporo International Communications Plaza** (Tel. 011-211-2105) is geared more toward long-term residents of Sapporo. It is on the third floor of the MN Building. They can supply information on hiking in the national parks as well. Visit both and stock up; once you hit the back roads, English material will not be available.

This is a good time to buy the atlas, a pocket English-Japanese/Japanese-English dictionary, and a copy of Paul Hunt's *Hiking in Japan*. In Sapporo, both the downtown Maruzen and Kinokuniya bookstores have English materials. Maruzen's selection is on the third floor and is more extensive than Kinokuniya's. The **Maruzen bookstore** (Tel. 011-241-7254) is near Mitsukoshi department store. It is daily open 10:00 A.M.–7:00 P.M. **Kinokuniya** (Tel. 011-231-2131) is near the wide Ōdōri Park boulevard, by the big TV tower. It is open daily 10:00 A.M.–10:00 P.M. (until 7:30 P.M. between April and August).

What to See and Do

Sapporo likes to consider itself one of the Three Great Brewery Cities in the world, along with Milwaukee and Munich.

Central Japan may be the land of saké, and southern Japan the land of *shōchū*, but here in Hokkaido it is beer that reigns supreme. Several breweries operate tours in Sapporo, with free samples included.

The venerable **Sapporo Brewery** runs a shuttle bus from the front of Gobankan Seibu department store (near Sapporo-eki) to its historic, red-brick brewery site. Founded in 1876, this is the oldest brewery in Japan. Tours run 8:40 A.M.–6:00 P.M. in June, July, and August, and 9:00 A.M.–5:00 P.M. during the rest of the year. Each 60–80-minute tour is free and includes samples at the end. The brewery is closed December 29–January 5. You could just show up, but they prefer that you call ahead (Tel. 011-731-4368). The tours are in Japanese, but if you can find nine other English speakers, they will try to arrange for an English-speaking guide.

Sapporo Brewery's arch-rival is **Kirin of Nagasaki**, which runs its own tour at their brewery in Chitose near Osatsu-eki on the Chitose Line. Stop on your way to or from the airport, if you like. Tours operate 10:00 A.M.–3:00 P.M. during the week, but close on Sundays, national holidays, and some Saturdays. The Kirin brewery also has a tropical dome housing thousands of orchids, over 200 kinds of tropical plants, and a garden of Hokkaido flora. The tropical dome is closed on the fourth Monday of each month. For more information call the brewery at 0123-24-5606. It is a 15-minute taxi ride from the airport to the Kirin brewery and tropical dome.

Suntory and Asahi breweries have their own tours as well, so if you work out the time schedule at the Sapporo tourist center you can make a circuit of breweries, enjoying free samples and comparing brands. It's a good way to spend an afternoon, though after the fourth tour your judgment may be slightly impaired.

If you would like an expansive—and expensive—**night view of Sapporo**, the Moiwayama Ropeway runs up Moiwayama (531 meters). The ropeway is southwest of the city and costs ¥1,300 round trip. Take the tram to the Fushimi-shōgakkō stop and walk west three blocks. You will come to a temple on your left, behind which the ropeway begins. Keep in mind, however, that the Hakodate night view is easier to get to and more impressive, so if you are on a tight budget and are planning a Hakodate trip anyway, save your night viewing for then.

Where to Stay

Near Sapporo-eki: Sapporo House Youth Hostel (Tel. 011-726-4235, 4236) is a seven-minute walk from the Nishi-dōri Kitaguchi exit of the main Sapporo-eki. When you leave this exit turn left (west) and walk three blocks. Turn left again and walk one block south. The hostel is a five-story Stalinist building that's hard to miss. It costs ¥2,670 per night and is closed December 31–January 1. Check in before 8:00 P.M. Curfews in effect. I really can't recommend staying here unless you are traveling alone and are absolutely strapped for cash.

The **Sapporo Washington Hotel I** (Tel. 011-251-3211) is across the street from Sapporo-eki. It has Japanese-style singles for ¥3,500 per night; Western-style rooms cost ¥4,000 per night. Breakfast is ¥600. In winter there is an additional ¥200 charge to cover heating costs. This is certainly one of the cheapest lodgings you will find, but be aware that Sapporo-eki is not in a very interesting or exciting area. After dark, the fun shifts south to the Susukino district. Don't go to the nearby Washington Hotel II by mistake; it costs much more.

The **Nakamura Ryokan** (Tel. 011-241-2111) is part of the Japanese Inn Group. It has single Japanese-style rooms at ¥7,000 per night and doubles for ¥13,000, without meals, plus tax. They accept American Express, VISA, and MasterCard. For people seeking a quieter place to stay, this is a good choice. It is a seven-minute walk from Sapporo-eki, near the Prefectural Government Office. From the station's main exit, cross the street and then walk west for three blocks (you will see the Washington

Hotel 1 on your way). After you pass the Sapporo Main Post Office, turn south. Three more blocks and you will pass the Hokkaido Prefectural Government Office building. Turn right on the next street and you will be at the ryokan. If you come to the botanical gardens, you've gone too far.

Susukino Entertainment District: Cross the open Ōdōri Park boulevard halfway to Susukino. (Ōdōri Park is Sapporo's main wide boulevard and the site of the city's Snow Festival.) A 25-minute walk south of Sapporo's main station takes you to the Susukino night-life district, where countless love hotels, most in the range of ¥6,000–¥8,000 per room overnight, beckon. (If you don't feel like walking, take the subway south two stops to the Susukino subway station.)

The **Sapporo International Inn Nada** (Tel. 011-551-5882) costs ¥9,000 for a single and ¥17,000 for a twin, which is a bit steep; from November to April, the rate drops to ¥7,210 and ¥13,596, respectively. It is to the west of the Susukino night-life district, about a ten-minute walk from the Susukino subway stop.

The **Susukino Green Hotel 3** (Tel. 011-511-7211) has singles for ¥8,000 per night; this price drops to ¥5,000 per night from October to April. It is two blocks south of the Susukino subway stop.

Note: Make sure you are in the Green Hotel 3. The other two are more expensive.

The **Sapporo Central Hotel** (Tel. 011-512-3121) is one block south and then west from the Susukino subway stop. It has singles for ¥6,000, but the management here does not warmly welcome foreign travelers. Go here only if you are desperate or have unusually thick skin.

One block north of the Central Hotel is the **Business Hotel Shinto** (Tel. 011-562-6611) which has twins only, for ¥10,300.

There are three capsule hotels in downtown Sapporo. The tourist offices can show you where these are located; otherwise, ask a nearby shopkeeper.

Niko Capsule (Tel. 011-231-2511) costs ¥3,000 per night; **Capsule Inn Sapporo** (Tel. 011-251-5571) costs ¥3,200 per night. Both of these capsule hotels are in Sapporo's center ward: Chūō-ku, Minami-3, near the Susukino district.

The **Capsule Inn Hokuō** (Tel. 011-531-2233) costs ¥4,400 per night, including breakfast. It is in Chūō-ku, Minami-6, Nishi-5 ward.

Escaping

You should be able to hitch in less than a day from Sapporo to Hakodate, via Shikotsuko. From downtown Sapporo take the subway south on the Nanboku-sen (line). The subway will emerge above ground; get off at Reienmae. Walk two blocks straight west and you will come to Highway 453. There will be an elementary school on the other side of the highway. On Highway 453 hitchhike south and with fingers crossed you should be at Shikotsuko within an hour.

Once at Shikotsuko, reverse the route back to reach Hakodate.

HAKODATE

At the southern tip of Hokkaido is the dusty, slightly seedy port town of Hakodate (population 307,000) whose strong Russian influence makes the city an interesting destination. The Russians were using Hakodate port as a landing base as far back as 1740; in 1854 Japan moved to counter Russian expansion by making Hakodate—like Nagasaki and Kobe—one of Japan's few open port cities. If you have to choose between spending time in Sapporo or Hakodate, pick Hakodate.

Where to Obtain Information

The **Hakodate Tourist Information Center** (Tel. 0138-27-3333) is located on the second floor of the Shashin Rekishikan photography museum in Motomachi Park (north of the Harisutosu Seikyōkai Russian Orthodox Church). The hours are 9:00 A.M.–7:00 P.M. April–October, and 9:00 A.M.–5:00 P.M. during the rest of the year. Another, smaller tourist center is in front of the station (Tel. 0138-23-5440).

What to See and Do

Hakodate attractions include the remains of a British-style, star-shaped fortress; syncretic Japanese-European architecture; streetcars; a Russian cemetery; a stately Russian Orthodox church; and the Chinese Chūka Kaikan (hall). The city is built on a bottleneck peninsula and the night view of the city lights is justly famous. Bicycles can be rented near the Kokusai Hotel. They cost ¥1,500 for three hours, ¥100 for each additional hour. Hakodate is well suited for strolling, but to see all of it, you should rent a bicycle.

Near Hakodate-eki is the boisterous **Asa-ichi** (morning market), which runs May–December, 5:00 A.M. to noon daily. Some shops stay open until 4:00 P.M., but the real excitement is earlier in the morning.

The Goryōkaku Star Fortress: All that remains of this fortress, the site of the shogun's supporters' last stand in 1869, is a wide park, the angular walls, and a small museum.

In spring, however, over 4,000 cherry trees on the grounds burst into bloom, which you should see if you are there during the right time. During July and August it is the site of Hakodate's **Goryōkaku Spectacle,** a laser show and outdoor theater that includes a reenactment of the Battle of Hakodate. Tickets are ¥1,800 if reserved ahead of time, ¥2,000 at the entrance. Call for more information (Tel. 0138-56-8601). On the third weekend of

May, the **Battle of Hakodate** is reenacted on an even grander scale. The fortress grounds are free to enter. In front of the moat is a tower and an elevator to take you to the top for a view of the fortress— at ¥520, it really isn't worth it.

If you have only a limited time in Hakodate, it would be better spent strolling through the old Motomachi District at the base of the mountain near the onion-domed Russian church.

The Night View from Hakodate-yama: In Japan, the JNTO carefully ranks a variety of tourist attractions: the Three Most Scenic Sites, the Five Best Landscape Gardens, the 100 Best Cherry Blossom Viewing Points, and so on. The night view from Hakodate-yama (mountain) is considered one of the Three Best Night Views in Japan—the other two are Kobe and Nagasaki.

For ¥1,130 round trip, the ropeway near the Harisutosu Sei-kyōkai Russian Orthodox Church takes you to the summit, 334 meters up. The ropeway runs 10:00 A.M.–10:00 P.M., May–October, and 10:00 A.M.–9:00 P.M. all other times. Go before 8:00 P.M. to enjoy the sunset. There is also a bus that runs from Hakodate-eki directly to the top of the mountain. The 30-minute ride on the Hakodate-yama Tozan bus costs ¥360 one way. Buses run ten times a day during the peak summer seasons, but don't run at all between November and late April.

The mountain is not especially high, and a mountain trail leads to the top for the fit and the broke. The hike takes about an hour, but the trail is closed from late October to late April. There is also a road that winds its way up, but it is too long to walk. You could hitch a ride up with one of the sightseers during the day, but if you can afford it, I recommend taking the ropeway instead. Then you can stay to see the night view, rather than having to beat it back down before dark.

Where to Stay

Near Hakodate-eki is the **Business Hotel Fantasu** (Tel. 0138-

26-7709), which, despite its name, is a capsule hotel. It costs ¥2,500 per night, meals not included.

Niceday Inn (Tel. 0138-22-5919) is an affordable place whose owner is sociable and speaks English. The rooms are both Japanese-style (tatami and futon) and bunk-bed style. It costs ¥3,000 per person, meals not included. Niceday Inn is a five-minute walk from Hakodate-eki, across the street from the Kokusai Hotel. The owner of Niceday Inn can offer advice on sightseeing in Hakodate as well. If Niceday is full, they may be able to advise you on other places.

A 12-minute walk toward downtown from Hakodate-eki takes you to **The Pension Hakodate Mura** (Tel. 0138-22-8105), a member of the Japanese Inn group. Located near the Jūjigai Densha tram stop, this hotel has Japanese- and Western-style rooms for ¥5,800 without a private bath. Breakfast will cost you ¥700 extra. American Express, Visa, and MasterCard are accepted at this Pension.

The **Hakodate Youth Guest House** (Tel. 0138-26-7892) looks more like a hotel than a hostel. New and very classy, it costs ¥3,500 per person, but increases to ¥4,500 July 1– September 30. Breakfast is ¥700; they don't serve dinner. It is south and west of the Hōrai-chō Densha tram stop, and just a ten-minute walk from the ropeway.

Escaping

Take a local train north and get off at either Kikyō or Onakayama stations. Highway 5 runs beside these stations to the east.

Note: The train tracks zigzag a bit after Onakayama, so don't wait. If you get off later, you may end up away from Highway 5 at a confusing angle. Do not hitch a ride from Hakodate's ferry port. I tried it, and spent the time watching cars roll off the ferry and bypass me.

ŌNUMA

North of Hakodate, about ten kilometers past Onakayama-eki, Highway 5 passes a series of lakes, an area collectively known as Ōnuma, a wetland dotted with hundreds of small islands. Try not to zip past Ōnuma without a side trip. To visit this scenic area, leave Highway 5 after you pass Ōnuma Zuidō-eki and then hitch-hike east along the southern shore of Konuma Lake. If you show an interest in visiting the Ōnuma area, the chances are very good that your driver will take you there. It is a very short detour.

Note: Ōnuma Zuidō-eki is not shown in the atlas.

What to See and Do

In the Ōnuma area, three lakes—**Ōnuma, Konuma,** and **Junsainuma**—converge to form a beautiful landscape full of water lilies, small islets, and island-hopping causeways. It is—and I quote—one of the "Three Most Beautiful Landscapes in Japan." The visitors' center is at Ōnuma Kōen, near the station. Paddle-boats and rowboats can be rented for ¥1,200. A road runs around Ōnuma Lake, and a footpath leads from the north shore of Ōnuma to the top of volcanic Komaga-take (1,133 meters). The moderate hike to the top takes about three hours and affords a good view of the lake area below.

Where to Stay

The **Exander Ōnuma Hostel** (Tel. 0138-67-3419) is a well-kept hostel in pleasant surroundings. The hostel, pronounced *iku-sandā*, is a ten-minute walk from either Ōnuma-eki or Ōnuma Kōen-eki, between the two and slightly to the east. If you are hitching in, ask to be dropped off at the Ōnuma Yūenchi—the hostel is across the road. Although ranked as a four-star hostel, it costs only ¥2,800 per night, and some English is spoken here. It is closed November 16–December 15. If you leave Hakodate in the late morning or early afternoon, you may want to spend the night here and then hitch out the next morning. They have bicycle rentals for exploring the lake area.

The **Higashi Ōnuma Camp-jō** is about 500 meters from Ōnuma Kōen-eki, and is well located for sightseeing. This free, *very* basic campsite has no toilets or water, and no tent rentals. There are enough services close by in the area to make this a good choice. The campsite is open from Golden Week (starting April 27) to the end of October.

Past the Ōnuma Camp-jō mentioned above, there are two other well-situated campsites:

1. South of the intersection of Highway 5 and 37 and west of Oshamanbe-eki is the **Oshamanbe Kōen Camp-jō** (Tel. 01377-2-5854), located 4 km from the center of Oshamanbe. The campsite is open from the beginning of April to the end of October. No charge if you bring your own tent. Five-man bungalows rent for ¥4,000 per night. This park has tennis courts, a baseball lot, and other recreational facilities.

2. Past Warabitai-eki and north of Highway 5 is the **Utasai Auto Camp-jō** (Tel. 01367-2-4546) which is open from the end of April to October 20. It costs ¥500 for a space, and ¥800 per person; facilities include a 24-hour coin laundry and showers. For anyone interested in paleontology, there are million-year-old fossil beds nearby.

TŌYAKO

Highway 5 turns inland at Oshamanbe. If you stay on the coast, you will follow Highway 37 around into Abuta. From here it is a short, 6-km hop north to Tōyako (lake). Mention to your driver that you are going to Tōyako and he or she will probably take you there.

Tōyako is well known for its two very active volcanoes. The smaller of the two, **Shōwa-shinzan** (mountain), first sputtered

out of a farmer's field in 1943 and grew to 402 meters. **Usu-zan,**
meanwhile, stands at 732 meters. Usu-zan last blew in 1977, in
a violent eruption that destroyed a cable car and showered the
surrounding area and towns with volcanic ash. A ropeway runs
up Usu-zan and costs ¥1,450 for a round-trip ticket. Alternatively,
hike to the summit in about two hours. It is a 500-meter, 15-
minute walk from Usu-eki to the start of the trail. From there it
is a 90-minute hike to the top; another walking path runs around
the mouth of the volcano.

There are **fireworks** every night on the south shore of Tōyako
April 25–October 31. In the center of the lake are several islands.
The largest, Naka-shima, is home to wild deer. Lake cruises to
Naka-shima and two of the smaller islands, both named after
Goddesses, Kannon-jima (Goddess of Mercy) and Benten-jima
(the Goddess of Art and Music), cost ¥1,100 and are not really
worth it. Spend your time climbing some of the hills instead. If
you rent a bicycle, you can ride around the lake in about three
hours.

Where to Stay

Shōwa-shinzan Youth Hostel (Tel. 0142-75-2283) is near the
volcanoes, in a very scenic location. They will take you to view
the fireworks on Tōyako for free. The hostel costs ¥3,000 per
night and has its own hot spring. They rent bicycles.

The **Usu Youth Hostel** (Tel. 0142-38-2411) is just to the west
of Usu-eki, south of Tōyako, near the start of the hiking path that
runs to the top of Usu-zan. The hostel is near the ocean, and the
beach is only a ten-minute walk. It costs ¥2,000 per night. If you
are staying at the Usu Hostel you can walk all the way from the
hostel to the volcano's edge.

On the southeast shore of the lake, east of the Shōwa-
shinzan Hostel is the **Takinoue Camp-jō.** Call Takigawa Shōten
(Tel. 0142-66-2068) to arrange a stay. It is open June 1–August 31
and costs ¥300 per person; no charge for a space. A five-man

tent rents for ¥850. On the east coast is the **Nakatōya Camp-jō** (Tel. 0142-66-2116), which is open July–August; rates are the same as Takinoue Camp-jō.

Escaping

If you are in a hurry to get to Sapporo, take Highway 230 and you can hitchhike all the way into Sapporo without any trouble. If you are not in a hurry, follow Highway 453 instead, across to Shikotsuko (lake).

SHIKOTSUKO

Pooled in an ancient volcanic caldera, Shikotsuko is just a short ride from the Shin-Chitose-kūkō airport area, so you may want to splurge on the ¥700, 45-minute bus ride instead. The lake area is hemmed in by mountains. To the south is **Tarumae-san** (1,038 meters), a live volcano, where you can hike up to the crater's edge. On the north shore of the lake is **Eniwa-dake** (1,320 meters), which offers a steep hike to the summit and a wide view of the lake. It takes almost four hours to reach the top of Eniwa-dake, but the view is worth it.

The main visitors' area is in the **tourist village of Shikotsu Kohan,** on the east side of the lake where Highway 453 nears the shore. An information center (Tel. 01232-5-2453) is located near the bus terminal and has maps and some English pamphlets.

Note: Shikotsu Kohan is not shown in the atlas.

What to See and Do

On the south side of Shikotsuko, below Highway 276, is the **Koke no Dōmon** moss canyon. This narrow, shaded walk was created by the fissures, lava flow from a nearby volcano. The water has gone and you can now walk through this 500-meter-long, three-story-high moss-covered canyon for free. The pathway is open only June–October, 9:00 A.M.–5:00 P.M. The moss canyon is located at the head of the hiking trail that leads from Highway 276 toward Tarumae-san mountain. Hitch to the mouth of the trail, explore the canyon, and then return to the highway and continue east. Alternatively, stay with the hiking trail all the way to the summit of Tarumae-san. Be warned! There are bears deeper into the woods along this trail, so make sure you are wearing a bell.

Note: Neither Tarumae-san nor the Koke-no-Dōmon moss canyon is shown in the atlas. The moss walk is located west of Fuppushi-dake, near the highway. It is very well known, and anyone driving along the south shore of Shikotsuko can drop you off at the start of the trail.

Where to Stay

Shikotsuko Lake Hostel (Tel. 0123-25-2311) is near the bus center in Shikotsu Kohan on the east side of the lake, south of Highway 453. The hostel costs ¥2,800 per night and has its own hot spring. The hostel is closed December 1–10 and May 16–19. Rent a bicycle from them to best explore the lake. During peak seasons, they also offer shuttle buses out to the Koke no Dōmon canyon and the trail head at Eniwa-dake.

On the west shore of Shikotsuko, north of where Highway 276 meets the lake, is the **Bifue Yaeijō campsite** (Tel. 0123-25-2752) which is open from May 1 to mid-October. It costs ¥300 per person. A five-man tent costs ¥1,500.

On the north side of the lake near the head of the trail up Eniwa-dake, is the **Poropinai Yaeijō campsite** (Tel. 0123-25-2755) which is also open from May 1 to mid-October. It also costs ¥300 per person. A three-man tent costs ¥1,200. Bargain "lodges" sleep six people and cost ¥2,400. If you are traveling as a couple, this works out to be *half* the cost of staying at the hostel—and with more privacy. If you are planning to continue on to Sapporo the following day, the Poropinai Yaeijō campsite is well suited for hitchhiking north on Highway 453. If you want to climb the mountain and then hitchhike into Sapporo the following day, this is a good place to stay.

On the east side of the lake, south of Shikotsu Kohan and near Highway 276, is the **Morappu Camp-jō** (Tel. 0123-25-2439), which is open from April 29 to mid-October. It costs ¥500 per person, no charge for a space. Tent rentals are inexplicably expensive here: ¥4,000 for a six-man tent.

Escaping

Anywhere along the lakeside is easy hitching. If you hitch up the northeast side of the lake on Highway 453 from Shikotsu Kohan, you can continue into Sapporo. If you camped at the Poropinai Yaeijō campsite you are in a perfect location for hitching out of the Shikotsuko region and into the big city. Once you get north of Shikotsu Kohan, most of the traffic will be flowing toward Sapporo.

If you are going to Shin-Chitose-kūkō instead, hitchhike east on the prefectural highway known as the Shikotsu-dōro (road) which runs from the east side of Shikotsuko to Chitose-eki.

Note: The prefectural highway number is either 37 or 16, depending when you get on. Refer to it as the Shikotsu-dōro. Or, just say Shin-Chitose-kūkō no hō (I'm going toward Shin-Chitose Airport.) A 45-minute, ¥700 bus runs from the lake to the airport, but hitching from the lake to the airport is fairly easy.

ERIMO-MISAKI

Virtually every guidebook on the market ignores Erimo-misaki (cape) and the southeastern coast of Hokkaido, since there is little public transportation available. As a result, the road to Erimo-misaki is rarely traveled by Westerners. The journey is fairly straightforward, but it will take you through some of Hokkaido's most rural areas.

Getting There

From Sapporo, there are two ways to reach Highway 235 toward the cape:

1. From Sapporo, take a local train south on the Chitose-sen line to Bibi-eki. If you are at the airport already, it is just one stop down. Walk west from Bibi-eki and you will come to Highway 36. Hitchhike south on Highway 36 to Highway 235.

2. Stay on the train until Numanohata-eki and then walk northeast on Highway 234 until you clear the station area. The intersection with Highway 235 is just 2 km from the station, so if you are feeling fit, you may just want to walk all the way to the start of Highway 235.

Note: This intersection is not accurately rendered in the atlas. Just make sure you end up pointed east on 235 and *not* north on 234.

En Route

As you hitchhike south on Highway 36 from Bibi-eki, you will soon pass Utonaiko (lake) on the east. Conservationists and bird-watchers might wish to stop and explore these lake marsh-lands, which are inhabited by swans and over 200 species of waterfowl.

Where to Stay

The **Utonaiko Youth Hostel** (Tel. 0144-58-2153) is on the north shore of Utonaiko and costs just ¥1,450. Between November and April, overnight costs increase to ¥1,600 to cover heating costs. To get to the hostel, hitch south on Highway 36 from Bibi-eki and turn toward the lake at the Youth Hostel Iriguchi *teiryūjo* (bus stop) across from the Shōwa Shell gas station. From this bus stop it is a ten-minute walk to the hostel, but your Japanese driver will probably drop you off right at the hostel door.

Escaping

South of Utonaiko, Highway 36 meets the tail end of Highway 234. Highway 234 makes a final "hook" and meets Highway 36, a junction not labeled very well in the atlas. Hitchhike southeast on 234, past Numanohata-eki, to Highway 235, which will take you to Erimo. It changes numbers along the way, but just stick with the coast and you will get to Erimo-misaki. If possible, try to clear the busy junction area by asking your Japanese driver to drop you off on Highway 235, east of Numanohata-eki. Just keep saying *Erimo-misaki no hō* (I'm going toward Cape Erimo-misaki) and you should be dropped off at the right spot. Make sure to include the suffix *-misaki*, or you may eventually be dropped off in the middle of Erimo-chō (town) instead.

The coastal highway to Erimo-misaki runs through a string of small fishing communities before reaching the lonely little town of Erimo. The highway number will change to 336, and does not go all the way down to Erimo-misaki, so you will need to take Prefectural Highway 97, shown in yellow but not numbered in the atlas. It is a 26-km trip down one side of Erimo-misaki and up the other.

Erimo-misaki is cold, exposed, and very windy most of the year; dress appropriately. At the tip of the cape is a scenic look-out and a lighthouse. On the rocky reef south of the cape live 300 or so sea leopards which you can view with the rental binocular from the Erimo Rest House. The cape offers beautiful sunrises and sunsets.

Where to Stay

If you can't make it to Erimo-misaki in one day, there are some options along the way.

The **Fun Horse Hostel in Nikappu** (Tel. 01464-7-2317) is on a farm near the mouth of the Nikappu-gawa (river), on the west bank. True to its name, you can go horseback riding here. The hostel is open March 1–October 31.

Inland from Monbetsu and marked on the atlas is the **Hidaka Kentucky Farm** (Tel. 01456-2-2192), which is open from the end of April to the beginning of November. It costs ¥2,000 for a space. There is no extra per-person charge if you are camping, but there is a ¥400 charge for visitors.

One kilometer from the cape, on the east side, is **Erimo-misaki Hostel** (Tel. 01466-3-1144) located beside an elementary school. The hostel is closed December 1–25; January 10–February 10; and April 10–25. For ¥2,600 per night (payable by VISA) you can enjoy nearby kayaking in the summer, and cross-country and downhill skiing in the winter.

Halfway down the east side of the cape, and near Hyakunin Hama (beach), is the **Erimo Machi Hyakunin Hama Auto Camp-jō** (Tel. 01466-4-2168). It is open April 20–October 20. It costs ¥300 per person. A four-man tent costs ¥1,000.

Escaping

The road from Erimo-misaki rejoins Highway 336 up the east coast. Hitchhike north and you will come to the hospitable town of Hiroo. From Hiroo, it will be hard to avoid being pulled into Obihiro (population 168,000), the major urban center in the area. North of Hiroo is the **Hiroo Camp-jō** (Tel. 01558-2-6486), which is open June 1–September 30. It costs ¥200 per person, and some tent rental is also available.

OBIHIRO

South of Obihiro, near the Obihiro-kūkō, is the **Guryukku Ōkoku German Kingdom,** a surreal tourist trap in the middle of rural Hokkaido. It costs ¥2,200 to enter and is apparently based on the tales of the Brothers Grimm. I skipped it. South of Obihiro-eki 1.5 km is the spacious Midorigaoka Kōen (park), which has a lake in the center and a famous 400-meter-long bench, the longest in the world, and the ultimate in lounging.

Where to Stay

If possible, try to pass right through Obihiro. There is no youth hostel in Obihiro; the closest is the **Ikeda Kitanokotan Hostel** (Tel. 01557-2-3666) in Ikeda, 20 km east of the city. Take the train to Toshibetsu-eki and walk one block south then one block west—about 500 meters altogether—and you will see the hostel, a two-story, Western-style building. The hostel has only 14 beds, so call before you set out. It doesn't accept families or groups over four, which is good news for independent travelers. It costs ¥2,800 and is closed January 16–27; April 5–20; May 11–21; and November 6–December 22. No smoking.

Escaping

If your ride is only going as far as Obihiro, ask to be dropped off on Highway 38 beside Nishi Obihiro-eki, to the west of the city center. Highway 38 runs right beside Nishi Obihiro-eki, parallel to the tracks. Hitchhike west on Highway 38 until it meets Highway 274 at Shimizu town. Get on Highway 274, and you can hitchhike through the mountains and right into Sapporo. You should be able to get from Obihiro to Sapporo in a day, with three or fewer rides. You may luck out. Your first driver may be going all the way to Sapporo. Still, I wouldn't advise using a Sapporo destination sign until you got much closer to Sapporo, otherwise you will be eliminating all the partial rides that assume you only want a ride *all the way* to Sapporo.

From Obihiro to Shin-Chitose-kūkō: Follow the instructions given above for escaping Obihiro to Sapporo, but ask to be let off at the intersection of Highway 274 and Highway 337—labeled the Dōō Expressway in the atlas. Hitchhike south and you will come to Chitose-eki. *Remember*: The airport is *south*, at Shin-Chitose-kūkō.

En Route

You can easily connect your Erimo-misaki journey with a trip through **Daisetsu National Park**. (The Daisetsu itinerary is given later in this chapter) To join it, hitchhike north from Obihiro on Highway 241. At Kami-Shihoro, Highway 241 meets Highway 273. Highway 273, known locally as the Nukabira-kokudō (road), will take you all the way to Sōunkyō Gorge, in the heart of the Daisetsu area.

Timing the Erimo-Misaki Loop: To do a loop south from Sapporo down to Erimo-misaki and then up through Obihiro and back into Sapporo should take only about five days, including a day and two nights of hiking and sightseeing at the cape itself. If you decide to hitchhike north from Obihiro and into the Sōunkyō Gorge area of Daisetsu National Park, add another three to four days.

THE NORTHWEST COAST

The coastal highway that runs from Ishikari (just north of Sapporo) to Wakkanai at the northern tip of Hokkaido is one of my favorites. If Jack Kerouac had ever come to northern Japan, he would have traveled this sad, forlorn stretch of road. The traffic is sparse but the rides are good; you won't be choking on any exhaust. As you continue north, you will see houses barricaded behind shanty-walls of lumber to protect them from the constant saltwater winds.

Like the road to Erimo-misaki, the northwest coast of Hokkaido is ignored by most guidebooks. There are no trains and the public transportation is scarce. As a hitchhiker, however, you will be in your element—beyond the range of mainstream tourists.

Getting There

From Sapporo, you want to get onto Highway 231. If you start at dawn prior to morning rush hour, you can hitchhike from within the city. Highway 5 runs right by the east end of Sapporo-eki. But be warned, Highway 5 soon turns sharply and joins the east-west axis of the Sasson Expressway. From there, you have to change onto Highway 231 through a complicated expressway interchange. Instead, clear the downtown core and get beyond the expressway and onto Highway 231 *before* you start hitchhiking. There are two ways to do this:

1. Take a local train from Sapporo-eki to Shin-Kotoni-eki on the Sasshō Line. From Shin-Kotoni-eki, walk ten minutes east to Highway 231. From there, hitchhike north.

2. Take the subway north to the end of the line at Azabu-eki, which puts you slightly closer to Highway 231. Shin-kotoni-eki mentioned above and the Azabu subway terminal are near each other. From the subway terminal, walk straight east three blocks and you will come to Highway 231. From there, hitchhike north.

Ishikari: Highway 231 runs to the east of Ishikari town. The wind-swept Ishikari coastline is hilly with dunes and grass, and is especially beautiful where the Ishikari River meets the sea. If you left Sapporo in the late afternoon, this open coastal area would be an ideal place to pitch a tent. If you leave Sapporo in the morning, however, you should be able to get all the way to Toyotomi before dark. If not, there are many places to stay along the way.

There are three inexpensive youth hostels along the coast between Ishikari and Wakkanai, all under ¥2,000 per night.

Shokanbetsu Hostel is in Mashike (Tel. 0164-53-2396), about 1 km from Mashike-eki; ask your driver to help you find it. A tennis court, a swimming pool, and a beach are nearby.

Bōyōdai Hostel in Obira (Tel. 01645-6-2631) is near a long beach, with a magnificent view of the Japan Sea at sunset. You can try your hand at ceramic art as well. The hostel is a five-minute walk to the highway, which makes it easy to resume hitchhiking the next morning.

If you are a bird-watcher, stay in Haboro at the **Haboro Hostel** (Tel. 01646-2-1460), which is part of a community sports center. From the hostel it is a 20-minute walk to the ferry terminal where tours depart for distant Yagishiri-tō and Teuri-tō islands, home to colonies of sea cormorants. Ferries to Teuri-tō take about one hour and 40 minutes and cost ¥4,380 round trip. The bird-watching season runs from May to the beginning of July. Ferry service is sporadic, but runs often during the summer. The weather on these islands can be miserable and cold well into May, so dress appropriately. There is a campsite on Yagishiri-tō island, but most of the birds are on Teuri-tō.

The **Green Hill Camp-jō** is south of Tomamae, below the junction of Highway 239 and Highway 232. Call the town office at 01646-4-2211. It is open July 1–August 31 and costs ¥100 per person to enter, and ¥410 for a space. Rent a four-man tent for ¥1,030.

The **Sunset Beach Camp-jō** (Tel. 01646-2-5080) is located on Sunset Beach in Haboro. There is no per-person entrance charge, but it costs ¥500 for a three-man tent space, ¥1,000 if you have a larger, four-man tent. There are no tent rentals available.

South of Enbetsu, near the Enbetsu-gawa (river), is the **Fujimigaoka Kōen**. Call the town office at 01632-7-2111. The free campsite is open May 1–October 31, and offers a distant view of the islands to the southwest.

Near the mouth of the Teshio River is the free **Kagaminuma Kōen campsite** (Tel. 01632-2-1830) which is open from the end of May to October 10. An eight-man tent rents for ¥1,000 per night. Showers and barbecues are also available; an additional ¥500 per person for barbecue materials—food not included—is charged.

What to See and Do

At Teshio, the highway turns inland. On an early weekend day with good weather, you can stay on the coast all the way up to the flower garden. This scenic route will be full of sightseers. The view of **Rishiri-tō** island, rising up from the sea, is unforgettable, especially when wreathed in a light mist.

Traffic up the coast is not reliable during the week or on the off-season. The safest way to get to the flower garden is to stay on the main highway when it turns inland at Teshio which brings you into Toyotomi, the gateway to the **Sarobetsu Gensei-kaen** (natural flower garden). Prefectural Highway 444 runs west from Toyotomi to the park area and marshland boardwalk. You can hitch out to the flower park and marshlands easily on a weekend because of the steady stream of flower viewers. Otherwise, take a bus from Toyotomi-eki—it's only a 15-minute, ¥380-ride.

Note: Prefectural Highway 444 from Toyotomi to the Sarobetsu Gensei-kaen is shown in yellow in the atlas, but it is not numbered. The Sarobetsu area has a short but brilliant summer. Winters are long and cold, so come between May and early October, when all the facilities and various rest houses are open. The Natural Flower Garden of Sarobetsu, home to over 100 kinds of wildflowers, is 7 km wide and 28 km long. Make sure you see the 1,200-year-old pine tree; it is inland, near the campsite at Kabutonuma lake, halfway between Toyotomi and Wakkanai. Even more exotic to Japanese tourists are the many sheep and cows grazing in the pastures inland, east of Toyotomi.

Where to Stay

The **Kabutonuma Park Camp-jō** (Tel. 0162-84-2425) is north of Toyotomi, and on the south side of Kabutonuma lake between Ashikawa-eki and Kabutonuma-eki. It is free and open May 1–October 30. Rent a six-man tent for ¥500. Five-man bungalows are also available (and highly recommended) for ¥700. The campsite has a coin laundry, and also has baths and showers for ¥200. Showers are 2:00 P.M.–7:00 P.M. There is an information center and some small shops as well that are open daily until 7:00 P.M.

TOYOTOMI

Toyotomi Onsen, the northernmost hot springs in Japan, is a small spa with a public bath in the center and many hot-spring hotels, ryokan, and *minshuku* in the vicinity. Though not a particularly inspiring place, it makes a nice stop if you need a break from the road.

Getting There

The hot springs of Toyotomi Onsen are a 6-km detour east of the town of Toyotomi on what is either Prefectural Highway 84, 724, or 1084, depending on where you get on and who you ask. Rather than refer to numbers, ask to be let off on the Hamatonbetsu-sen road. Even better, just ask "Toyotomi Onsen?"

Note: The secondary highway that runs from Toyotomi to Toyotomi Onsen is shown in green but not numbered in the atlas. It is easy to find.

Where to Stay

There are no youth hostels at Toyotomi Onsen, but there are enough places that somebody will have a room. Prices average ¥5,000–¥6,000. Ask to see the hot spring before you check in.

Try **Murakami Minshuku** (Tel. 0162-82-1152), **Wada Minshuku** (Tel. 0162-82-1847), or **Kikuchi Ryokan** (Tel. 0162-82-1244), all around ¥5,000 with no meals. If you want to splurge, try **Kawashima Ryokan** (Tel. 0162-82-1248), which costs ¥7,000–¥10,000 per night.

WAKKANAI

Wakkanai is the northernmost city in Japan, with some 50,000 people living on this distant hook of land along the eastern shore of a small peninsula. At the tip of Nosappu-misaki, north of the city, are several shrines, *minshuku*, and a scenic view of the offshore islands—breathtaking at sunset. The main reason anyone comes to Wakkanai is to catch a ferry to the islands of Rishiri-tō and Rebun-tō, which, together with the wild Sarobetsu coast, make up Japan's most northerly national park. It is a good idea to stay in the Toyotomi area so that you can arrive early in Wakkanai the next morning to connect with a ferry to the islands without having to spend a night.

Where to Stay

Should you need to stay in Wakkanai, the **Wakkanai Youth Hostel** (Tel. 0162-23-7162, 7179) has views of the Russian island of Sakhalin as well as Rishiri-tō. The hostel is a 12-minute walk from Minami Wakkanai-eki and costs ¥2,800 per night.

At ¥3,100 a night, the **Wakkanai Moshiripa** (Tel. 0162-24-0180) is slightly more expensive, but they take VISA. It is a five-minute walk from Wakkanai-eki. Closed during November.

The **Wakkanai Shinrin Kōen Campsite** is inland, 1 km west of the Wakkanai station/port area. Call the city office at 0162-23-6161 for more information before heading out. The quickest route is through Wakkanai Rei-en graveyards. Bring all your food and supplies with you because this free campsite has no facilities. The next morning you can walk back down to the ferry port and be on your way to Rishiri-tō and Rebun-tō. No tent rentals.

RISHIRI-TŌ and REBUN-TŌ

These two islands, shaped like a bagel and a sausage, offer contrasting attractions, but both are renowned for their rugged scenery, splendid coasts, and scenic hikes. They are so well known that the suffix -tō, meaning "island," is not commonly used and most people you talk to will just say "Rebun" or "Rishiri." I have followed suit. Try to visit Rishiri and Rebun between June and September, when the weather is not stormy. I spent several cold days in mid-May huddled in the Rishiri Green Hill Youth Hostel, waiting for a ferry out.

Getting There

The ferry service from Wakkanai changes depending on weather conditions, so check in advance. If it is stormy, ask your driver to call ahead for you to confirm ferry times. Off-season ferries are especially erratic, and high seas cause frequent cancellations and occasionally leave travelers stranded out on the islands.

Ferry runs are most regular between June and August. From Wakkanai-kō (port), most ferries go first to Rishiri and then to Rebun. Ferries to Rishiri cost ¥3,700–¥4,320 depending on which run you take. A direct ferry to Rebun costs ¥4,120.

Rishiri: The two main ports are Oshidomari-kō (port) in the town of Rishirifuji-chō and Katsugata-kō in the town of Rishiri-chō. Make sure you keep the port names and their respective towns straight. The atlas lists only the towns. It does show the ferry routes, but does not label the ports.

Rishiri can be circled by bicycle comfortably in a day, with stops at melancholy ghost towns along the way. I tried hitchhiking, and after an hour and only three vehicles, I got a ride with a very forlorn housewife whose world seemed to end at the island's edge. A rented bicycle is easy to arrange at the Oshidomari-kō or at the youth hostel. The run around the edge of the island is 55 km long, and for the most part the road is level and the cycling is easy. With sightseeing stops along the way, it should only take about five or six hours to complete.

The hike to the summit of **Rishiri-zan** (1,719 meters) is a full day's outing, so take food and water with you. The view from the top is panoramic, and you should be able to see the Russian island of Sakhalin, where a devastating earthquake in 1995 wiped an entire town off the map. There is a basic mountain shelter near the top, so if you have heavy, warm clothing and a good sleeping bag, you can stay to watch the sun set on the Sea of Japan and then watch it rise again over Hokkaido the following dawn. Otherwise, head back down before dark.

As the ferry comes in to the Oshidomari-kō (in Rishirifuji-chō), you will see the towering cliff of Peshi-misaki. On a clear day, the view is reminiscent of a Scottish Highland coast with a town nestled beneath wind-swept, treeless cliffs. Southeast of Rishirifuji-cho are the murky green ponds of the Himuenuma marshlands.

Where to Stay

Unless pitching a tent, your only option is the **Green Hill Hostel** (Tel. 01638-2-2507), a half-hour walk west along the main road from the ferry port at Oshidomari-kō. You may want to splurge on a taxi. The Green Hill Hostel is a large, well-kept building with its own dramatic ocean view and cliff-side sea-gulls. It costs ¥2,500 per night; they also rent bicycles, indispensable in touring the island.

Note: If you want to stay at the hostel (recommended) make sure that your ferry is going to Oshidomari-kō (port) in Rishiri-fuji-chō.

Inland, up the mountain from the Oshidomari-kō, is the **Rishiri Yaeijō Campsite** (Tel. 01638-2-2394), open May 15–October 15. It is free with your own tent, though you can rent a four-man tent for ¥2,000. At the Katsugata-kō, near the lighthouse in the park located on the spur of land that juts out from shore, is another free campsite. Another campsite is located on the southeast coast of Rishiri, near the smaller Oniwaki-kō.

Beyond these designated spots, there are several scenic look-outs and lots of empty space to pitch a tent on the sly. Make sure you bring food with you if you set out to circle the island, because restaurants and provisions are scarce once you leave the main towns.

Rebun really is the end of Japan, the very last island of the chain. The main ferry ports are Kafuka-kō at the south end of the island and Funadomari-kō at the north. Neither ferry port is labeled in the atlas, but the ferry routes are shown.

Rebun has one main road up the east side, another road across its northern peninsula, and a hiking trail down the west side. The trail is called "The Eight-Hour (*hachijikan*) Hiking Course," but I've never made it in less than ten. The hike should not be undertaken without proper supplies and clothing. The hostels can explain the course and provide maps. Leave at dawn to finish before dusk. The hike itself is wonderfully varied: small coves, beaches, grassy views, sea-shacks, half-forgotten shrines, stone pillars, open ocean, agate deposits, good bird-watching opportunities, and fields of wildflowers. It is fitting that the last possible walk you can take in Japan is also one of the most beautiful. On the east coast of the island are views of Rishiri rising up from the far horizon.

Warning: The stream water on Rebun is *not* safe to drink. Bring enough water with you and do not be tempted by the apparently crystal clear streams—they are infected with fox-borne parasites.

Where to Stay

There are three hostels on Rebun, each charging ¥2,600. **Rebun Hostel** (Tel. 01638-6-1608) is a short 15-minute walk north along the main road from the Kafuka-kō at the southern end of the island. No alcohol allowed. Bicycle rentals are available.

Conveniently nestled at the start of a trail entrance is the **Momoiwa-Sō Youth Hostel** (Tel. 01638-6-1421, 1390). It is across the peninsula from the port, on the southwest side of the island. If you have a reservation, you can call from Kafuka-kō and they will come and pick you up. The hostel is open only June 1–September 30. Bicycle rentals are available.

At the north end of the island and a 20-minute walk from Funadomari-kō is the **Funadomari Hostel** (Tel. 01638-7-2717) near Kushu lake. If you have a reservation, they will pick you up at Funadomari-kō. If your ferry comes to Kafuka-kō on the south end of Rebun, you may spend a couple of hours waiting for a ride. Instead, take a bus north to Funadomari. One usually connects with incoming ferries. The Funadomari Hostel is open only May 1–October 15. No bicycle rentals.

Camping

Near the Funadomari Hostel, on the northwest shore of the Kushu lake, is the **Kushu Camp-jō** campsite (Tel. 01638-7-2073), which is open from June to September. No charge.

About 4.5 km north of Kafuka-kō, on the east side of the island is the **Midori-ga-oka Camp-jō,** which is also free of charge.

Escaping

Your visit to Rebun and Rishiri was a break from hitchhiking. Now it is time to resume your journey by thumb. If you are returning directly to Sapporo you will find that it is a *much* quicker ride going south. Although it took you a day and a half to get from Sapporo to Wakkanai, it will take less than a day going back. Large cities act like gravity wells, and none more so than Sapporo.

If you are not ready to return to Sapporo, continue down the even lonelier northeast coast of Hokkaido. From Wakkanai, the highway leads to **Sōya-misaki,** the northernmost point of mainland Japan—but otherwise unremarkable. Stop to dip your hand into the Sea of Okhotsk; it is rare that a cape lookout is so low along the water.

This may be your chance to see the Russian island of Sakhalin, which is purportedly visible from Sōya. I have never seen Sakhalin from Sōya. The first time it was "too hazy," the second time it was "too sunny." I suspect that Sakhalin viewing was dreamed up by local merchants to draw tourists in.

There are no designated campsites at Sōya-misaki, but there are several *minshuku*. Try the **Minshuku Saihoku-no-yado** (Tel. 0162-76-2408), which is—surprise—the northernmost *minshuku* in Japan. It costs ¥6,000 with two meals.

Escaping

From Sōya-misaki, the highway follows the coast southward. There are no trains and few buses, and you will be on one of the most remote roads in Japan. Traffic is sparse, but the cars that do pass are often college students, fishermen, or other adventurous sightseers who will take you for long, scenic rides down the coast. Because the area is so remote, and non-Japanese visitors so rare, the sympathy factor works greatly in your favor.

En Route

North of Hamatonbetsu is the **Beniya Gensei-kaen** (natural flower park) with over 100 kinds of wildflowers and a view of the Sea of Okhotsk. The flowers are at their best between the end of June and the beginning of August.

Where to Stay

There is a **Youth Hostel** in Hamatonbetsu (Tel. 01634-2-3108). It is closed December 1–24, and it costs ¥2,300 per night. They take VISA. Unless its late in the day, there is no need to stop in Hamatonbetsu; continue south to Monbetsu .

North of Esashi, near Usutaibe-misaki is the **Usutaibe Senjōiwa Camp-jō**. Call the town office (Tel. 01636-2-1234 *naisen* 273) to arrange a stay. No charge. It is open June 1–October 31.

SAROMAKO

After Monbetsu (population 31,000), the traffic picks up. The road between Monbetsu and Abashiri takes you past Saromako (lake) and Notoroko, two vast saltwater lagoons often over-looked by many guidebooks in English. In the atlas, Saromako is divided among several pages with neither spear of land proper-ly labeled. Ryūgū Gaidō, the southeastern spear of land, is 20 km long. Traffic is only allowed to the start of the peninsula; you will need to hike it or rent bicycles. Bicycles cost ¥500 and can be rented at the Wakka Nature Center. You should be able to find an after-dark secluded spot along the grassy, vine-tangled, windy peninsula of Ryūgū Gaidō to pitch a tent. Make sure you bring food and water with you if you plan on camping farther down the land spear. Both have designated campsites, but you should be able to camp in any secluded spot.

Two spears of land separate Saromako from the ocean:

1. The northwestern spear of Ryūgū-dai has a road that runs down to the Sanri Hama (beach) and campsite. Halfway down the peninsula is the **Saroma Gensei-kaen** (natural flower park), which is marked in the atlas.

2. The southeastern spear of Ryūgū Kaidō features the **Wakka Gensei-kaen**. The road runs only to the start of the eastern spear, after which a very long hiking/biking path leads down to the tip. This is a beautiful place, with lots of discreet areas to pitch a tent.

What to See and Do

An interesting but easy-to-miss diversion along Highway 238 is **Sangosō Gunraku**, one of only four inland coral beds in Japan.

Abashiri (population 43,000) boasts the **Abashiri Keimusho** (prison), located north of Abashiriko, where Highway 238 meets Highway 39. For the Japanese, this working prison has the same aura as Alcatraz or Siberia: a distant, cold place far from home and filled with daring escape attempts. You can buy crafts and wood-carvings made by the inmates. Two kilometers south of the present site is the prison museum, the **Hakubutsukan Abashiri Kangoku**. The original buildings and walls were moved here and incorporated into the museum. The entrance is a stiff ¥1,030 to tour the re-created interiors.

Stop by the **Hoppō Minzoku Hakubutsukan** (museum) in Okhotsk Kōen which has interesting displays of Ainu costumes and culture. The museum compares the Ainu with seven other northern aboriginal groups, including the Inuit of Alaska and Canada's Far North, and the Laplanders of Finland. This well-known museum is open 9:30 A.M.–4:30 P.M.; if you are hitching into Abashiri, your driver should be able to find it easily. If not, ask to be dropped off at Abashiri-eki; from there it is a 15-minute bus ride to the museum. Buses leave every hour. Admission is ¥250, and English explanations are provided. Call 0152-45-3888 for information.

Yet another natural wildflower park, the **Koshimizu Genseikaen,** is on the shore near the scenic lookout west of Hama-Koshimizu-eki. I confess that I was a bit saturated with flower viewing and went right by without stopping.

Where to Stay

Camping: On the east shore of Komukeko (lake), not far from Monbetsu-kūkō (airport), is the **Komuke Kokusai Camp-jō** (Tel. 01582-8-2146), which is open from the end of April to the end of October. It costs ¥200 per person. Tent rentals are available.

At the tip of the peninsula on Ryūgū-dai, the western spear of land separating Saromako from the sea, is the **Sanri Hama Camp-jō** (Tel. 01586-8-2455) which is open July 1–September 15.

It costs ¥300 per person. No tent rentals. Bungalows cost ¥4,000. This campsite is well situated; facilities include a small shop on the campground open 8:00 A.M.–5:30 P.M. and a small restaurant about a kilometer away that is open during the camping season.

On the eastern side of Saromako, in Tokoro and across the road from the Tokyu Resort Hotel, is the **Saroma Kohan Shizen-kyūyōrin Camp-jō** (Tel. 0152-61-3150) which is open June 15– September 15 and costs ¥300 per person. No tent rentals. Cabin bungalows are available for ¥3,000.

Just above the Saroma Kohan Youth Hostel, on the small hook of land called **Kimua-neppu-saki** that juts out into the lake, is another campsite.

Northeast of Notoroko, just south of the lighthouse at Notoro-misaki, is the scenic **Misaki Camp-jō** campsite (Tel. 0152-44-6645), which is open July 1–August 31. It costs ¥300 per person. Rent a five-man bungalow for ¥3,000.

South of the Hoppō Minzoku Ainu museum, in Okhotsk Kōen, is the **Tent Land Camp-jō** (Tel. 0152-45-2277). It is open April 29–October 31, and you must call ahead for a reservation. It costs ¥1,000 per person and ¥500 for a tent space. Tent rentals are available. This campsite is north of Yobito-eki, east of Abashiriko, on the road that runs parallel to Highway 39.

Hostels: The **Saroma Kohan Hostel** (Tel. 01587-6-2515) is located about 1 km northwest of the Saroma Ōhashi bridge, near the eastern end of Saromako. It costs ¥2,600; they take VISA. The owners speak some English and rent bicycles as well. The people at this hostel will take you out to the highway when you leave, making it easy to resume hitching the next day. The hostel is near the shore and has some nice walks. Closed May16–19 and November 10–19.

The **Abashiri Ryūhyō-no-oka Hostel** (Tel. 0152-43-8558) is north of Abashiri, toward Notoro-misaki. It costs ¥3,100 per night. It is near the Misaki Camp-jō listed earlier, so if it rains or if the campsite is closed, you can beat a hasty retreat to this hostel.

The **Gensei-Kaen Hostel** (Tel. 0152-46-2630) is south of Kitahama-eki near the east end of Tōfutsuko (lake). Closed November 10–January 20 and April 10–25. It costs ¥2,800 per night.

On the west end of Tōfutsuko, south of Hama-Koshimizu-eki, 1 km off the highway and near the lake shore, is the **Okhotsk-Koshimizu Hostel** (Tel. 0152-64-2011). Closed November 5–14, and May 16–19. It costs ¥2,600 per night.

DAISETSU-ZAN NATIONAL PARK

Located in the heart of Hokkaido, Daisetsu-zan is Japan's largest national park. The high volcanic peaks of Daisetsu are the highest—and coldest—in Hokkaido. The park, often called "the Alaska of Japan," is filled with steep canyons, sheer cliffs, high plateaus, hiking trails, campsites, hostels, and abundant wildlife. Hitchhiking in and around the edges of Daisetsu is excellent because much of the traffic is made up of hikers, students, and families on outings. Deeper into the mountains, it becomes more a hiking destination than a hitchhiking one.

Note: The borders of Daisetsu-zan National Park are not designated in the atlas. Roughly speaking, the main park area is bounded by Highway 273 on the east, Highway 39 on the north, Highway 237 on the west, and Highway 38 to the south.

Getting There

From the Saromako area, you can reach Daisetsu by hitching southwest from Yūbetsu on Highway 242. Highway 242 meets Highway 333 just after Engaru. You *could* stay on Highway 242 south to Rubeshibe, and then west on Highway 39 into Daisetsu. This is a direct route and the traffic along Highway 39 is consistent. However, I recommend turning west sooner, on Highway

333, a route that follows the train line (in case you get stranded); there are several campsites along the way.

If you want to hitchhike into Daisetsu-zan's main area—the **Sōunkyō Gorge and Hot Springs**—hitchhike west on Highway 333 until you reach Highway 39 just south of Kamikawa. Turn southeast on 39 and you will easily hitch a ride into the Sōunkyō Gorge area. The traffic along Highway 39 into Sōunkyō Gorge is always good. If you want to go to the Asahi-dake area, stay on Highway 333 and you will go straight into Asahikawa (population 360,000), Hokkaido's second largest city. **Asahikawa** is the gateway to western Daisetsu-zan. It is a modern city with little to offer casual visitors. It is also a tough city to escape. Don't bother trying to hitchhike *out* of central Asahikawa; instead take a bus into the Asahi-dake region.

Where to Stay

After you turn west on Highway 333, you pass through the town of Maruseppu. South of the town, toward the Maruseppu Onsen, is the **Shinrin Kōen Ikoi-no-mori Camp-jō** (Tel. 01584-7-2466) which is open from April 29 to the last Sunday of October. It costs ¥300 per person and tent rentals are available. For steam-engine enthusiasts, an old locomotive runs through the park.

Farther west along Highway 333, and then a ten-minute drive south from Oku Shirataki-eki, is the **Shirataki Kōgen Camp-jō** (Tel. 01584-8-2803), which is open all year, but only for large groups during the winter. No charge. Bungalow-cabins can be rented for ¥1,540. Tent rentals are also available.

Highway 333 meets Highway 273. North on Highway 273, just past the tunnel and to the west, is the **Uki-Uki Land Camp-jō**, which is open from the middle of May to the end of October. Call the town office (Tel. 015829-2111) for general information. No charge if you have your own tent. Bungalow-cabin rentals are available; you must call first (Tel. 015829-2454). No tent rentals.

SŌUNKYŌ GORGE

In the northwest corner of the park is the main visitors' area near the Sōunkyō Onsen. The gorge is 8 km long—the largest and longest in Japan—and the *onsen* area is more or less halfway down it. Highway 39, also known as the Daisetsu-kokudō (road), runs along it.

What to See and Do

The gorge is best viewed on foot or by bicycle on a path that runs along the highway for much of the way. Don't hitchhike through, because just when it gets interesting, the highway disappears into a tunnel. The bicycle/hiking path eventually branches off and leads you deep into Kobako and Ōbako canyons. Bicycles can be rented at several places in the *onsen* area, usually for around ¥1,500 a day. Try the **Aka Hotsu Enterprise** (Tel. 0168-5-3517), which charges ¥1,200 a day. Ask at the Kankō Information Center beside the bus center for more information, including directions to nearby youth hostels.

Instead of bicycling, you may want to hike through the gorge and then hitchhike back on Highway 39. It is not a very long or especially difficult walk. But bicycling is more fun.

About 3 km south of Sōunkyō Onsen along Highway 39 are the Husband-and-Wife waterfalls, Ryusei-no-taki and Ginga-no-taki. These thin, high-falling waterfalls flow down the steep mountain sides, separated by clefts in the stone wall. The best place to admire them is from the Sōbakudai viewpoint. Near the end of the gorge are two steep-walled natural enclosures called Kobako and Ōbako, meaning "little box" and "big box."

Farther down Highway 39 is another gorge with rugged walls and several waterfalls, including the Kinshi-no-taki (falls), which are marked in the atlas.

Kuro-dake: The Sōunkyō Ropeway up Kuro-dake (mountain)

is nearly a mile long. For ¥1,500 round trip, it puts you at the Fifth Station, the last service and supply center, so stock up now and use the toilet before continuing to the summit. From the Fifth Station, a chairlift takes you the rest of the way up for an additional ¥500 round trip. From there you can hike the one-hour trail to the summit of Kuro-dake, almost 2,000 meters above sea level. There are some shelters and lots of places to pitch a free-standing tent, but the top of Kuro-dake is a cold and windy place to spend the night. I would advise retreating to lower climes. The ropeway and lift do not operate March 1–30.

If you are a hardy hiker you can cross the mountains from the top of Kuro-dake to Asahi-dake and then take the Asahi-dake Ropeway down to the other side. There are youth hostels at the base of either ropeway, and by hiking across the top of Daisetsu-zan National Park you will certainly have cut off some mileage from your hitching, but be advised: this is a serious, seven-hour, all-day hike. You will have to carry all your bags and supplies with you.

Paul Hunt's guidebook *Hiking in Japan* has a detailed section on Daisetsu-zan. The heart of the park is more of a hiker's destination than a hitchhiker's. For hitchhikers, Sōunkyō Gorge and Kuro-dake are more readily accessible.

Where to Stay

The **Sōunkyō Hostel** (Tel. 01658-5-3418) is a seven-minute walk from Sōunkyō Bus Center, and costs ¥2,800 per night. No alcohol allowed. This hostel is near the Sōunkyō Ropeway that runs up Kuro-dake.

The **Ginsenkaku Hostel** (Tel. 01658-5-3003, 3501) is close to Sōunkyō Hostel mentioned above, and is just five minutes from the bus center. It also costs ¥ 2,800 per night.

North of Sōunkyō Gorge, just off Highway 39, is the **Sōunkyō Seishōnen Ryokō Mura Campsite** (Tel. 01658-5-3368), which is open May 1–October 31. It costs ¥360 per person to enter. To pitch a three-man tent costs ¥300. No tent rentals available, but blankets can be rented.

ASAHI-DAKE

At 2,290 meters, Asahi-dake is the highest mountain in Hokkaido. You can hike across from the top of the Sōunkyō Ropeway or hitchhike into Asahikawa on Highway 39 and take a bus from Asahikawa into the Asahi-dake Onsen area. If you are staying at the hostel, the bus ticket will be refunded.

What to See and Do
The hot-spring spa area of Asahidake Onsen is a less visited, more rugged place than the visitor-jammed area around Sōunkyō. This is a chilly, damp, cold, and magnificent mountain, so dress warmly. The ropeway runs from Asahi-dake Onsen to Sugatami Station in two shifts. An outdoor hot spring (*rotenburo*) marks the halfway point—it also attracts bears in the morning and evening, so be on guard. The full ropeway run costs ¥2,600 round trip. Smouldering Asahi-dake looms above, and a one-hour hiking trail leads you to Sugatami-no-ike, a sulfurous pond with a small sheltered hut. From this pond it is another two hours to the top.

Where to Stay
I highly recommend a stay at **Daisetsuzan Shirakaba-sō Hostel** (Tel. 0166-97-2246), which is near several hiking trails, cross-country ski trails, and the ropeway. The hostel is in a rustic Canadian-style log cabin, and it has its own *rotenburo*. It costs ¥2,600 a night plus ¥600 for breakfast. You can take a bus from Asahikawa-eki to Asahidake Onsen and get off at Camp jō-mae *teiryūjo* (bus stop), near the hostel. The bus ride takes about one hour and 40 minutes, but only three buses run each day. Save your ticket receipt and the owner of the hostel will reimburse

you. The hostel owners can lend you compasses and supply anti-bear bells and maps to the area. A highly recommended hike is through the forests to the even *more* remote hot-spring area of Tenninkyō. The hostel can supply details, and the trail head is well marked.

DAISETSU-ZAN

From Sapporo to the Asahidake Onsen Area: If you are going directly from Sapporo to the Asahidake Onsen area, hitch-hike to Asahikawa first. Hitchhiking between Sapporo and Asahi-kawa involves going between Hokkaido's two largest cities. The traffic flow is steady—now is the time to use a sign saying "Asahikawa-shi" in order to get a ride all the way. If you choose to hitch along the highways instead of the expressway, you should still be able to get from Sapporo to Asahikawa in about three hours. To escape Sapporo, take a local train north on the Hakodate Line to Ōasa-eki and then hitchhike northeast on Highway 12 (in the same direction the train is going).

A second alternative is to take a subway to the end of the line to Shin-Sapporo-eki. Highway 12 runs beside it and if you are patient enough you *can* hitch a ride, though you are still very much in the thick of things.

Sapporo to Sōunkyō from the South: If you are not going to the Asahidake Onsen area, you can avoid the more congested route leading into Asahikawa by coming in from the south and then up the east side of the park. From Sapporo take a local train to Kami-Nopporo-eki on the Chitose Line. From Kami-Nopporo, walk north and in a few minutes you will come to Highway 274. Turn and hitchhike east on Highway 274 across to Shihoro. (It is a long ride from Sapporo to Shihoro, so make sure you set out early in the day.)

At Shihoro, hitch north on Highway 241, which will take you

to Highway 273, which leads right into the Sōunkyō Gorge. This is the safest way to get to Daisetsu-zan, because you stay on national highways the entire way.

En Route

If it is getting late, you may want to stop on your way to Daisetsu-zan. On Highway 274, about 15 km west of Shimizu, is the **Shimizu Machi Camp-jō** (Tel. 01566-2-3994), open from the beginning of July to mid-September. There is no per-person entry charge and no tent rentals. ¥510 for a space. A six-person bungalow costs ¥2,060; call ahead to reserve.

SHIRETOKO

If, instead of turning inland toward Daisetsu-zan National Park, you continue down the northeastern shore of Hokkaido, you will eventually come to the untamed seacoast of the Shiretoko-hantō. Usually referred to simply as Shiretoko, the peninsula juts out from Hokkaido like a heel spur, and it offers rugged coastlines, steep cliffs, seaside waterfalls, and one of the best natural outdoor baths in Japan. This is a beautiful place, called "The End of the Earth" in Japanese. In many ways, it is a more interesting destination than Daisetsu-zan National Park. If you are not captivated by mountains, and prefer coast, Shiretoko is a better destination.

Shiretoko is home to a rare, protected breed of sea eagles; they favor the southeastern side of the peninsula, around the town of Rausu, but if you take a boat cruise along the west coast you may still see some of these magnificent birds circling in the air. From Shiretoko you can also see the hotly disputed Northern Territories.

En Route

As you hitchhike to the End of the Earth, you will pass

through the small logging town of Shari (population 15,000). If it is late in the afternoon, spend a night in Shari and then head out early the following morning. The traffic to Shiretoko is not consistent. The **Shari Youth Hostel** (Tel. 01522-3-2220) is just around the corner from Shari-eki and costs ¥2,600 per night. VISA is accepted. The hostel is closed November 1–May 31. The next morning head into Utoro.

On your way in to Utoro, stop at the seaside Oshinkoshin-no-taki (waterfalls) near Highway 334 , about 7 km south of Utoro at Oshinkoshin-zaki. These falls are the highest in the Shiretoko region.

Utoro: Most of Shiretoko is a national park, but the highway goes only halfway up the peninsula. Along the peninsula is the fishing village of Utoro, which has tried to turn itself into a high-priced tourist town, with mixed results. You can arrange expensive boat tours along the spectacular Shiretoko coast—prices start at ¥3,000.

Bicycle rentals are available for ¥1,500 per day at **Bonzu Home** in the center of town, near the Utoro bus terminal. You can rent a mountain bike from the **Shiretoko Youth Hostel** for ¥1,500 a day between May and October. Mountain bikes are reserved for hostel guests, but if there are not many guests they will probably rent one to you. Show them your passport and let them write down the information if it will help reassure them that you aren't a bicycle thief.

Where to Stay

The **Shiretoko Hostel** (Tel. 01522-4-2034) is north of Utoro Onsen. At ¥3,100 it is slightly more expensive than most, but it does have a large hot-spring bath. Check out the giant sea-eagle mural on the side of the building. They accept VISA, and as mentioned earlier, they rent mountain bikes.

Near the Shiretoko Hostel is the **Shiretoko Yaeijō Campsite**

(Tel. 01522-4-2722), which is open from mid-June to the end of September. It costs ¥300 per person. There are no tent rentals, but you can rent a four-man bungalow for ¥3,000.

Iwaobetsu: If you reach Utoro early in the day, you should continue up the peninsula on Prefectural Highway 95, aiming for the small fishing village of Iwaobetsu. This road, shown in yellow but not numbered in the atlas, will take you into the most beautiful and unspoiled region of Shiretoko.

What to See and Do:

The **Shiretoko Go-ko** are five, bottom-fed, spring-filled lakes that drain into the ocean. A walking path and boardwalk winds its way around the lakes. (Watch out for bears!)

Save the Five Lakes stroll for later and instead grab a towel and head for the Kamuiwakka waterfalls, one of Japan's finest natural outdoor hot springs, the **Kamuiwakkayu-no-taki**. It's free, it's warm, and it's mixed, so leave your inhibitions behind. These hot-water waterfalls are about 15 km down the road from the hostel. Catch a bus and get off at the Shiretoko Ōhashi (bridge), by the Kamuiwakka-no-taki *teiryūjo*. To get to the *roten-buro*, scramble upstream for about 30 minutes. You will feel the water getting warmer and warmer as you go, and eventually you will come to a series of thermal pools cupped in the rock, fed by a hot, sulfuric waterfall that slides down the rock face and fills the pools. The water is heated by volcanic **Iō-zan** (1,563 meters). Strip and climb into one of the most beautifully located outdoor hot springs in Japan. The higher pools offer a glimpse of distant ocean and a view of the mountains.

After a hot bath *au naturel*, you may feel ready to try a hike up the trail to the top of Iō-zan. It is a full day's walk up Iō-zan and back again, so you may want to make the hike first and then relax in the hot springs in the late afternoon on your way down.

Another mountain hike leads up **Rausu-dake** (1,661 meters), which offers an equally splendid view. The trail head is at the Iwaobetsu Onsen *teiryūjo* (bus stop) near the campsite. If you are planning on making this hike, stay at the campsite (listed below) beside Iwaobetsu Onsen instead of at the hostel.

The trail soon comes to two scenic outlooks in a row: **Okhotsk Tenbōdai** and **Daini Tenbōdai.** If you still feel energetic, push on and you will pass through fields of wildflowers and alpine forests to the top of the mountain itself. Make sure you bring all your supplies with you for the hike, as well as a small bell to wear to scare away bears.

Most hikers just go to the top of Rausu-dake and then come back down again, but the trail continues down the other side, and meets the highway that runs between Iwaobetsu and Rausu. This is a solid five-hour hike through a very secluded area. If you only want a light mountain walk, do not attempt to cross over the mountain. If you do decide to hike across Rausu-dake to the highway, you may want to make a detour to the fishing port of Rausu. To get to Rausu, hitch east on Highway 334, called the Shiretoko Ōdan-dōro (road), through the twists and turns of the Shiretoko Pass. It's a nice enough ride, but the trip to Rausu is *not* a must-see and is really only for people with a lot of time on their hands.

Where to Stay

As you come up from Utoro along the coastal highway you will pass near the **Shiretoko-Iwaobetsu Hostel** (Tel. 01522-4-2311), which costs ¥2,800 a night and is open April 29–October 25. (Do not confuse this with the Shiretoko Hostel in Utoro mentioned earlier.) Bicycle rentals are available for ¥300 a day. This hostel is about 9 km from Utoro near the Iwaobetsu *teiryūjo.* From there, the trail head up Rausu-dake is about an hour's walk; they can supply hiking information. The first car by will probably give you a lift, but you could even walk it in an hour or two.

If you have trouble getting to Iwaobetsu, or if it's getting dark, you can call from Utoro and they will fetch you, but try to hitch-hike in and save them the trouble. As mentioned, they rent bicycles which will come in handy if you want to see the Five Lakes, which are about 6 km farther down the road from the hostel.

There is a **campsite** at Iwaobetsu Onsen, which is even nearer to the start of the Rausu-dake hiking trail. Arrangements for the campsite can be made at the hot-spring office, but this may change soon. In any case, just show up and pitch a tent.

On the highway into Rausu, in the Rausu Onsen area, is the **Kokusetsu Rausu Camp-jō**. It is very basic, but free. This may change, however, as there is talk of upgrading it.

Inland from Rausu town, near Rausu Chomin Ski-jō, is the **Rinkan Hiroba Camp-jō,** which is also free, but unless you are already in the area, it is not really worth the effort to get here.

If you get stranded on the wrong side of Shiretoko Peninsula, the spartan **Rausu Hostel** (Tel. 01538-7-2145) near the Hon-machi Noriba bus stop is marginally better than spending the night in a barn. It costs ¥2,400 per night.

AKAN NATIONAL PARK

From the Shiretoko Peninsula you can return to Sapporo via Akan National Park. Backtrack from Utoro on Highway 334 until you come to Highway 391, inland at Koshimizu. Turn south on 391 and you can hitchhike directly into the Kussharoko (lake) area of Akan. Or you can come in from Abashiri on the scenic Abashiri Kawayu-sen highway.

If, however, you want to hitchhike from Abashiri to Kussha-roko lake in one go, you are better off taking Highway 39 south from Abashiri to Bihoro and then hitching along Highway 243, also known as the Bihoro-kokudō. This will take you south through the Bihoro Tōge (pass). The hairpin turns of the Bihoro Pass make for a dramatic entrance to the park.

Note: The Abashiri Kawayu-sen highway is shown in green but

is not labeled in the atlas. Kawayu is the name of the hot-spring resort area by the lake, at the end of the route. The highway runs from Abashiri through the village of Higashi-Mokoto and past the scenic lookout of Mokotoyama. There are two strategically located campsites along the way.

What to See and Do

Kussharoko is home of Kusshi, a sea monster similar to that of Loch Ness fame, Canada's Ogopogo, and Kagoshima's Isshi. You can see a tourist likeness of Kussharoko's monster near Kawayu Onsen, west of Kawayu-eki. The area around the lake is very thermally active, with warm sands and hot-spring pits capable of boiling eggs, which are sold to tourists.

Wakoto Onsen, on the south shore of the lake, is the main visitors' center. There are two campsites here, but they need reservations far in advance. Overpriced boat cruises leave from Ikenoyu Onsen on the east shore; the boats circle Naka-jima (island) and leave you lighter of wallet and vaguely bored.

Where to Stay

Near Mokotoyama, north of Kussharoko and west of the highway, is the **Mokotoyama Shizen Kyūyōrin Yaeijō** campsite. Call the town office (Tel. 0152-62-2311) for more information. It is open July 1–August 31 and costs ¥300 per person. Five-man bungalow-cabins are available for ¥3,090. The other campsite, farther north and to the east in the Mokotoyama Onsen area, is the **Mokotoyama Onsen Camp-jō** (Tel. 0152-66-3111), which is open May 1–September 30. It costs ¥200 per person. No tent rentals are available.

On the east shore of Kussharoko, west from Kawayu-eki, is the **Auto Camp Kussharo** (Tel. 01548-3-2575), which is open May 20–September 30 and costs ¥300 per person. Tent rentals are also available. There is a *rotenburo* in the campsite that you can use anytime.

Farther south along the shore of the lake, in the Sunayu Onsen area, is the **Sunayu Camp-jō,** which is open from the end of June to the beginning of September. Tent rentals are available.

AKANKO

To hitch from Kussharoko to Akanko you will have to pass through Teshikaga. Three national highways meet near Teshikaga, and it can get confusing; make sure you get dropped off on Highway 241, pointed west.

Highway 241 west from Teshikaga is also called the Ōdan-kokudō (road). It becomes a wonderfully scenic route once it leaves the Teshikaga area and starts winding its way toward Akanko. The view at Sokodai is particularly good.

Akan Kohan is the main visitor/tourist center and includes several lakeside hot springs and bubbling hot mud pits. A boat cruise runs from Akan Kohan Onsen on the south side of Akanko to tiny Chiurui-jima and then down the coast. The 90-minute ride costs ¥1,000. East of Akanko, just 3 km along the highway, are two wooded ponds called **Tarō-ko** and **Jirō-ko**—which is the equivalent of naming them Lake Joe and Lake Fred. A walking path connects the two; another path leads from the lakes up to the top of **Oakan-dake** (1,371 meters). The Joe-and-Fred hike up Oakan-dake is an easy, scenic, and pleasant way to spend an afternoon.

More dramatic is the hike up **Meakan-dake,** a sulfurously active volcano south of Akanko. Hitch southwest on Highway 241 and then in to Onnetō. Paul Hunt describes this thrilling hike in *Hiking in Japan*.

Where to Stay

The **Akan Angel Hostel** (Tel. 0154-67-2309, 2954) is a pleasant enough place near the eastern shore of tourist-thronged

Akanko. It costs ¥2,600 per night and has its own hot spring. Some English is spoken.

Mashūko Hostel (Tel. 01548-2-3098) is named for Mashūko (lake), but isn't in a particularly scenic location. The hostel is in the crossroads town of Teshikaga, about 3 km south of the inter-section of Highways 241, 243, and 391, right beside The Great Bear Restaurant. The hostel is closed December 1–20 and costs ¥3,000 per night during peak seasons.

Note: Although this hostel is outside the main park area, if it's late in the day you may want to stay here anyway. The next morning you can hitch west on scenic Highway 241 (also known as the Ōdan-kokudō) to Akanko.

The **Akan Kohan Camp-jō** (Tel. 0154-67-3263) in Akan Kohan is near Highway 240 and about 200 meters west of the Ainu tourist village. This campsite costs ¥200 per person between July and August, otherwise it's free. A five-man tent costs ¥1,600, but they are available in the summer only. This campsite is near the Akan Angel Hostel; if the campsite is full, walk west on Highway 240. The hostel will be to the north.

Timing: To budget your time safely, count on the following: At least two days from Sapporo to either Rishiri or Rebun Island, followed by four to five days on the islands. Two days to get from Wakkanai to the Shiretoko Peninsula, and another two days in the Iwaobetsu area. Two days to get from the Shiretoko Peninsula to Sapporo, three if you want to spend time in Akan National Park. Thus, a Grand Tour of Northern Hokkaido—from Sapporo up to Rishiri and Rebun, then down to the Shiretoko Peninsula and across Akan National Park back to Sapporo—will take at least two weeks. To avoid feeling rushed or having to cut your journey short, allow just over two weeks to be safe. In Hokkaido, the more time you have, the better.

If you decide to turn inland at Yūbetsu and hitchhike into Daisetsu-zan National Park instead of visiting the Shiretoko

Peninsula, you should add three or four days of hiking and sight-seeing, and then another day to get back to Sapporo. Thus, for a journey up to Rishiri and Rebun, and then back through Daisetsu, count on 15 days.

These are extended tours, of course. You can break them up if you don't have the time. A simple trip across from Sapporo to Shiretoko and back should only take about six days. A journey from Sapporo up to Rishiri and Rebun, and then back, would take only a week. In Hokkaido, more than anywhere else in Japan, it is important to have a day or two leeway in your schedule. The roads are more open and the speed limits faster, which makes for ideal hitchhiking, but Hokkaido is a big place. In the atlas, Hokkaido is drawn to a smaller scale than the rest of Japan; as a result, the distances in Hokkaido are much greater than they appear.

Tohoku and the
Niigata Coast

If Hokkaido is the New Frontier, Tohoku is the Old Frontier:
Japan's Deep North, a land of mendicant monks and wandering
poets, a land rich in tradition and folklore. It remains a remote
area to most Japanese people, but the remoteness is more psy-
chological than physical.

With coastal roads, mountain hot springs, monasteries and
sacred mountains, a single extant castle, and a desolate volcanic landscape, Tohoku is well suited for the adventurous
hitchhiker. A large, valley-like plain runs up the middle of
Tohoku, from Sendai to Towadako (lake). The majority of the
population lives along the coast or in this central plain; the rest
of Tohoku is mountainous and empty. The interior highlands
have some of the lowest population densities in Japan.

Tohoku has always been the realm of the long-distance traveler; the priestly poet Bashō immortalizes his Tohoku travels in
1690 with a haiku-laced travel narrative entitled *Oku no Hosomichi*
(The Narrow Road to the Deep North).

Bashō only skirted the edge of Tohoku, but then, he had to
walk most of the way in straw sandals. You, as a hitchhiker,

will be going far deeper into Tohoku and you will be traveling in air-conditioned vehicles. In the mountain interiors, along the Iwate coast, and in the outlying peninsulas, hitchhiking is often the most efficient way to travel, short of renting a car yourself.

The Three Best Hitchhiking Destinations in Tohoku are 1) Kinkasan Island, 2) the Miyagi–Iwate coast, and 3) the Dread Mountain of Osorezan. I have also included a side trip to the Three Sacred Mountains of Dewa Sanzan. The Niigata coast and Sado Island are part of this itinerary, even though they are not technically a part of Tohoku. Tohoku's Three Famous Sites are 1) Matsushima, 2) the Golden Pavilion of Hiraizumi, and 3) the castle-town of Hirosaki. Although they do not necessarily lend themselves to hitchhiking, I have included all three of these sites in this itinerary so that you will not feel you have missed anything.

THE SENDAI–AOMORI LOOP

Both Sendai and Aomori have international airports, but Sendai has more connections, so I have chosen it as the starting point.

SENDAI

Sendai (population 900,000) is the largest city in Tohoku. It was founded during Japan's tumultuous seventeenth century by the great feudal warlord Date Masamune, the "One-Eyed Dragon," whose image still graces tourist trinkets. Unfortunately, like many of Japan's major cities, much of Sendai was leveled by fire-bombing during World War II. The city was rebuilt on a spacious grid pattern with wide tree-lined avenues, similar to those in Sapporo. Many cities in Japan call themselves "green," but Sendai is one of the few places to live up to its own publicity.

Getting There

If you want to begin your visit to Japan with a tour of Tohoku, fly into Sendai-kūkō (airport) and follow this itinerary. Sendai-kūkō is south of the city. Highway 4 is a long, 2.5 km-hike west from the airport. If you have the time and energy you can walk out to the highway and then hitchhike into the city center on Highway 4. I didn't bother; instead, I took a connecting bus that runs from Sendai-kūkō to Sendai-eki for ¥890. Sendai is also on the Shinkan-sen (Bullet Train) route just two hours from Tokyo at ¥10,390, but there is no reason to spend that kind of money.

─────────────── KEY TO MAP ───────────────

1. Sendai
2. Matsushima-wan
3. Oku-Matsushima
4. Ishinomaki
5. Ayukawa
6. Kinkasan Island
7. Onagawa
8. Kesennuma
9. Rikuzen-takata
10. Goishi Kaigan
11. The Dai-Kannon
12. Kamaishi
13. Miyako
14. Omoto
15. Ryūsendō
16. Rikuchū Kaigan
17. Kuji
18. Kabushima Nesting Grounds
19. Hachinohe
20. Misawa
21. Ogawarako
22. Noheji

23. Mutsu
24. Osore-zan and Usorisanko
25. The Yagen Valley
26. Sai-mura
27. Hotoke-ga-ura
28. Wakinosawa-mura
29. Natsudomari-hantō
30. Aomori
31. Hirosaki
32. Iwaki-san
33. Hakkōda-san
34. The Oirase Valley
35. Towadako
36. Yasumiya
37. The Ōyu Stone Circle
38. Morioka
39. Iwate-san
40. Tazawako
41. Hiraizumi
42. Ōdate
43. Noshiro

44A. Hachirōgata-chōseichi
44. Monzen-mura
45. Oga Onsen Area
46. Akita
47. Jūroku Rakan Stone Buddhas
48. Sakata
49. Tobi-shima
50. Tsuruoka
51. Haguro-san
52. Gas-san
53. Yudono-san
54. Dainichibō and Chūrenji
55. Murakami
56. Niigata
57. Ryōtsu
58. Aikawa Gold Mines
59. Senkaku-wan
60. Ogi
61. Sado-ga-shima

TOHOKU and the NIIGATA COAST

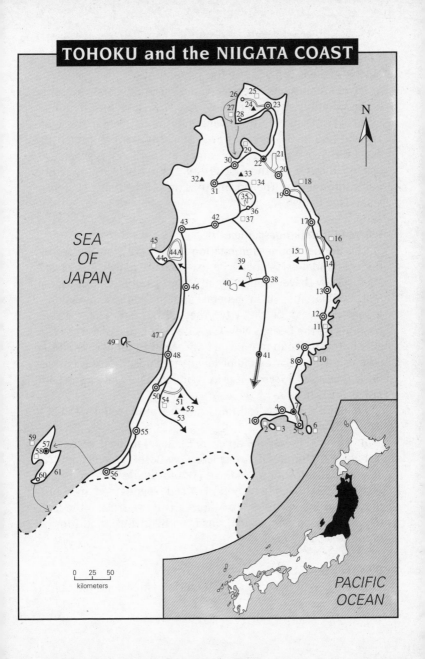

N

SEA
OF
JAPAN

PACIFIC
OCEAN

0   25   50
kilometers

Remember: You can hitchhike between major Japanese cities quickly and easily if you use the expressways.

If you hitchhike into Sendai on the Tohoku Expressway, ask to be dropped off at the Sendai–Miyagi IC east of the city, where most of the traffic will be flowing into the city center. If you are arriving late in the day, however, you may want to get off the expressway one intersection earlier, at the Sendai–Minami IC, and go directly for the Dōchu-An Youth Hostel without first going into the city. The Dōchu-An is one of the finest hostels in Japan (see below).

Where to Obtain Information:

The **Sendai Tourist Information Center** (TIC) on the second floor of Sendai-eki is open 8:30 A.M.–8:00 P.M. daily (Tel. 022-222-4069). They have English maps and pamphlets of Sendai, Matsushima, Tohoku in general, and the Yamadera Buddhist monastery west of the city. They also offer ¥200-discount coupons for the **Leaves New Capsule Hotel,** one of the few capsule hotels in Japan that has a floor reserved for women. Make sure to pick up the excellent language phrase booklet entitled *Sendai-Matsushima Tourist's Handbook* and the JNTO maps and pamphlets for Hiraizumi.

Sendai has its own toll-free **English Hot Line**: Tel. 0120-222-800. Call before 6:00 P.M.

If you need to buy the atlas, an English-Japanese pocket dictionary, Weatherhill's *Exploring Tohoku*, or Bashō's travel narrative, stop in at the downtown **Maruzen Bookstore** near the south end of the Higashi Ichiban-chodōri Arcade pedestrian mall. The most pleasant way to get to Maruzen is to walk down the leafy, tree-lined Aoba-dōri, which runs from Sendai-eki, and turn left onto the walking mall.

What to See and Do

At the end of Sendai's wide Aoba-dori (street) are the obligatory castle ruins of Aoba-jō, with an original turret. The Ōsaki Hachiman Jinja (shrine) dates from the city's glory days of the seventeenth century. The Aoba-jō Shiryōtenjikan museum has a display of swords, helmets, and armor from the time of the Warring States (Sengoku Jidai), but with a ¥700 admission, it is for samurai aficionados only.

Where to Stay

Although it is a pleasant enough place, you should really try to get out of Sendai as quickly as possible and over to the Matsushima Youth Hostel. However, if you do decide to spend the night in Sendai, there are four hostels, three of which have English speakers on staff.

Hostels: The Japanese-style **Dōchu-An Hostel** (Tel. 022-247-0511) is one of the best hostels in Japan. Although situated in the southern suburbs of Sendai close to the airport, the hostel is surprisingly rural. It is built in a reconstructed farmhouse, complete with a thatched-roof entrance gate, and is as well kept and rustic as any ryokan. It costs ¥3,100 per night. English is spoken—they even have English newspapers available.

To get there from the airport, take a bus to Tatekoshi-eki and then take the train three stops to Nagamachi-eki. From there it is a ¥700 taxi ride to the hostel. If you are coming from downtown, the hostel is a ten-minute walk east from Tomisawa *chikatetsu*-eki (subway station). It is actually located between the Tomisawa subway and Nagamachi-eki mentioned above.

If you are hitching into Sendai from Hiraizumi on the Tohoku Expressway, you can bypass downtown Sendai by getting off at the Sendai–Minami IC and then hitching east on the highway. Tell the driver you want to go either to the Nagamachi-eki or to the Tomisawa *chikatetsu*-eki.

The Japanese-style **Chitose Hostel** (Tel. 022-222-6329) is downtown, a 15-minute walk from the Higashi-guchi (east exit) of the main Sendai-eki. English is spoken, and the hostel has an international telephone. Closed December 30–January 5. ¥3,000 per night.

The **Sendai Onnai Hostel** (Tel. 022-234-3922) is near the Tohoku Kai Byōin (hospital) only a 15-minute bus ride (No. 24) from Sendai-eki; ask to get off at the hospital. English is also spoken at this hostel, which is in a good location for exploring the ruins of Aoba-jō. ¥2,500 per night.

Sendai Akamon Hostel (Tel. 022-264-1405) is a 40-minute walk from Sendai-eki, west through downtown and then north along the west side of the Hirose-gawa (river). The hostel is beside the river near the Nakanose-bashi bus stop. The park and castle ruins of Aoba-jō are to the south of the hostel. Closed December 28–January 3. ¥2,300 per night.

Japanese Inn Group: Behind the central post office is the **Japanese Inn Aisaki** (Tel. 022-264-0700), a member of the Japanese Inn Group. It is a 12-minute walk from Sendai-eki. Japanese- and Western-style rooms, without a private bath, cost ¥4,500. American Express, VISA, and MasterCard accepted.

Capsules: The new, well-kept **Leaves Capsule Hotel** (pronounced "reebooze kapuseru") is in the downtown area (Tel. 022-261-8020). If you are a woman this may be one of your few chances to stay in a capsule hotel. The capsules cost ¥3,100 per night for an upper berth, ¥3,300 for a lower. The Tourist Information Center in Sendai Station offers ¥200-discount tickets for Leaves, and they can also show you where it is on an English map. Leaves is a five-minute taxi ride or 15-minute walk from Sendai-eki. Alternatively, take the subway to Kōtōdai Kōen-eki and exit from the Minamai San-ban Deguchi (exit south 3). From there it is a three-minute walk.

Camping: The **Sendai Jōgi Outdoor Sports Park** (Tel. 022-271-8004) requires a reservation at least a day before. They charge ¥500 per person and ¥2,000 for a spot. It is a 20-minute ride west from the Sendai–Miyagi IC, on Highway 48, and then north ten minutes along the Okura-gawa road. The campsite is at the north side of the Okura Dam, which puts you well out of town if you are planning to head east toward Matsushima. It is better to stop here on your way back instead. Coming in from Hiraizumi (to the north) on the Tohoku Expressway, ask to be let off at the Sendai–Miyagi IC and then hitch west. Tell people you are headed toward the Okura Dam.

MATSUSHIMA

Matsushima is one of Japan's Three Most Scenic Spots—the Bridge of Heaven at Ama-no-Hashidate and Miyajima Shrine near Hiroshima are the other two. Matsushima Bay is dotted with over 260, small pine-covered islands in odd shapes and sizes, and tour boats ply the waters constantly.

For all the hype, the main harbor area is disappointing and the hotels are outrageously expensive. Fortunately, Matsushima's youth hostel is east of the main tourist zone in a quieter, unspoiled area. When Bashō came here, he was reportedly so taken by the beauty of the place that the only 5-7-5 syllabic poem he could come up with was—in my own approximate translation of the Japanese—as follows: "Matsushima, ah! Ah-ahh, Matsushima, ah. Matsushima, ah!" What can I say? The man was a genius.

Getting There

There is no point trying to hitchhike from downtown Sendai to Matsushima. For ¥310, take the 30-minute train which runs from the basement of Sendai-eki.

Note: In Matsushima, the main sightseeing area is near JR Matsushima-kaigan-eki. Don't buy a ticket to Matsushima-eki, which is farther east and on a separate train line.

Where to Obtain Information

More than one guidebook has mistakenly thought that the small Japanese tourist office at the Matsushima wharf is the main tourist center. It isn't. **The tourist center** is in front of Matsushima-kaigan-eki and maintains information in English, French, Spanish, German, Chinese, and Korean. Office hours vary, but normally it is open 10:00 A.M.–4:00 P.M. There is usually an English speaker on duty.

What to See and Do

The **cruises of Matsushima Bay** leave every hour and cost ¥1,400. They are underwhelming to say the least. There are two routes, one that circles the bay and then returns to the main wharf and another that crosses the bay to Shiogama. If you are determined to see the islands in Matsushima Bay, make it part of your trip. When coming in, get off at Shiogama-eki and take the ferry across to Matsushima.

There are a number of interesting places to visit on shore in Matsushima; the English pamphlet gives full details. Because several of them close around 4:00 P.M. or 5:00 P.M., explore the coast first and take a boat cruise later.

Zuigan-ji Zen temple was rebuilt in 1606 in the more baroque style of the Momoyama period. The approach to the temple leads through a forested park, lined on one side by meditation caves carved out of the rock face by very bored monks. Admission to the temple and grounds is ¥500.

Godai-dō is a small pavilion first built in 807, but later rebuilt in 1607. It is on a tiny tuft of an island connected by a bridge known as **En-musubi-no-hashi,** or Love-Match Bridge. Legend has it that many a love blossomed here after a kind gentleman helped his female companion up the steep precipice.

Oshima is a small island connected to the mainland by a short vermilion Moon-Crossing Bridge. It also has small meditation caves carved into the rock, giving it a certain Cro-Magnon charm.

The view from **Matsushima Tower** is worth seeing. However, the tower seems to be an optical illusion; though it looks near, it is actually a long walk from the bay and is nearer to Matsushima-eki. The tower closes at 6:00 P.M. and costs ¥400. Keep in mind that a similar view can be had for free from Otakamori in Oku-Matsushima, a short bicycle ride from the hostel.

Note: The "castle" near the bay is really a theme ryokan and in no way authentic.

OKU-MATSUSHIMA

This is the quieter, eastern side of Matsushima. Rent a bicycle at the hostel and then spend a lazy morning or afternoon exploring its various fishing villages and beaches. During the off-season you will have the wide open eastern beach all to yourself. I went the week right after Golden Week and the area was empty and relaxing.

What to See and Do

When bicycling around the Oku-Matsushima area, make sure to visit the narrow, cramped village of **Tsukihama** tucked into a nook by the sea. Though the beaches can be a little dirty in the off-season, this picturesque village should not be missed.

A short bicycle ride from the hostel takes you to **Otakamori Hill**. Hike to the top for a beautiful view of the islands in the bay. Sunsets from Otakamori are stunning.

The eastern side of Oku-Matsushima is the most attractive, and most of it can be seen only by boat, a far more interesting boat ride than the bigger tourist ones in Matsushima Bay. The Oku-Matsushima cruise begins not far from the hostel, near the bridge that connects Oku-Matsushima with the mainland. (Oku-Matsushima is an island, though this is not always clear on maps.) Unlike the large ferries to the west, the Oku-Matsushima cruise is on a small boat and travels much closer to the islands and rock formations.

Using odd mathematics, charges for the **Oku-Matsushima cruise** are as follows: ¥4,500 per person if there is only one passenger; ¥4,500 per person if there are two passengers; and ¥1,500 per person if there are three or more passengers. The main thing to remember is that if you are solo or in a couple, wait until there at least three people before taking the cruise.

Where to Stay

In the forested parklands between Oku-Matsushima and the mainland is the **Pi-La Matsushima Youth Hostel** (Tel. 0225-88-222), a modern, well-kept, friendly place where some English is spoken. Take advantage of available bicycyle rental; the Oku-Matsushima area is fairly big and best explored on two wheels. The hostel is a 20-minute walk from Nobiru-eki. From the station walk straight out, over the bridge, and keep walking until you see signs pointing you off to the right, into the forested area and toward the hostel. If you are arriving after dark or are simply exhausted, spend the ¥600 or so and take a taxi directly from Nobiru-eki to the hostel.

Escaping

The stretch of road known as Matsushima Kankō dōro runs past Nobiru-eki and along the river. This is the most accessible and best suited for hitching east out of the Matsushima area.

Much of the traffic is headed for Ishinomaki (population 127,000), so you may want to make a sign that says "Ishi-No-Maki" to spare yourself the short hops. Once you get a ride make sure you explain that you are ultimately headed for Kinkasan. Ask to be let off east of the Ishinomaki city center. If you do get dropped off in the middle of town, ask to be taken to Ishino-maki-eki. From there you can take a bus east, out of town. Don't bother trying to walk out beyond the city limits from the station. Ishinomaki goes on forever.

When I came from Oku-Matsushima, I got one ride all the way to Ishinomaki. I was dropped off east of downtown on Highway 398, in front of the hillside graveyard just beyond the river. My choice of hitchhiking locations may have unnerved some drivers. It was a long, hot, muggy day and it took a long time to get a ride. If you want to preserve your strength, or if you are new at hitchhiking, you can spare yourself much aggravation by taking a train from either Nobiru-eki or Ishinomaki-eki all the way to Watanoha-eki. This puts you near the road that runs south down the Oshika-hantō (peninsula).

Hitching Down the Oshika-hantō: There are two roads suitable for hitching run down the peninsula: **Prefectural Highway** (Number 2 or 7 depending when you get on), not far from Watanoha-eki, which runs down the west side of the peninsula, through fishing villages and into Ayukawa port. This is the "working" road of Oshika. Expect to ride with fishermen and maybe even a whaler or two.

There is also the **Ojika Cobalt Line,** a skyline that begins farther east, in Onagawa, and runs down the center of the peninsula. To avoid backtracking, hitchhike *down* the west coast highway and then *up* the skyline. Or even better, hitchhike down and then take a *ferry* back from Kinkasan Island to Onagawa.

En Route

On the way down the prefectural highway, you will pass near the site of the mysterious **Jūichimen Kannon,** a statue of the Buddhist Goddess of Mercy. This wooden statue, dating possibly to the Kamakura period (1185–1333), was found washed up on the beach nearby. It stands three meters high and was carved from a single block of wood. No one knows how or why it came to rest on the shore of this distant peninsula. If you mention it to your driver, he or she will gladly stop for a visit. There is a campsite along the way as well. If it's late in the day, ask to be dropped off. The way to the campsite is well marked by road signs.

You must leave the Oku-Matsushima area early in the day in order to connect with a ferry from Ayukawa to Kinkasan. There is also a single ferry that leaves once a day from the Ishinomaki port to Ayukawa at 9:30 A.M. in the morning. Take care: the port in Ishinomaki is far from Ishinomaki-eki. If you are running out of time, you can take a bus from Ishinomaki to Ayukawa. The Ayukawa bus leaves from the Number 2 bus stop in front of Ishinomaki-eki. The 1:45 P.M. bus is the last one that connects with a Kinkasan ferry.

AYUKAWA

Hitchhiking down the Oshika-hantō takes you through fishing villages and over high mountain vistas and into the whaling port of Ayukawa. From Ayukawa a ferry takes you out to Kinkasan.

Note: The bustling port town of Ayukawa is not shown in the atlas, because technically the entire southern peninsula revolves around the town of Oshika-chō. The small town of Ayukawa is closer to the sea; ferries depart from here. Although Kinkasan is the main hitchhiker's destination, the small port town of Ayukawa has its own unique character and attractions.

What to See and Do

For ¥600, pan for gold for 30 minutes at **Ayukawa's Sakintori Taiken** (experience), near the port. Any gold you manage to find you can keep. Gold panning is open from the end of April to the beginning of November.

The large whaling boat that has been dragged up onto dry land marks the entrance to the **Ayukawa Whaleland,** which costs

¥1,000 to enter. A brief English pamphlet is provided, and your ticket allows you to roam around the whaling ship. The ship itself is well presented; the crew and captain's cabins are maintained exactly as they were, without any repainting or tidying up. There are whale videos, whale songs, and even preserved whale penises on display. The museum also has its own chamber of horrors, but if you have a weak stomach you may want to skip this "conservation" museum.

The **Dariya Shokudō** restaurant has raw whale meat (*kujira sashimi*) for ¥1,000. Fried whale meat (*kujira kara-age*) is ¥1,500. A full-course whale steak (*kujira sutēki teishoku*) is ¥2,000. I thoroughly enjoyed my whale meal, except for the sharp pangs of guilt and remorse that followed from eating an endangered species.

Escaping

The ferry from Ayukawa to Kinkasan Island costs ¥880 one way and runs every hour, on the half-hour, 8:30 A.M.–3:30 P.M. If you are hitching make sure you leave the Oku-Matsushima area before 8:00 A.M. to avoid missing the last ferry out. This should give you some time in Ayukawa to wander about before catching your ferry. If possible, get the earliest ferry available. If you take the 2:30 P.M. ferry to Kinkasan, it will *just* give you enough time to check into the shrine's lodgings, climb to the mountain summit, and be back in time for a bath and supper. The 1:30 P.M. ferry from Ayukawa is even better. If you miss the ferry, the **Ayukawa Kokumin-shukusha** (Tel. 022-545-2281) is out of town, but a shuttle bus will pick you up if you make arrangements at the ferry port visitors' center. It costs ¥6,500 with two meals.

KINKASAN

Kinkasan boasts wild monkeys, deer, and—best of all after the tourist strip of Matsushima—silence. A night on Kinkasan ("golden flower") island offers the traveler a chance to experience Shinto rites firsthand, as well as to explore one of the most sacred places in northern Japan. An ancient shrine complex is built into the forests of Kinkasan. A hiking trail leads to a smaller shrine at the summit.

The steep hills and forests of this secluded island at the end of the Oshika-hantō is an antidote to Matsushima. Not much happens on Kinkasan, a quiet, spiritual place.

A few understocked shops are cluttered around the Kinkasan port. They close down at 4:00 P.M. so if you need to stock up, be quick. A large red torii gate to the left of port is the entrance to the steep road that leads to **Koganeyama Jinja** (also called Kinkasan Jinja). This shrine is dedicated to the gods of money circulation, and it is said that if you worship at Kinkasan for three years in a row, all your financial worries will be over. The deer that live on the grounds are considered messengers of the gods. The shrine complex is tranquil, especially after the last ferry for the mainland departs with all the day-trippers.

Behind the shrine, past a small cement dam, a rough path follows the jumbled boulders of a mountain stream. At times the path is the stream; eventually it leads through the woods to a ridge, veers right, and runs to the very top of Kinkasan. Keep careful track of the path you take so that you can retrace it on your way back to the shrine. Don't try to take spontaneous shortcuts on Kinkasan; the trails are marked but not *well* marked. It will take you a little over an hour to get from the main shrine to the summit. If you are hiking after lunch, you will probably have the path to the summit of Kinkasan all to yourself. Along the way you will see genuine wild monkeys; they are nervous when you approach and will either hiss or run away when they see you. At the top of the mountain is a small, weather-beaten shrine and a high view of the island. A small stone-carved X marks the actual summit.

From the summit you retrace your steps back to the main

shrine, or you can continue down the other side of Kinkasan to the remote Senjōjiki coast. From there, follow the gravel road to the right and it will take you back around to ferry port. Do not attempt to cross Kinkasan late in the day—this is a full day's hike.

The easiest hike is simply up to the top and back down again on the same path. This is a nice afternoon hike. If you take the 2:30 P.M. ferry (or earlier) to Kinkasan, you can climb to the top and return just in time for a bath and supper. If you are going to do anything more elaborate make sure you obtain a trail map from the ferry port or the shrine.

Where to Stay

For a glimpse inside the living faith of Shinto, stay in the shrine complex itself, at the **Kinkasan Jinja Pilgrims' Lodging House** (Tel. 0225-45-2301). A night's lodgings with two meals and morning rites will cost ¥9,000. It is money well spent, because staying at the shrine gives you a chance to wake up on Kinkasan; morning rites make your stay even more memorable.

The pilgrims' service takes place in the large shrine connected via a hallway with the hotel-style building. Make sure you get there before 6:20 A.M. The ceremony begins at 6:30 A.M.—*sharp*—but there is a satiny white vest you will need to put on before entering. Sit right up front so that the priest can bless you without having to cross the room. During the ceremony, follow the other pilgrims' lead. The paper blessing is for purity, the small golden bells are for success.

The only other rooms available on Kinkasan are at the **Abe Ryokan** (Tel. 0225-45-3081), which costs ¥6,500 with two meals.

Escaping

From Kinkasan, rather than hitching back up again, I recommend taking a ferry to Onagawa directly. This will cost you more, but it will put you farther up the road and save you several hours of hitching. Ferries from Kinkasan to Onagawa run every hour 9:00 A.M.–4:00 P.M. with some extra runs during peak season. The Onagawa ferry costs ¥1,600 one way and makes the high-speed run between Kinkasan and Onagawa in half an hour.

If you do want to hitch, take the Cobalt Line north to where it meets Highway 398 at Onagawa, a town thinly spread along 398. You may want to take a bus east of the ferry port before beginning. Once you clear the town the road begins to rise and you enter forested coastline dotted with coastal villages.

At the edge of Ogatsu, east of the highway, the highway does a quick zigzag. Stick to 398 and head toward Kitakami, the next town down the road. At Ogatsu, I hitched in front of the bus stop by an abandoned rail car/ice cream stand at the end of the zigzag and was picked up in 20 minutes. There are no trains and practically no buses between Ogatsu and Shizugawa (north of Kitakami), so you are now in the hitchhikers' domain.

When you get to Shizugawa you will have reached Highway 45. Congratulations! This highway runs north along the Miyagi–Iwate coast, and it is one of the best hitchhiking roads in Japan.

THE MIYAGI–IWATE COAST

For some reason, guidebooks often downplay the attraction of the Miyagi–Iwate coast and suggest that visitors not spend a lot of time exploring it. If you only pop in and out you *will* be disappointed. The more you explore the unspoiled coastline of this remote prefecture, the more beautiful it becomes. Along the Miyagi–Iwate coast you will find unspoiled scenery, hidden fishing villages, and a side of Japan that most tourists miss.

Small cities dot the wide highways along the coast, providing convenient places to rest and replenish supplies. Many scenic lookouts provide excellent places for discreet camping.

When hitchhiking this coast, it is easy to go too fast, since the

highway was built for speed and misses some of the more interesting side roads and peninsulas. Stick with the shoreline whenever possible, even when it means going off the main highway.
Explore the many fjords and peninsulas. Hitchhike down the
smaller branch roads. Some of the most beautiful small shrines
in Japan are located on just such lonely outposts between sea
and land. These shrines lack the splendor of Nikko or the aesthetics of Kyoto, but they blend with the landscape, where the
natural surroundings are as important as the architecture.

KESENNUMA AREA

Kesennuma (population 65,000) is an active port city built in
a narrow fjord. I liked the look of Kesennuma, but unless you are
fascinated by sea traffic, you can easily bypass it by staying on
the highway and hitching straight through. If you do venture into
Kesennuma you may want to take one of the frequent ferries out
to Oshima Island wedged into the bay.

What to See and Do

Karakuwa and **Osaki-misaki**: Tumbled stone stacks, 16
meters high, and waves that roll like boiling water mark the east
coast of the Karakuwa Peninsula. The names in Japanese are
Ore-ishi (the broken stone pillar) and Ōgama-hanzō (the boiling
water) and they make for an interesting ride. If it is in the
evening ask to be dropped off at Karakuwa Hostel (below).

Dairiseki Kaigan: North of Kesennuma, and tucked in just
under Highway 45 and not visible from the road is a small, picturesque cove at Dairiseki Kaigan. Working fishermen haul up
small boats, and a walking path leads in and out among the
white stone formations. This is a pleasant place for a stroll and
a stretch. Mention it just after you clear Kesennuma and your
driver will gladly make the detour.

Where to Stay

The **Karakuwa Hostel** (Tel. 02263-2-2490) is on the peninsula near the Ezokari *teiryūjo* (bus stop). It costs ¥2,800 per night and some English is spoken. Ferries run between the peninsula to the city port, and from there to Ōshima. The hostel has complete ferry schedules if you want to visit the island.

RIKUZENTAKATA

If I were ever asked to design the perfect city for hitchhikers, I would come up with Rikuzentakata. The city (population 29,000) has a wide highway running straight through it; between the highway and the sea is a swath of pine forest and **Takata-matsubara** beach. The forest makes for fine strolling, and pitching a tent in among the trees is apparently free in the off-season.

What to See and Do

A 15-minute bicycle ride from the hostel takes you to **Kōshō-ji**, the Sōdo-shū Zen sect's temple, where you can practice Zen meditation. Call before going to make sure there is time and space available (Tel. 0192-55-3063). Please do not pursue this in a frivolous manner. A temple visit should be arranged only if you are genuinely interested in Zen meditation.

Where to Stay

The **Rikuzentakata Hostel** (Tel. 0192-55-4246) is nestled among the trees just a short walk to Highway 45. This same stretch of highway has several restaurants and shops along the way with many parking lots—always a good choice for hitchhiking—as well as a *bentō* shop for the budget-minded. The youth hostel is closed June 6–15. It costs ¥2,500 a night.

If you have a tent, walk out to the beach first and look over the beachside campsite before you decide. The designated camping site is between the old Western-style wood building and the toilets. If it rains, you can beat a hasty retreat to the nearby hostel.

GOISHI KAIGAN

North and east of Rikuzentakata is a peninsula of Ōfunato-wan (bay), an area you should not skip.

Getting There

Highway 45 bypasses the peninsula entirely, so make sure you get onto Prefectural Highway 38 (shown in green but not labeled in the atlas). This highway follows the train tracks down the peninsula and joins Prefectural Highway 275. Follow 275 to the three-arched formation of Anatōshi-iso. These numbers don't really concern you: Tell your driver that you are headed to Anatōshi-iso and you will be understood.

What to See and Do

Most tourist pamphlets mention the stone-arch formation of **Anatōshi-iso,** located in a secluded spot that invites discreet, free camping. There are no shops or modern distractions at all, so make sure you bring drinks and breakfast. You will pass a public toilet on the path down—bring tissues.

If you leave Rikuzentakata in the mid-afternoon, you may want to explore the Goishi Kaigan (coast) and then ask someone to drop you off at the Anatōshi-iso lookout. A night spent here is both a minor adventure and very relaxing. Throughout the night, you will hear the constant hiss and sigh of the waves in the cove below. Feudal lords once collected the smooth black stones from this area for Go, a Japanese board game that uses both black and white stones.

East of Anatōshi-iso is the actual **Goishi Kaigan**. A path leads past several natural stone formations, one of which is called the Kaminari Iwa (thunder rock), where waves crash with the sound of thunder. Behind the Goishi-zaki Tōdai (lighthouse) is a carved stone Go board; walk farther along to collect your own Go stones for a souvenir. During the summer, boat tours run up and down the coast between **Hosoura-kō** and **Ebisu-hama**. Call 0192-29-2888 for information and schedules.

Where to Stay

If you don't wish to camp at Anatōshi-iso lookout, there is a campsite near the Thunder Rock walking path. **Goishi-zaki Camp-jō** costs ¥500 per person and a space charge of ¥500. Five-man tent rentals are available for ¥1,500.

KAMAISHI

Lovers of kitsch will delight in Kamaishi (population 53,000). As you approach the city, a 49-meter high, 12-story white statue of Kannon, the Goddess of Mercy, looms into sight. Similar to the Statue of Liberty—though much smaller—you can climb inside her and look out over the bay. Interestingly enough, the observation platform is right under her ample bosom—"A symbol of her maternal affection," my host insisted.

Admission to the **Dai-Kannon** is a hefty ¥850, which includes entrance to the stupa which contains a relic of the Buddha Himself. A small shard of bone, not on display, was given to Kamaishi in 1975 by the high priest of Kelaniya temple in Sri Lanka.

The Kamaishi Dai-Kannon was built in 1970 to comfort the souls of those lost to tidal waves and earthquakes. She is also a jealous deity, and a notice posted at the front gate warns that couples who visit the Dai-Kannon together may soon break up. If you are traveling with your loved one, don't despair. In the basement of the stupa, amid the statues of famous Japanese monks and saints, is a fiery demon-like character called **Aizen Myōō**, who rekindles passion and brings couples back together.

From the Dai-Kannon, the highway plunges you into Kamaishi. There are reportedly only two major bridge market-places in the world. One is in Italy, the other is here. The Kyōjō Ichiba market in Kamaishi is held every day except the 5th, 15th, 20th, and 25th of the month.

TODOGA-SAKI

This peninsula is the easternmost point of Honshu and, hence, the place where the sun first rises in the Land of the Rising Sun. A lighthouse marks the point.

Where to Stay

If you want to be the first to see the sun rise in Japan, you can stay at the **Aneyoshi Camp-jō,** which is just south of Todoga-saki. It costs ¥200 per person. No tent rentals. Open all year.

MIYAKO AND JŌDOGA-HAMA

Miyako (population 60,000) is the largest city and main center for sightseeing along the Rikuchu coast.

Where to Obtain Information

The **Miyako Kankō Kyōkai Tourist Information Center** (Tel. 0193-62-3574) is just in front of Miyako-eki. This is removed from the main sightseeing area, which is farther west at Jōdoga-hama (beach). The Miyako TIC has a listing of 17 different hotels in Miyako that are part of the International Tourist Association. They can help you arrange reservations. (It is best to make the reservations through the TIC office, rather than calling yourself.)

What to See and Do

The main attraction is the **Jōdoga-hama** area, north of the city center. The name means "Paradise Beach," and it really is beautiful, with its white sands and shaded forests. It can get very busy on the weekends, so try to arrive during a weekday. Even then, there is a lot to explore beyond the concentrated main area. The parking lot is a good place to inquire about rides heading north toward Kuji.

A 40-minute minicruise from Jōdoga-hama costs ¥1,000. It takes you up the coast to **Rōsoku Iwa,** the "Candlestick Rock," a towering 40-meter-high stone column that has been designated a national natural treasure. The sea-spraying **Shiofukiana** is another national treasure, and is shown in the atlas. Waves underground can force waterspouts as high as 30 meters into the air.

Note: You can hitch to the Shiofukiana area on Highway 45 if you don't want to take the boat tour. Highway 45 north of Miyako is also called the Hama-kaidō (road). Later try to get off the highway at Tarō and take the secondary road that runs east, out to Cape Misaki. (But be aware that this road is not the simple loop that the atlas makes it appear to be.) This will take you past the dramatic rock formations of Sanō Iwa. Farther along, near the cape itself, is a campsite (see below). This small hook of land is often missed by travelers, so make an effort to see it.

Where to Stay

You can call the Miyako Hotel and Inn Assistance number (Tel. 0193-62-4060); an English speaker is not always available to help, so you may have to ask your driver to be your go-between.

The **Suehiro-kan Hostel** (Tel. 0193-62-1555) is a three-minute walk from Miyako-eki. Walk straight away from the station and turn right at the first main intersection. The hostel is down just a bit and on your right. It costs ¥2,800 per night.

East of Tarō, on the north side of Masaki, is the **Numa-no-Hama Camp-jō** (Tel. 0193-87-2473), which is open July 1–October 30. It costs ¥300 per person and ¥500 for a space. Tent rentals are ¥1,500 for a four-man tent. This campsite has custodians only during July and August. If you need to rent a tent at other times during the season, call the **Masaki Lodge** (Tel. 0193-87-2771).

Escaping

Highway 45 meets Highway 455 at the town of Omoto (only the train station is labeled in the atlas). The peninsula to the south is called Kuma-no-hana, or "Bear's Nose," because of its shape. From the **Kuma-no-hana Observatory** you can view a sea cave from across the tops of the pine trees. At the end of this peninsula is the **Moshi Tōdai** (lighthouse).

The nearby Moshi-hama is known for its fossilized shell deposits; the fossils of a 30-ton dinosaur were discovered in 1978.

RYŪSENDŌ CAVE

After you cross the Omoto-gawa (river), hitchhike west on Highway 455 into the hills. There is steady traffic and good hitching along this road. At Iwaizumi, you will come to Ryūsen-dō, one of the three largest limestone caves in Japan, still being explored today.

The caves are over 5 km in length, though only about 700 meters are open to the public. They are home to five species of bats, including one called *usagi-kōmori* (rabbit-bats), so named because of their long ears.

Ryūsendō is renowned for its unusually clear and deep ponds. Plastic bottles of this calcium-rich water are for sale in the cave's souvenir shop. Admission to the caves is ¥820. They are open daily 8:30 A.M.–5:00 P.M.

Where to Stay

Just north of the caves, on the main prefectural highway, is the **Ryūsendō Seishōnen Ryokō Mura** campsite (Tel. 0194-22-

4255), which is open May 1–October 31. It costs ¥300 per person. Rent a four-man tent for ¥410 or a six-man bungalow for ¥2,470.

Escaping

You can return to the coast, or, if you are feeling bold, you can strike out on Prefectural Highway 8 north which runs by the caves and campsite and will take you to Akkadō Cave, through Yamane Onsen and then into Kuji.

This lonely, peaceful route from the Ryūsendō Caves to Kuji is 55 km long, and makes a nice alternative if you want a change of pace from the coast. Unfortunately, if you take the mountain route to Kuji, you miss some of the most rugged coastline in all of Rikuchū Kaigan. The question is, are you a mountain person or a coast person, a cave person or a sea person?

Note: Prefectural Highway 8 from Ryūsendō and Kuji is shown in green but not numbered in the Shobunsha road atlas.

RIKUCHŪ KAIGAN SCENIC COAST

In the heart of the Rikuchū Kaigan is the village of Shimano-koshi; you will have to leave the main highway to get here. The port is a ten-minute walk from Shimanokoshi-eki, but as a hitch-hiker you have the advantage over train schedules.

The **Kitayamazaki Meguri Kankōsen** sightseeing cruises depart from Shimanokoshi-kō (port). For ¥1,200, these 45-minute cruises take you past Benten-zaki and the ridged cliffs of the Kitayamazaki coast with its stone arches and pillars. Service operates from mid-April to the beginning of November. If you are only going to spend money on one coastal boat ride, this is the one. The JNTO has dubbed this area, with no small amount of hyperbole, the "Alps on the Ocean," and also "the most beautiful scenery on the north half of the Iwate coast."

The black-tailed gulls that nest here are a protected species and apparently rare, though it doesn't feel like it. Some Japanese refer to them as *umi neko*, or "sea cats," after their distinct mewing calls. You can hold out some bread to entice them into swooping down and eating out of your hand.

Where to Stay

There are two campsites in the Rikuchū Kaigan area. North and east of Tanohata-eki, near the coast is the **Aketo Camp-jō**; call the Tanohata village office for information (Tel. 0194-34-2111). The campsite is open April–October, and costs ¥300 per person. No tent rentals.

At the other end, 2 km east of Fudai-eki on the Fudai-hama Kaisui-yokujo beach, is the **Fudai-hama Camp-jo**. If you have any questions, call the Fudai village office (Tel.0194-35-2111). The campsite is open May–October and costs ¥200 per person. No tent rentals.

TANESASHI KAIGAN SCENIC COAST

As Highway 45 approaches Hachinohe, it veers inland shortly after Taneichi. Get off the highway and onto the coastal road, called the Umi Neko Line (shown in green in the atlas), and you will pass the beautiful Tanesashi Kaigan, with its sand dunes and open beaches.

There is a designated campsite here, though it is easy enough to pitch a tent anywhere along the shore. During the off-season, this is a relaxing, secluded area. It also your farewell to the east coast of Tohoku.

North of Tanesashi Kaigan is a prime bird-watching zone. If you want to see black-tailed gulls nesting, ask to be shown to noisy **Kabu-shima**. Take an umbrella to guard against bird droppings. Kabu-shima is east of Hachinohe harbor and near Same-eki.

Where to Stay

South of Hachinohe, in Taneichi town, is the **Edoga-hama Camp-jō** on the coast near Taneichi-eki. Call the town office for more information (Tel. 0194-65-2111). It is open only July 8–August 20. It costs ¥200 per person. No tent rentals.

HACHINOHE CITY

Unless you are craving urban entertainment, it is best to skip this sprawling, industrial port city (population 243,000). There are a lot of Americans and other foreigners living in Hachinohe, which reportedly gives it a lively night life. If you do decide to go into Hachinohe, I don't advise trying to hitchhike out. Instead take a train north, out of the city, past Misawa to Kamikita.

Whether hitching along the coast or on Highway 45 toward the city, you can avoid downtown Hachinohe by asking your driver to take you to the Hachinohe Kita Bypass. This will put you past the city without having to go in.

What to See and Do

West from Hachinohe on Highway 104 is one of the oldest shrines in Tohoku, the venerable **Kushibiki Hachimangū** grand shrine, which dates from 1648 and is surrounded by a forest of 700-year-old Japanese cedar trees. If the day is young, this shrine is worth a visit. When you hitchhike into Hachinohe, ask to be dropped off at Highway 104 instead of the bypass. Drop a hint that you are heading to the Kushibiki Hachimangū and you will probably be taken all the way there; it is only about 5 km east of the intersection of the bypass and Highway 104.

Where to Stay

Above Hachinohe, north of Shimoda and less than a kilometer from Mukaiyama-eki, is the **Kawayu Green Hostel** (Tel. 0178-56-2756); the proprietors speak some English. This is an excellent hostel, with fresh milk and vegetables from their working farm. It costs ¥3,000 per night; they also offer an excellent Japanese barbecue for ¥1,500. Afterwards, soak in their *rotenburo*. The hostel is closed January 11–February 13.

Escaping

To get from Hachinohe to Osore-zan (Dread Mountain), take a local train north, past Misawa, to Kogawara-eki—or anywhere else that catches your fancy. The Tohoku-sen from Hachinohe runs alongside Prefectural Highway 8. This highway will take you into Noheji.

Note: Prefectural Highway 8 through Kamikita is shown in green but not numbered in the atlas. At Noheji, ask to be dropped off east of town, on Highway 279. Hitchhike on this highway and it will take you all the way to Mutsu, the gateway to Osore-zan.

En Route

If it is late in the day and you want to escape Hachinohe to a campsite, take the train from Hachinohe to Kamikita-eki. A few kilometers southeast of the station, on the shore of Ogawarako (lake), is the **Ogawara Kosui-yokujō Camp-jō** (Tel. 0176-56-3525). It is 30-minute hike from Kamikata-eki, but you should be able to hitch a ride. The site is open April 15 to the end of November. There is no charge to set up your own tent, but there are no tent rentals.

SHIMOKITA AND OSORE-ZAN

Poised above Tohoku like an ax is the Shimokita, known also—appropriately—as Masakari-hantō, the Ax-Handle Peninsula. Try to spend at least a few days exploring Shimokita.

Shimokita is the home of the world's most northerly monkeys. In addition, there are many rustic hot springs, several of which are outside and mixed: women, men, and—in Wakino-sawa—even the occasional monkey. The main attraction in Shimokita is the Osore-zan area, with its volcanic lake and sulfurous landscape said to be the entrance to the afterlife. Make sure to try the delicious local specialty, *botan nabe*, wild boar meat cooked in a pot with vegetables.

Where to Stay

Halfway up the Ax-Handle of Shimokita is the town of Yokohama, where you may want to camp on your way in. If you are hitchhiking in May, you will be greeted with the sight of hundreds of acres of blooming, bright yellow rapeseed—now given the more innocuous name "canola."

The **Hamanasu Kōen campsite** (Tel. 0175-78-3286) in Yokohama is near Mutsu-Yokohama-eki and not far from the beach. Yokohama bills itself as "A Windsurfer's Paradise!" This campsite is conveniently located, hitching in is easy and—best of all—it's free. No tent rentals.

MUTSU

This city of 50,000 is the main center and gateway to Shimokita. Mutsu is strictly functional, but it is a good place to stock up before heading across the interior of Shimokita.

Where to Obtain Information

The **Mutsu International Relations Association** puts out a small English booklet in a sincere effort to make Shimokita accessible to non-Japanese guests. Call 0175-22-5012 if you need assistance or information.

What to See and Do

If you are coming through Mutsu in August, make sure you see the nighttime spectacle of the **Tanabu Matsuri** (August

18–20), based on Kyoto's Gion festival. The Ōminato **Nebuta** at the beginning of August is a smaller-scale version of Hirosaki and Aomori's Nebuta festivals.

Where to Stay

The Kaisuiyokujō Camp is in Mutsu. Call the **Matsukazesō Ryokan** (Tel. 0175-24-2695) in the Shimokita Onsen area for arrangements. It is open from mid-July to mid-September.

SHIRIYA-ZAKI

At the northeast tip of the Shimokita Peninsula is the low-lying, wind-swept coast of Shiriya-zaki (cape). Watch for wild horses.

Where to Stay

Find an empty spot and pitch a tent. Otherwise, the **Shiriya-zaki Hostel** (Tel. 0175-47-2941) is in the village of Higashidōri-mura, about 5 km from the cape lighthouse. It costs ¥2,800 and is open April 1–October 31.

OSORE-ZAN AND USORISANKO

Northwest of Mutsu is **Osore-zan,** the Dread Mountain. Pooled in a volcanic crater in the center of eight rolling hills are the acidic blue-green waters of **Usorisanko** (lake).

Note: The entire area around the lake is called Osore-zan. The actual mountain, Osore-zan, is farther west.

The Osore-zan area is traditionally the entranceway to Heaven and Hell, complete with a River Styx, the Sanzu-no-Kawa, which souls are said to cross after death. It is here that the beloved saint Jizō helps the souls of dead children in their long and lonely journey. Stone Jizō statues and sad offerings for the souls of children add to the forlorn atmosphere.

The Sanzu-no-Kawa runs beside Bodai-ji (labeled "Jizōdō" in the atlas).

What to See and Do

The **Osore-zan Temple area** is open only from May to the end October and costs ¥300 to enter.

There are two festivals in which blind shamans, *itako*, contact the souls of the dead for bereaved relatives. The summer communion is in July and is very crowded.

THE YAGEN VALLEY

If you continue north from Osore-zan on the Asunaro Skyline, you will come to the secluded hot-spring town of Yagen. Farther west in Oku-Yagen are the mixed baths and open-air hot springs of **Kappa-no-yu**. From here the road continues through the stunning scenery of the Yagen Valley. If you are traveling during autumn, avoid the crowds of the Oirase Valley (see below) and come to Yagen instead. The autumn colors are just as brilliant, and the Yagen Valley, with its mountain streams and waterfalls, is one of the prettiest hitchhiking roads in Japan. Make sure you hitch this road on the weekend. There is enough traffic between Osore-zan and Oku-Yagen that hitching isn't a problem during the week, but it can get sparse *after* Oku-Yagen, as you go west through the valley.

Where to Stay

There is no youth hostel in the Osore-zan area, but there are several campsites. Highly recommended is the **Yagen Yaeijo** campsite near the Yagen Onsen hot springs. Call the town office in Ōhata (Tel. 0175-34-2111) for more information. The campsite is open April 29–November 3 and costs ¥300 per person. There are no tent rentals, but there is a toilet and a kitchen. Local deer and hot springs make this an inviting location.

From Yagen, hitch west along the Ōhata-gawa Ravine on the Asunaro Skyline, which will take you all the way to the small village of **Sai-mura**.

THE AX BLADE

Take a ferry from Sai-mura down the "blade edge" of Shimokita to Wakinosawa-mura past the rugged, breathtaking coast of **Hotoke-ga-ura**, the Buddha's Shore. Limestone cliffs plunge 100 meters into the sea and shark-fin islands and knife-edged pillars are scattered along the inlets. Many of the stone pillars resemble either the saint Jizō or the Buddha (*hotoke*), which is how the coast got its name. This ferry makes a great coastal cruise and combination travel jaunt, because once it works its way down the shore, it continues on to Aomori.

The ferry from Sai-mura to Aomori costs ¥3,400 and takes about two and a half hours. It's a working ferry that runs twice a day, calling at isolated little fishing villages along the way—an interesting and affordable cruise. Departure times change, so call ahead to the **Sai-mura ferry port** (Tel. 0175-38-2255).

Note: If you are planning only a short trip from Aomori to Shimokita and then back, you should reverse the order. Take the ferry up the coast to Sai-mura. From Sai-mura hitchhike east through the Yagen Valley and down to Osore-zan and then into Mutsu. From Mutsu you can hitchhike down the ax handle and back into Aomori without much trouble. It is always better to hitchhike *into* a major city, and taking the ferry out and hitching back is a good strategy.

WAKINOSAWA-MURA

If you have some extra time, take the ferry from Sai-mura but get off at Wakinosawa-mura instead. The village of Wakinosawa is at the bottom of the ax blade.

What to See and Do

In Wakinosawa-mura, the view of choice is the whale-shaped **Tai-jima** (island) off the coast; cruise around it for ¥1,000 in a glass-bottom boat.

The snow monkeys, which seem to embody the Japanese virtue of *gaman* ("endurance"), are the main attraction. In this snowy, harsh land the monkeys manage to thrive, though they do look a bit glum. Visit the **Wakinosawa Yaen Kōen** wild monkey park near Kaizaki (in the area marked Anama-yama in the atlas). To hint to your driver, just keep saying *saru*, which means "monkey"—or *yasei no saru*, "wild monkeys"—and your driver will get the idea.

Where to Stay

The **Wakinosawa Youth Hostel** (Tel. 0175-44-2341) is near the ferry port, only two minutes from the beach. Look for the high pointed roof. It costs ¥2,800 and is closed December 30–January 2. No alcohol allowed.

West of the village center of Wakkinosawa-mura, toward Hokkai-misaki and near the Wakkinosawa-kō (port), is the **Kaizaki Camp-jō** (Tel. 0175-44-3252), which is open May–October. It costs ¥410 for a space. There is no electricity here and the campsite is 6 km from the ferry port. Make sure you hitch in during daylight hours. A walking path leads from the parking lot to the campsite.

Escaping

Either take the ferry the next day or hitch back into Mutsu along coastal Highway 338 east. The rides along Highway 338 are not great, but after Kawauchi, the traffic picks up.

THE NATSUDOMARI PENINSULA

If, instead of taking the ferry, you hitchhike back to Aomori, you will pass the Natsudomari-hantō (peninsula), north of Hiranai. Natsudomari is a nice spot, seldom visited by Westerners, but popular with the Japanese as a place for a weekend getaway. Spending the night in one of the many campsites clustered on this peninsula will save a couple ¥7,000 or more over a night in Aomori. If it is late in the day you may want to leave Highway 4 and hitchhike up the coast of Natsudomari instead of going into Aomori.

Where to Stay

Natsudomari Hantō Shirasuna Kaigan Camp-jō belongs to a *kokumin-shukusha* (Tel. 0177-59-2155). The forested beaches and ocean view of this campsite near Hanakukuri-zaki make it an attractive place to stay before heading into the city. It is open May 1–October 30, and costs ¥400 per person and ¥500 for a space. No tent rentals.

The **Ōshima Tsubakiyama Camp-jō** (Tel. 0177-59-2012) is near Tsubaki Jinja and is in a good location for visiting both the shrine and the Ōshima hook of land. It is open May 1– September 30. It is a bargain at ¥300 for a space, with no extra per-person charge. No tent rentals.

The third site is the **Natsudomari Auto Camp** (Tel. 0177-59-2546) on the northwestern side of the peninsula. It is open only July 1–August 31.

Escaping

It is a short hop to hitchhike from Natsudomari into Aomori. If you want to visit the hills and pine forests of this peninsula's northern tip, take your time. Once you get back onto Highway 4 most of the traffic will be flowing into Aomori.

AOMORI

This large, harbor city (population 295,000) is the northern gateway of Tohoku; ferries connect it to Hokkaido. Like Sapporo, the prefectural capital of Aomori is a young metropolis.

Aomori is a booster of the prefecture's most famous crop—apples. The city's new bridge has support beams in the shape of an **A** to signify both apples and Aomori, as does the A-shaped ASPA building built in front of the bridge. After the bridge, this triangular glass building is the landmark of Aomori and is only a ten-minute walk from Aomori-eki.

Where to Obtain Information

Inside the ASPA building is a **Tourist Information Center** on the first floor. Some English pamphlets are available, but the services are limited.

If you are beginning your journey in Aomori and want to buy an atlas or a pocket Japanese-English English-Japanese dictionary, the **Narita Honten** bookstore is a ten-minute walk from Aomori-eki down Shin-machi Street. It is open until 8:00 P.M. and has English maps and books on the second floor.

What to See and Do

There isn't a great deal to do in Aomori, but it makes a nice break from hitching. Across from Aomori-eki and to the right (past the police box) is the **Shinmachi market district,** which can be lively enough in the morning to warrant a stroll.

If you want a night view of Aomori, go to the **ASPA Building**. There is an observation deck, but be warned: there is an ¥800 fee, and the night views of Aomori are kind of bland—the most interesting piece of the skyline is the ASPA building, and you're in it. If you arrive during Aomori's raucous **Nebuta Festival** you will see a city as rowdy as any in Japan. Unfortunately, accommodations are very difficult—almost impossible—to arrange on short notice during the Nebuta Festival. You may have to stay up all night and then catch a couple of hours' sleep in a love hotel.

Where to Stay

There are no youth hostels in Aomori. The **Aomori Sunrise Hotel** (Tel. 0177-73-7211) is a five-minute walk from the station, straight down Shin-machi. Singles start at ¥5,665. Right across the station is the Sun Friend Building. Look for a small English sign near the top floor, under what looks like a bunch of bananas. On the fourth floor is the **Sun Capsule Hotel,** which costs ¥3,000 a night. Refresh in the sauna and public bath located in the basement, then buy some nibbles from the food store on the first floor.

Escaping

The local train from Aomori to Hirosaki is only ¥640 and takes about an hour. But Hirosaki-eki is not conveniently located for exploring the castle grounds or getting to the hostel. If you want to arrive in Hirosaki under the protection of a Japanese driver—and save a few hundred yen—hitchhike instead.

I took the train from Aomori-eki to Tsugaru Shinjō-eki, which is still within the residential area. Though not an ideal site, I still got a ride out to the highway without any trouble. The narrow two-lane road that runs beside the station soon passes under the Aomori Kanjō Bypass and meets Highway 7. Once you get onto Highway 7, hitching into Hirosaki is easy.

HIROSAKI

Hirosaki (population 177,000) is a seedy, slightly faded city that boasts the only extant castle in Tohoku, Hirosaki-jō, built in 1611 and rebuilt in 1810. The castle's perfectly preserved concentric moats and four extant watchtowers and gates make this a unique site. Unlike most castle-towns, the castle does not dominate the skyline. As you approach, you may mistake one of the watchtowers for the castle; they are of similar size.

Hirosaki is renowned for its many older Western-style buildings and churches, though these are more of interest to Japanese visitors. Architecturally, many of them have deft touches of Japanese style blended into more dominant Western architecture; the effect is very subtle and will probably be intriguing only to people with a solid architectural background.

Where to Obtain Information

Ask to be dropped off the **Ōtemon Shiritsu Kankōkan Sightseeing Square and Information Center** (Tel. 0172-37-5501), which is open until 5:00 P.M. This spacious, newly built complex incorporates several old Western-style buildings and is located south of the castle grounds. The youth hostel is behind it, a few blocks south. Hirosaki is a notoriously confusing place, so ask the people at the Ōtemon Information Center to help you locate the hostel on a map before you head out. They also have the usual English pamphlets, as well as some English-version video blurbs on Hirosaki.

There is a second tourist information center in front of the station, and though helpful, their English is limited. Some English pamphlets and maps are available, but most of them can be obtained in Aomori before starting out. Hirosaki-eki is on the other side of town from the castle, temples, and hostel, so if you are dropped off at the station you will need to take a bus. The bus fare in Hirosaki is a uniform ¥160.

What to See and Do

The best way to see Hirosaki is on a bicycle, and the youth hostel has some old junkers for rent at the cheapest rates in town. Even if you are not staying at the youth hostel, you can still rent bicycles from them. Avoid the overpriced rental shop near the station.

Hirosaki Castle is the site of several seasonal festivals; the most famous is the **Sakura Matsuri** celebration of cherry blossoms held between April 25 and May 6. The castle is well known for the beauty of its cherry blossoms and is considered—and I quote—one of the "Three Best Cherry-Blossom Viewing Sites in Japan."

Autumn is also a good time to visit, especially in early October when the maple trees have turned red in a blaze of glory.

The city's **Nebuta Festival** is a more restrained version of Aomori's and is held during the first week of August. The giant illuminated floats are on display at the **Nebuta Mura craft center** at the northeast corner of the castle grounds.

Near the Ōtemon Information Center, and of interest to coin collectors, is the **Aomori Ginkō Kinenkan** (memorial bank), which has old Japanese money on display. Take note of the building though, a Renaissance-inspired wooden structure built in 1904. It is one block south of the park; you will probably pass it on your way to and from the pagoda and the castle.

The 33 **Temple Row of Zenrin** is a wide residential street flanked by Zen temples. A smaller, parallel street of temples runs beside it to the right. At the end of the avenue is **Chōshō-ji**, with its large wooden gate, darkened altars, and "nightingale hall," whereby would-be intruders are foiled with purposefully built squeaking floorboards. (Japan's most famous "nightingale hall" is in Nijōjō in Kyoto.) For any ghouls out there, Chōshō-ji also contains the tomb and mummified remains of a young prince who was discovered buried under a schoolyard after 100 years in the ground. His body was remarkably well preserved and it is put on display between April 22 and May 7, during the Cherry Blossom Festival.

Hirosaki's pagoda was built in 1667, and is located at the bottom of the newer Shin-Teramachi Temple Row on a bluff looking over the city. Pay ¥100 and you can ring the bell three times for fortune and longevity.

From the pagoda runs **Shin-Teramachi**, a busy street lined with newer temples belonging to the Nichiren sect. This is not a very impressive street, especially after visiting the older temples along Zenrin.

The music of the *tsugaru shamisen*, a specialty of western Aomori prefecture, is known as "Japanese bluegrass." To see Hirosaki at its rollicking best, go to the **Live House,** a restaurant near Hirosaki-eki, where the lively, banjo-like *tsugaru-shamisen* music is played. Just ask "Tsugaru shamisen?" and most people will direct you to the spot. Live House is run by a family of musicians, and the patriarch has his own line of CDs and cassettes available. His son is the current all-Japan *tsugaru-shamisen* champion.

Where to Stay

The **Hirosaki Youth Hostel** (Tel. 0172-33-7066) is not far from the entrance to the 33 Temple Avenue of Zenrin. The cost is a modest ¥2,800 per night. The hostel is in a good strategic location for sightseeing, but rent a bicycle. Take Bus 51 or 61 from stop number 3 in front of Hirosaki-eki and get off at the Hirosaki Daigaku Byōin. From there, continue walking straight down the street (the street will jog a bit to the right) and look for a small YH sign pointing to the left, down a side alley. The information office in the station can give you a map and show you the bus route and hostel location. Remember to get a Japanese map of Hirosaki as well, to cross-reference the cartoon-like English one.

If you want to stay in a temple, try **Henshō-ji** (Tel. 0172-32-8714) at the other end of the Shin-Teramachi Temple Row from the pagoda. The lodgings are in a newer temple, and not especially evocative, but you can visit the inner altar during your stay. Lodgings cost ¥6,000, including two meals. You should make a reservation, and you may be asked to send a ¥1,000 deposit.

The **Hirosaki Ryokan Hotel Kumiai Reservation Center** (Tel. 0172-34-2657) can arrange accommodations, but unless you speak some Japanese, you will have to ask your driver to call for you.

Escaping

From Hirosaki-eki, take a local train on the private Kōnan line from track 5. The train rattles across the plains and eventually crosses the Kuroishi Bypass. The stop before the bypass is Tsugaru-Onoe. The stop just north of the bypass is Inakadate; the station is not shown in the atlas.

I got off at Tsugaru-Onoe station, which is right in the middle of Onoe. Prefectural Highway 13 runs through town, to the east of the tracks. Ask someone to point you to the Onoe Yūbinkyoku (post office), where a bilingual highway sign will help you to orient yourself. Walk north on Prefectural Highway 13 to clear the town. Stick out a thumb and hitch north to the Kuroishi Bypass—just a short jump. Once you get on the bypass, hitch east toward Kuroishi Onsen.

If I had to do it again, I would take the train one more stop to Inakadate instead and then walk *south* to the Kuroishi Bypass before I started hitching. Live and learn.

HAKKŌDA-SAN

The term Hakkōda-san refers to both the central peak and the entire range. Hakkōda-san (1,585 meters) is just south of Aomori and east of Hirosaki. It is ringed with hot springs and marshes, has several campsites and hiking paths, and draws lots of traffic from Aomori during the summer. This is good news for hitchhikers, but at times traffic can reach gridlock levels and you may face the surreal situation of an outdoor, wilderness traffic jam.

The mountain is best known as the grisly site of a winter death march by an army-training patrol of the 5th Regiment in 1904 that left almost 200 soldiers dead when they were caught in a blizzard. Jiro Nitta recreates the events in his harrowing work, *Death March on Mount Hakkoda* (Stone Bridge Press).

What to See and Do

The **Hakkōda Ropeway** runs up the west side of Tamoyachi-yama (1,324 meters). It costs ¥980 one way and ¥1,650 round trip. Hiking trails lead from the top of the ropeway. If you want to save money, you could take the ropeway up and then walk down. Or, if you are feeling fit, skip the ropeway entirely and make the three-hour hike up Tamoyachi-yama on foot. The trail begins in the Sukaya Onsen area, crosses the marshland boardwalk, and sweeps up the mountain.

There are several popular hot springs in the Hakkōda-san area. Most cost only a few hundred yen, and many are steeped in history. **Yachi Onsen** has been around for 400 years and was once the retreat of samurai and noblemen. West of Yachi on Highway 103 is the **Suiden-numa** (marshlands) with a good view of autumn maple leaves and Hakkōda-san. The **Sukayu Onsen** hot springs (written "sugakura" in the atlas) include huge bathing ponds, some of which are mixed. To the south of Yachi, toward Towadako Onsen, is **Tsuta Onsen** with its old wooden building and nearby mountain ponds and walking path.

Where to Stay

In the Sukayu Onsen area is the **Sukayu Camp-jō** (Tel. 0177-38-6400). It costs ¥200 per person. No tent rentals. Bungalows are ¥2,500 for a six-tatami-mat cabin.

THE OIRASE VALLEY

The waterfalls and roadside stream of this beautiful green valley make this one of the prettiest walks in Japan. The footpath runs right beside the road for most of the way, so if it starts to rain or you start to get tired, all you have to do is step out and hold up a thumb. The valley is filled with slow-driving sight-seers, so hitchhiking is never a problem. In autumn, when the leaves are ablaze, the valley becomes very congested on the weekends. Walk the entire way, however, and you will often escape the crowds that gather around the waterfalls.

The best part of the Oirase Valley is between the Ishigado vis-itors' center at the north end of the valley and Nenokuchi on the east shore of the lake. At Ishigado look for the giant slab rock where a witch used to live; it is near the start of the trail and there is a sign in English.

From Ishigedo, the walking path runs along the mossy, boul-der-strewn stream and past several waterfalls. It is an easy, four-hour walk from **Ishigedo** to **Nenokuchi** (or vice versa). From Nenokuchi, you can walk north along the Oirase Valley and then hitchhike back. This way you will get to see the Oirase twice, once on foot and once by car. You can leave your bags in Nenokuchi and pick them up on the way back. The path is reserved for walkers. Bicyclists have to share the narrow highway road with trucks and cars.

Note: The Ishigedo rest area is not shown in the atlas. It is roughly a third of the way down the road between Yakeyama and Nenokuchi.

Getting There

There are two ways to reach the Oirase Valley. From Hakkōda-san, hitchhike south through Towadako Onsen. If it is already after lunch, you may want to stay in the **Oirase Youth Hostel** in Yakeyama, north of the Oirase Valley, and then make the walk the following morning.

A more direct route from Hirosaki to the Towadako–Oirase Valley area is to take Highway 102, also known as the Towada-michi (road). Stay on the bypass after it turns into Highway 102 and it will take you right down to Towadako. This route takes you past a sweeping view of the **Aseishikawa Dam**. Halfway down is a flat and uninspiring campsite. Though not beautiful, this site puts you right beside the highway to Towadako (lake)—a very strategic place to stop if it is late in the day. If you are friendly with the other campers you may be able to arrange a ride the next morning without even having to hitchhike.

Where to Stay

North of Ishigedo, in Yakeyama, is the **Oirase Hostel** (Tel. 0176-74-2031). It is west on Highway 102, and is a good place to stop if you want to visit the Oirase Valley the following day. It costs ¥2,800 per night. No alcohol allowed. To get from the hostel to the start of the Oirase Valley walk, you will have to hitch south to the Ishigedo refreshment area. Most of the hostel guests will be heading for the Oirase as well, so you should be able to arrange a ride to Ishigedo with one of them.

TOWADAKO

Towadako is a deep caldera lake formed by a series of volcanic eruptions. Two peninsulas, a high, mountainous "thumb" on the east, and a lower, longer "finger" on the west, jut into the lake. Kura-yama (the "thumb") is best seen from the highway. The main visitors' center is in the tourist village of **Yasumiya,** which is on the west side of the "finger." It is a long ride from Yasumiya to the Oirase Valley.

Note: Yasumiya, the main community on the lake, is not labeled in the atlas. It is located just south of Towada Jinja, which is labeled. Yasumiya and the Oirase are prime nature getaways for families from the city.

What to See and Do

Towadako offers the usual overpriced **boat cruises**. They take a little over an hour and cost ¥1,300. There are two courses. The A Course runs from Yasumiya, does a loop, and then returns.

The B Course runs back and forth between Nenokuchi and Yasumiya. If you are determined to take a boast cruise, you should at least make it pay off. After hiking the Oirase Valley, take the B Course from Nenokuchi to Yasumiya. This way you can use the boat cruise as transportation.

The famous statue of two women touching hands is on the shore of Towadako, at Yasumiya. The story behind the statue is a poignant one. You may notice that the two **Maidens of the Lake** look like the same woman. They are. Her name was Chieko, and her story is retold by her poet–sculptor husband Kōtarō Takamura in a collection of verse entitled *Chieko's Sky*. She suffered from schizophrenia and depression. Adding to her troubles was her artist–husband, who took her away from her Tohoku country home to Tokyo. Deeply homesick, she mourned that "There is no sky in Tokyo," and in that phrase she summed up the longing and nostalgia that the many displaced residents have for Japan's Deep North.

Farther into the woods is **Towada Jinja,** which was first enshrined in 807 (none of the original site remains) and has iron sandals on display instead of the more typical straw variety. You can walk to the shrine from the Chieko statues, and then leave by the wooded entrance path.

Where to Stay
Camping: There are four campsites spaced around the edge of Towadako—make sure you are dropped off at the right one!

The **Oide Camp-jō** (Tel. 0176-75-2368, 2079) is located on the south side of the lake, west of Yasumiya and just in front of the Towada Youth Hostel. Whether you are going east, south, or north, this campsite is well located for hitchhiking. They are open April 25–November 3 and charge ¥300 per person and ¥200 for a space. Highway 103 turns inland into the mountains just to the west of the Oide campsite. If you are following this itinerary south, this is the highway on which you will hitch out.

The **Utarube Yaei-jō** (Tel. 0176-75-2477) is located near Highway 103, on the eastern neck of land joining Kura-yama to the shore. It is open July and August and costs ¥300 per person. No tent rentals.

The **Nenokuchi Camp** (Tel. 0176-75-2503) is big, busy, well known, and located near the start of the Oirase Valley walk. It is near the shore, north of the Nenokuchi, along Highway 102. Open from the end of June to the end of August. They charge ¥600 per person, no extra charge for a tent space. Bungalow cabins are available for ¥5,500.

On the northwest shore is **Takinosawa Camp** (Tel. 0176-75-2341), open May 1–October 31. It costs ¥200 per person. Tent rentals are available during the summer season only: ¥1,500 for a five-man tent. Takinosawa is not very conveniently located for sightseeing, but if it's late in the day as you are coming from Hirosaki, you may want to stay here.

Hostels: There are two conveniently located hostels in the Towadako area, both on the southern side of the lake.

The **Hakubutsukan Hostel** (Tel. 0176-75-2002) near the Yasumiya-kō is actually inside the Grand Hotel; the hostel rooms were originally hotel rooms. The rooms are excellent and cost just ¥3,000 per night. VISA accepted. I came through just after Golden Week and I had a full, hotel-style room with fresh linens and a color TV all to myself.

West of Yasumiya, across the highway from the shore, is the **Towada Youth Hostel** (Tel. 0176-75-2603), which costs ¥2,200 per night and is open May 1–October 31. This is in a much quieter and prettier location. The Oide campsite is nearby.

Escaping

Just past the Towada Youth Hostel, Highway 103 turns south and snakes its way up into the mountains, presenting several splendid farewell vistas of Towadako. Hitch at the intersection because the highway quickly becomes steep and twisty. Highway 103 comes down into the drab little hot-spring town of Ōyu.

En Route

About 5 km west of Ōyu are the **Ōyu Stone Circles**—a *very* miniature Stonehenge—worth a side trip. Your driver will probably drive you out.

The turnoff toward the Stone Circles is marked in English and Japanese. There are two stone circles, one on either side of the highway.

These circles, standing for over 3,000 years, seem to be in line with Kuromori-yama to the north, which forms a dramatic backdrop and is thought to be an ancient stone pyramid.

Whether Kuromori-yama is a pyramid or merely a pointy mountain is debatable. The man who runs the Ōyu Youth Hostel was downright jingoistic and even insisted—against all evidence and common sense—that the concept of pyramid-building went *from* Japan *to* Central and South America.

Try to leave Towadako early so that you can see the stone circles and then take the expressway down to Morioka the same day. If possible, avoid spending the night in Ōyu.

Where to Stay

The **Kuromori-sō Youth Hostel** (Tel. 0186-37-2144) is just a short walk from the Ōyu bus station beside the river. It costs ¥2,700 per night. The hostel's hot spring costs ¥100 more whether you want it or not. Order the breakfast because little is open in Ōyu during the morning. The **Izumi Café,** at the intersection that leads from Highway 103 to the Stone Circle, makes a delicious bowl of beef stew.

Escaping

From Ōyu, hitch south on Highway 103 to the Towada IC on

the Tohoku Expressway, which will take you down to Morioka in about two hours. Get off at the Morioka IC and you will be west of the Morioka city center.

Alternatively, take Highway 282 from Ōyu to Morioka, a route that looks congested on road maps but is uncluttered and fairly rural. I chose to hitchhike to Morioka along the expressway and I regret it. It was fast enough, but the whole way down I saw fascinating glimpses of villages and farmlands whip past, out of reach. Highway 282 follows the expressway most of the way, so if you set out you can always change your mind and join the expressway at the next IC.

MORIOKA

From the busy Morioka IC you can hitchhike into Morioka on Highway 46, which takes you right past the downtown core. Ask to be dropped off at Morioka-eki. If you are hitching down on the highway you will be coming in from the other side of town. Again, ask to be dropped off at the station.

Morioka (population 275,000) is a lively, upbeat city that manages to mix the best of the old with the new. The city once had a castle—the grounds are now a park—and it is still a center of traditional folk crafts in Tohoku. It is also a very modern city with a compact downtown core good for strolling and night life.

For some reason, the Lonely Planet Guide did not appreciate Morioka. The crafts and folk arts of the Konya-chō (the Dyer's Row) alone make the city worth a visit. It should be noted that Exploring Tohoku and Gateway to Japan both give Morioka very favorable reviews.

Where to Obtain Information
The **Morioka Tourist Information Center** is on the second floor of Morioka-eki, and is open 9:00 A.M.–7:00 P.M. daily. The

English pamphlet/map of Morioka is useful in planning a short walking tour of the city.

What to See and Do

Many of Morioka's sites are near the station. I would recommend first walking down to see the *ishiwari-zakura*, the 300-year-old "rock-splitting cherry tree," located in front of the courthouse. This cherry tree split a boulder as it grew, which makes for a dramatic juxtaposition: the ephemeral cherry tree, a symbol of all that is passing in life, having broken sheer bedrock. Some spoilsports have suggested that maybe the boulder was already split and the tree just grew in the crack. Either way, it is an evocative symbol for most Japanese and has been designated a National Treasure.

From the courthouse, continue down the street and then turn right toward **Sakurayama Jinja**. The road leading to the shrine is crowded with small shops and red lanterns. As dusk falls this shrine-front shop zone glows with light and laughter. The shrine's object of veneration is a towering boulder to the rear of the main building. Behind the shrine is the castle park commemorating Morioka Castle; the structure was built in 1633, but in 1874 it was sold and subsequently torn down during Japan's Meiji modernization. The park serves as a testimony to the trauma of Japan's initial contact with the West. In a secluded cove of the park, across from Bishamon-bashi (bridge), is the **firefly** (*hotaru*) **viewing spot**.

Across the Nakatsu-gawa from the Castle Park is **Konya-chō**, the Dyer's Row. This narrow street begins at the Old Iwate Bank and continues down to Kami-no-hashi, and is lined with small craft houses, traditional sweet shops, coffeehouses, and a secondhand store.

Morioka has taken a lead in reviving and maintaining the folk crafts of northern Japan, and one of its finest crafts is the cast-iron kettleware called *nanbu tetsubin*. Small ornaments and amulets made by renowned craftsmen are sold for as little as ¥800—portable, indestructible souvenirs.

North of downtown and east of Kami Morioka-eki, is the Mitsui area, with over a dozen temples. In **Hōn-ji** temple there are 500 statues of Buddhist disciples, including among their ranks the unlikely duo of Marco Polo and Kublai Khan.

For diners, the Morioka specialty is *wanko-soba*, noodles eaten in small mouth-sized portions that are quickly tossed into your bowl by a server who stands beside you. The challenge is to see how many of the tiny bowlfuls you can eat at one sitting—40 bowls is a respectable total. When you have had enough, you have to clamp the lid on your bowl before the server can put more in. If she beats you to it you are expected to eat the noodles—to waste them would be rude. So again you have to try to put the lid on before she can serve you and again she tries to beat you at it.

Guests often challenge each other to *wanko-soba* eating contests, with participants keeping score with matchsticks. I ended up in one such contest, with my ravenous appetite pitted against that of a short, middle-aged salaryman. Because it was assumed I was a typically voracious Westerner, the betting was heavily in my favor. I lost, of course—no one can slurp back noodles like a Japanese salaryman. Try the **Wanko-ya Restaurant** (Tel. 0196-24-4626) in the Konya-machi area of Morioka. It costs ¥2,000 for all you can eat, so starve yourself before going. Closed Mondays.

Another popular *wanko-soba* shop is near the red-bricked Old Iwate Bank. To find it, go across from the bank to the other old Western building. Just behind this building, on the next street over, is the **Azumaya Restaurant** (Tel. 0196-22-2252). The price starts at ¥2,000.

Where to Stay

The **Morioka Hostel** (Tel. 0196-62-2220) is in the northwest area of the city, near Takamatsu Pond and not far from Highway

4. It costs ¥2,800 per night; no alcohol allowed. The hostel is not a convenient place to stay if you want to visit downtown Morioka. But if you are planning to bypass the city—or if you are coming into Morioka late in the day—you will hitchhike in on Highway 4 (Highway 282 turns into Highway 4 as it approaches Morioka) and pass by the hostel. The hostel is well located for hitchhiking *out* of Morioka, too.

The **Ryokan Kumagai** (Tel. 0196-51-3020) is a member of the Japanese Inn Group and offers a typically Japanese surrounding for ¥4,500 (single) and ¥8,000 (double). They take American Express, VISA, and MasterCard. The ryokan is an eight-minute walk from Morioka-eki. From the station, cross the river and take the main road that angles right. The ryokan is near the Zen-rinkan.

Across from Morioka-eki is the **Morioka Capsule**; berths cost ¥2,500 per night.

The Hachimangū shrine's lodging house is called **Sakura Kaikan** (Tel. 0196-51-8411) and it costs ¥6,500 a night with two meals. This shrine is nicely located near the Highway 4 Bypass, making hitching out of Morioka the next morning easy.

Escaping

If you spent the night in the Morioka Hostel, you can hitch on Highway 4 all the way to Hiraizumi in about three hours. The expressway will be twice as fast. Highway 4 runs from Morioka to Hiraizumi, but the quickest way is to hitch on the expressway to the Hiraizumi–Maesawa IC exit. This expressway route will put you back on Highway 4 about 1 km north of Chūson-ji (temple) and the Golden Pavilion. If you intend to stay at the hostel in Hiraizumi, ask your driver to drop you off at Mōtsū-ji instead.

HIRAIZUMI

The small town of Hiraizumi (population 9,700) was once the center of the northern Heian court of the Northern Fujiwara, a semi-autonomous kingdom whose capital at Hiraizumi rivaled Kyoto in power and grandeur. Marco Polo heard legends of the Golden Pavilion and sought a passage to Japan in his quest. The saga of the Northern Fujiwara lasted just over a century, from 1089 to 1190. During that time, Hiraizumi was the northern outpost of Japanese culture.

When the poet Bashō came through in the seventeenth century, the place was already a forsaken, faded spot. Reflecting on the passage of time and ambition, Bashō sat in a thatched-roof hut near the Benkei-dō pavilion at Chūson-ji and penned one of the most famous haiku in Japanese history: *Summer grass—all that remains of warrior dreams.*

What to See and Do

Today, a handful of sites remain testimony to the city's former glory days. The Golden Hall, or **Konjiki-dō,** of the Chūson-ji temple complex is the most famous cultural treasure in Tohoku. It was built in 1124 to hold the mummified bodies of the first three Fujiwara lords and is resplendent in gold and mother-of-pearl inlays that are meant to evoke the paradise promised by Amida Buddha. This small piece of paradise is at the end of the Chūson-ji grounds, at the top of a steep path that runs through the forest, and is flanked by wooden pavilions—and crowds of tourists. On the way up you will pass the Sankōzō Treasure Hall on your left, which contains Buddhist imagery and art.

You may be disappointed when you visit the Golden Pavilion. It must have looked stunning in its original open-air position, but sealed behind glass and crowded with hundreds of schoolchildren, it seems more like a museum piece than an object of grandeur. It costs ¥500 to enter the Chūson-ji grounds; your ticket includes entry to the Sankōzō Treasury Hall. Chūson-ji is open from 8:00 A.M to 4:30 P.M. or 5:00 P.M., depending on the season. Arrive before 8:00 A.M. to beat the convoys of tour buses that begin pulling up.

Mōtsū-ji: Though once a grand temple and garden, today only the central pond and the foundation stones remain. Between May 1 and 5, the temple hosts the costumed **Fujiwara Matsuri Festival,** as well as the **Kyokusui-no-en** floating poetry contest. Participants sit along a small stream and must compose lines of verse before the floating tray reaches them, a tradition introduced to Japan from Korea.

Takkoku no Iwaya Cave Temple: A 900-year-old relief carving of a Buddha is still visible on the cliff face next to this temple. Embedded in a cave is the temple dedicated to the Unified Buddha, as well as the samurai-god Bishamonten, defender of the faith.

There are no buses to Takkoku-no-Iwaya, and taxis are expensive. You can hitch out and back from Mōtsū-ji on the road that runs by the entrance. Or rent a bicycle at the station or the hostel, and enjoy a beautiful ride, out past thatched-roof Tohoku farmhouses and rice fields. It's only a 6-km ride, and after you see the temple, you can continue on to Genbikei Gorge.

Where to Stay

The **Mōtsū-ji Youth Hostel** (Tel. 0191-46-2331) is an eight-minute walk straight from Hiraizumi-eki. If you are hitching in, just ask your driver to drop you off at Mōtsū-ji. If you say "youth hostel" they may become confused, because many people do not realize that this famous temple has a hostel on its grounds. The hostel costs ¥2,700 a night, which includes the entrance fee to the temple grounds. It is closed December 30– January 3. The proprietors at Mōtsū-ji were fairly strict about shower times and curfews.

Escaping

From Hiraizumi it is better to take the expressway back to Sendai. Hitchhike back to the Hiraizumi IC and then take the Tohoku Expressway south to Sendai. The loop is complete.

If you are staying at the **Dōchu-An Youth Hostel** south of Sendai—a good idea if you are flying out the next day—get off at the Sendai–Minami IC. See the previous section on Sendai for more details. If you are going into downtown Sendai, get off at the Sendai–Miyagi IC instead.

Note: If you want to go to the Three Sacred Mountains of Dewa Sanzan—described in the following section—hitchhike west from the Sendai–Miyagi IC, *away* from Sendai and through Tendō. This will take you along the scenic Futakuchi-kaidō (road) and past the mountain Buddhist monastery of Yamadera. The Sendai Tourist Information Office has English pamphlets and maps of Yamadera if you want to include it in your travel plans.

NIIGATA AND THE NORTHWEST COAST

Instead of coming down the center of Tohoku, you can cross over and hitchhike down the west coast instead. This will take you to the Oga Peninsula, Sado Island, and—if you continue—right down to the Ama-no-Hashidate "Bridge of Heaven." You can then enter Kyoto from the back door. This may seem like a roundabout way of including Kyoto in your travel plans, but Kyoto is best approached from the rear. The northwest coast of Honshu has open highways well suited for hitchhikers. The eastern side of central Honshu is too crowded to hitchhike effectively.

Do you remember the Ōyu Stone Circle? Well, instead of joining the expressway at the Towadako IC, stay on Highway 103 and you will come to Ōdate. Make sure you get dropped off as far west of town as possible, on Highway 7.

Ōdate is home of the **Akita Inu Kaikan** (dog museum). Akita prefecture is known for its breed of dog, the Akita, which is renowned for its loyalty and intelligence, and Ōdate is the main center of dog breeding in Akita. Hachikō—the dog who loyally waited for his master to return outside of Shibuya Station in Tokyo for ten years, unaware that he had died and would never come home—was an Akita. If you are already familiar with the statue of Hachikō in Tokyo, you might want to see the other, lesser-known statue to Hachikō in Ōdate.

From Ōdate, Highway 7 will take you to Noshiro (population 57,000), an easy city to bypass, because the highway sweeps past it to the south. From Noshiro, Highway 7 south is a busy run, with a lot of traffic flowing into Akita.

OGA-HANTŌ

This is a quiet corner of Japan, rich with the folklore of the Namahage Demons. The **Namahage** come out at New Year's Eve and in winter festivals. These wild men in red masks and straw capes terrorize children and adults alike in a frightening ritual meant to cure people of "winter laziness." Like so many creatures of Japanese folklore and religion, the Namahage are placated with saké.

In summertime the demons are quiet, but even without them, the Oga Peninsula makes an interesting two-day side trip. The peninsula's rolling grassy hills, crumbling cliffs, quiet forests, and distinct folklore make it an interesting off-the-beaten-path destination. Even though it is relatively remote, there is still enough traffic into the city of Oga (population 35,000) to make hitchhiking viable.

The peninsula can be a cold, harsh place during the off-season; it is best to visit between June and September. The north side of the peninsula around Oga Onsen is well developed. The south side around Monzen-mura is quieter. Note that the Oga place-name is applied to several points on the peninsula: Oga station (Oga-eki), Oga city (Oga-shi), the Oga Hot Springs (Oga Onsen), and of course the entire peninsula is called Oga-hantō. Make sure you explain clearly where you are going.

Note: The village of Monzen-mura is not marked on the atlas. It is near Tateyama-zaki.

What to See and Do

In the Oga Onsen Nyūdōzaki (cape) area you can watch craftsmen make the Namahage demon masks at the **Ishikawa Kōbō** craft production center (Tel. 0185-38-2218). You need to call ahead for a reservation. The masks are impressive—and very expensive. Prices begin at ¥9,000.

Near the Monzen Youth Hostel, west along the coast, is an eerie spot. The village of Monzen was once being tormented by Five Demons (Go-Hiki Namahage). The villagers made a pact with them: If the demons could build 1,000 steps to the **Goshadō** shrine in one night, the villagers would give them a young woman every year. The demons hooted and hollered and set about their work. But just as the demons were about to put in the last step, an especially canny villager imitated the crow of a rooster and the devils, fearing dawn, ran away. Peace returned to the village. In a wooded grove you can count the steps to Goshadō—there are 999.

Where to Stay

In Oga Onsen, near the sea, is the **Oga Seaside Hostel** (Tel. 0185-33-3125). It costs ¥2,500 per night. Ask to be dropped off at the Oga Grand Hotel; the hostel is 200 meters from the hotel, toward the shore. It is closed February 19–28. If you wish to spend New Year's on Oga, be warned: the infamous Namahage Demons of Oga will be "breaking in" to the Oga Seaside Hostel on December 31 to terrorize (and celebrate with) the guests.

Nearby, the **Oga Kokumin-shukusha** (Tel. 0185-33-3181) has rooms beginning at ¥5,500 including two meals. If you include breakfast and supper at the hostel, the two places are almost the same cost. If you haven't already made a reservation, you may want to check out both the hostel and the *kokumin-shukusha* before deciding which one you prefer.

On the south coast of the peninsula, about 12 km west along the coast from the station and near the Monzen *teiryūjo*, is the **Monzen Youth Hostel** (Tel. 0185-27-2823), which costs ¥3,000 a night. Bicycle rentals are available.

AKITA

For some reason, Akita (population 300,000) is usually dismissed as a travel destination. Neon lights sparkle along the riverside and make the downtown night-life district fun, bright, and inviting. Even better, Akita has a 24-hour **Mister Donut** near the station, which, after camping on the Oga Peninsula, was like discovering civilization again.

If you are in the area August 4–7, a trip to Akita is *definitely* in order to witness the spectacle of the city's **Kantō Matsuri,** one of Tohoku's major festivals. The highlight of the festival involves men balancing and twirling high poles lit with dozens of paper lanterns. It's a wild spectacle. It is also extremely hard to find rooms at this time. Even the love hotels fill up, and you may have to stay up all night—the 24-hour Mister Donut can come in handy!

What to See and Do

There isn't a great deal to do in Akita unless you arrive in time for the festival, but it makes a good break from rural hitchhiking. If you missed Akita's famous Kantō Matsuri, go to the **Neburi Nagashikan Exhibition Hall** and try your hand at balancing the swaying towers of lanterns used during the festival. It makes for a great photo, and entrance is just ¥100. The hall is west, across the river from **Senshū Kōen,** and a block north of the Washington Hotel.

Where to Stay

If you do end up in Akita, the **Tourist Information Center** near the station can arrange accommodations; there are several lower-priced business hotels in the station area.

The **Hawaii Hotel** (Tel. 0188-33-1111) is a three-minute walk from Akita-eki (toward the river and night-life area). The Hawaii has singles for ¥4,000 per night without a private bath, or ¥5,700 with a private bath. If you check in before 7:00 P.M. you get a ¥1,000 discount on rooms with a private bath.

The **Kohama Ryokan** (Tel. 0188-32-5739) is a member of the Japanese Inn Group and has Japanese-style rooms for ¥4,500 for one person, and ¥8,500 for two, without meals. They take American Express, VISA, and MasterCard. The ryokan is in an older wooden building near Akita-eki; from the station, turn left and walk down the street past Mister Donut. The ryokan will be on your right. It's only a five-minute walk, so don't go too far.

Escaping

To hitch out of Akita you need to get to the Akita-Kita Bypass and then hitch south on Highway 7. The bypass runs far to the west of downtown, about 4 km from Akita-eki. Take the train one stop south to Ugo Ushijima-eki, which will put you beside Highway 13. Hitchhike *north* on 13 up to where it meets Highway 7. Then hitchhike *south* on Highway 7.

En Route

South along the coast—at the prefectural boundary line between Akita and Yamagata—is Misaki Kōen, a popular park with rolling hills and a seaside view.

Farther south from this park—along the highway and near Fukura-eki—is a rugged, ten-meter-high stone landscape that has been transformed into strikingly organic sculpted images of 16 Buddhist deities. This site is named **Jūroku Rakan** and is not listed in any English guidebook I can find. The stone carvings were begun in 1868 by the monks at a nearby temple, to comfort the souls of fishermen lost in a gale. Stumbling across this carved landscape took me by surprise. Even better, there is a campsite just beside it. (See below.) You will be hitchhiking right past the Jūroku Rakan. The spot is well marked and is a popular spot for Japanese drivers. If you want more information, contact the **Yuza-machi Kankō Kyōkai Visitors' Office** (Tel. 0234-30-2211); be prepared to speak in Japanese.

Where to Stay

Just below the 16 Stone Buddhas of the Jūroku Rakan, and near the intersection of highways 7 and 345, is the **Nishi-Hama Camp-jō** (Tel. 0234-77-3331). The next morning you can hitch south on Highway 345 all the way into the Dewa Sanzan mountains. There are hot springs in nearby Yunota.

SAKATA

Sakata (population 100,000) is a sister city of Tsuruoka, which in turn is the gateway to the mountains of Dewa Sanzan. The two cities are similar in size and blend into each other. Most people just pass right through Sakata and Tsuruoka on their way to Dewa Sanzan, but if you do find yourself in either city there are a couple of places worth visiting.

Note: If you want to take a boat trip down the **Mogami-kyō** river gorge you should turn east at Sakata. Highway 7 turns into the Sakata Bypass. Once it crosses the Mogami River it meets Highway 47, which runs southeast. This highway will eventually take you inland through the heart of the Mogami-Kyō river gorge. Boat rides depart from the village of Tozawa.

What to See and Do

Rent bikes for free at the Bussankan Museum, the Jusco store, and Shimizuya. This makes visiting the photo gallery south of the city easier and will save on taxi fares. In Sakata, the sunset near the small six-sided wooden Rokkaku Tōdai lighthouse in **Hiyoriyama Kōen** is said to be more beautiful than anywhere else in Tohoku. Coming up the east side of Tohoku you enjoyed seeing the sunrise, now coming down the west side of Tohoku, it is the sunsets that are impressive. This park is near Sakata port, west of Sakata-eki. Camping inside the park is prohibited.

For a taste of the macabre, go to **Kaikō-ji** temple, just east of the entrance to Hiyoriyama park, which has two mummified monks (*soku-shin-butsu*).

For those interested in contemporary Japanese photography, the **Domon Ken Kinenkan** is dedicated to the acclaimed works of Domon Ken, who chronicled the postwar years of Japan. His photographs represent Italian neo-realism imbued with Japanese sensibilities. The gallery is on the banks of the Mogami River, south of the city. It is open 9:00 A.M.– 4:30 P.M. daily except Monday. Admission is ¥500.

Where to Stay

The **Hotel Alpha One Sakata** (Tel. 0234-22-6111), is a basic business hotel near Sakata-eki. It has singles from ¥5,350 to ¥6,250 per night and doubles for ¥11,200 per night.

South of Sakata, with a view of the Shōnai airport runway, is the **Yūhi-no-oka Auto Camp** (Tel. 0234-92-4570), which is open from the fourth Saturday of April to the first Sunday in November. Costs are ¥400 a person and ¥3,000 for a space. There are only three or four flights a day into Shōnai, so the campsite isn't noisy. It is hard to hitchhike to, because it is 18 km south of the city and traffic only picks up just before or after a flight.

TOBI-SHIMA

From Sakata-kō ferries run to Tobi-shima (island) once or

twice a day and cost ¥2,000 and take 90 minutes. Call 0234-22-3911 for schedule updates.

This place is for people who *really* want to get away from it all. The island is 10 km in circumference, and the main attractions are bird watching and fishing. From Tobi-shima you can charter fishermen to take you out to the smaller islands.

There are several *minshuku* and ryokan, including the oddly named **Youth Hostel Sawaguchi Ryokan** (Tel. 0234-95-2246) which is a seven-minute walk from the port and near Enfuku-ji. Make sure you call this hostel before setting out for the island. It costs ¥2,200 June 1–September 30, and ¥2,000 during the off-season. Bicycle rentals are available, and the hostel can help you arrange boat rides to the smaller islands. The hostel is open April 1–October 31.

TSURUOKA

Tsuruoka (population 100,000) is the usual gateway to Dewa Sanzan.

What to See and Do

The **Tsuruoka Chidō Hakubutsukan** (museum), west of the castle ruins, is dedicated to fishing and agricultural history. Six historical buildings from the Meiji era (1868–1912)—old clan houses and police stations—have been moved to this area, so if you have an interest in West-East blends of architecture this will be worth your time to visit. The **Sakai House** has old Japanese armor on display; it is open 9:00 A.M.–4:30 P.M. daily. Admission is ¥520.

East of Tsuruoka is **Nangaku-ji,** a temple that houses the mummified remains of a priest who is said to have attained Buddhahood in 1868. If you want to visit this temple first, you can hitchhike directly to it, without going into downtown

Tsuruoka. The temple is at the end of the Tsuruoka Bypass, between Highway 7 and Highway 345. Keep in mind that if you follow this itinerary, you will also pass by the temple grounds on your way out of Tsuruoka, so you may want to save it for *after* your visit to Dewa Sanzan.

Where to Stay

A short walk from the station is another **Hotel Alpha One** (Tel. 0235-25-1212). It has singles from ¥6,000 to ¥6,960 and doubles for ¥12,680.

The misnamed **Tsuruoka Hostel** (Tel. 0235-73-3205) is far from the mountains and is near the coast, southwest of the city. You will pass by the hostel on your way south, before you get to Sanze-eki. This hostel is located in a quasi-national park, only a five-minute walk from the ocean. Cycling in the area from here is good. This hostel is not in a convenient location for trips going into the mountains, but it makes a good place to stay after visiting Dewa Sanzan, on your way south to Niigata. It costs ¥2,600 per night. Closed May 27–June 5.

DEWA SANZAN

These three mountains—**Yudono-san, Haguro-san,** and **Gassan**—are three of the holiest peaks in Japan, and home of the Shugendō sect, an eclectic mix of Shinto and Buddhist mysticism. The followers of Shugendō, mountain monks called *yamabushi*, have a history that dates back over 1,000 years.

The *yamabushi* today are a friendly lot, blowing their conch shells and enjoying the role they play. Many are "part-time," mystics, but a good number still do take part in the rigorous mountain training. Don't hesitate to take the photograph of any you come upon; there is no taboo against it.

Think of the Dewa Sanzan mountain route as a circle broken on the east side. Tsuruoka is on the west side of the circle. From there you can either hitch north to Haguro-san and Gas-san, or you can hitch south instead, past Chūren-ji temple to Yudono-san. To complete the circle you will have to hike across the mountaintop from Gas-san to Yudono-san (or vice versa). The hike from Gas-san to Yudono-san is not difficult, but it is long and it will take a full day's outing to complete. Wear good hiking shoes and warm clothes. In late June it was still cold up at the top, and there are patches of snow that never melt. Make sure to bring adequate rain gear. The main mountain hiking trail from Gas-san is open only from the beginning of July to the first week of October, and even then the end of the season can be cold and drizzly.

If you don't make the full hike, you will have to backtrack. If you aren't obsessive about seeing all three holy mountains (though I strongly recommend that you do) or if simply short of time, you may want to skip Gas-san, which is the least accessible of the three.

Because of the constant flow of hikers, pilgrims, and sightseers into the Dewa Sanzan area, hitching in and out is easy—and much simpler than trying to coordinate the various bus times and routes. If you are lucky you will hook up with Japanese pilgrims and you can hike the route with them. As a hitchhiker, you can ask your last driver of the day for help in arranging lodgings. Approaching a pilgrims' lodging in the company of a Japanese person will make everything much smoother.

Note: In the atlas, the Dewa Sanzan area is not well represented. It is divided between two different pages and Haguro-san is not labeled at all. This is a serious omission. To locate Haguro-san in the atlas, look for Dewa-Sanzan Jinja, which is on the mountain. The village of Tōge, where most of the pilgrim lodgings are, is not shown either; it is just west of Dewa Sanzan Jinja.

Haguro-san is the easiest of the three mountains to reach. From Tsuruoka hitchhike east on Prefectural Highway 47 through the town of Haguro-machi. This highway is shown in green but not numbered in the atlas. If you are coming south from Sakata on Highway 7, ask to be dropped off east of the Tsuruoka on Prefectural Highway 47, across the river if possible. If you explain that you are headed for Haguro-san, they will point you in the right direction. It is only a short, 12-km ride west to the Haguro-san lodgings in Tōge, so if you are very nice your driver may decide to take you all the way in to Haguro-san.

At the top of Haguro-san, **Dewa Sanzan Jinja** honors the gods of all three mountains. You can hitch right to the summit on the Hagurosan-dōro toll road (¥400) and then walk down the mountain on the footpath from the shrine. However, I recommend walking up the wooded path instead. It is good exercise, and it helps to give you the sense of physical effort that a pilgrimage should entail. The one-hour walk is memorable.

The path up to the shrine begins at the parking lot of the Haguro Sentā bus stop. This is also a pilgrims' lodging area, so if you stay here, you can hike up early the next morning and beat most of the crowds. An old wooden Buddhist gate marks the start of the trail. You will cross a small bridge and soon come to a pagoda, which has been standing since 1372. From the pagoda, 2,446 steps lead through a steep, 300-year-old forest of cedars. Halfway up is a teahouse that serves refreshments—a side path from the teahouse leads out to an old abandoned temple pavilion where the poet Bashō once stayed. Have a cup of tea and then continue on to the shrine complex at the top. When I went, there were still patches of snow in the shadows and the crowds were thin. The walk takes an hour.

The shrine at the top is an example of Buddhist architecture that was forced to house the more "purely Japanese" Shinto religion. Across from the main hall is the **Kagami-ike** (mirror pond), so named because female pilgrims in the Meiji era used to toss their mirrors into it as a demonstration of their desire to abandon earthly vanities. Some of the mirrors have been retrieved and are now on display in the Rekishi Hakubutsukan (museum) nearby.

Gas-san (1,980 meters) is the highest of the three mountains and attracts more of the "real" pilgrims and fewer of the day-trippers. From Haguro-san a road runs south toward Gas-san. Almost all the traffic is going to the head of the trail, which begins at Hachi Gōme, the Eighth Hiking Station. From there, it is a three-hour hike across some marshes, a plateau, and then up a steep hike to the shrine at the summit.

From the top of Gas-san it is another three-hour hike down the other side to Yudono-san Jinja. All said, it is a good full-day hike from Hachi Gōme (eighth station), up one side of Gas-san, down the other, and on to Yudono-san.

En Route

On the way to Yudono-san, just north of Highway 112, are the **Chūren-ji** and **Dainichibō** temples where the mummified remains of devout *yamabushi* monks are on display. English explanations of these "living Buddha mummies" are available at Chūren-ji. From Chūren-ji you can walk to Dainichibō temple.

Note: Only Dainichibō temple is shown on the atlas; Chūren-ji is to the west.

Yudono-san (1,500 meters) was once a prohibited mountain, and today it is still the most sacred of the three. You can hike across the mountains from Gas-san, or you can hitchhike in on Highway 112. You will have to take the ¥400 toll road north from Highway 112. You should offer to pay this, even if your driver was going there anyway. At the end of the toll road is a bus, charging around ¥200 more to whisk you farther up the mountain. From there, it is a 30-minute walk to **Yudono-san Jinja** (shrine) at the top.

Note: If you are coming into Yudono-san on the hiking trail

from Gas-san, you can avoid the bus and walk downhill to where the toll road starts. In the parking lot you should be able to find a ride back toward Tsuruoka.

At the **Yudono-san Jinja,** the object of veneration is a large boulder with a natural hot spring running over it. It was once forbidden to tell anyone what you saw here, but Japanese and English guidebooks have broken this taboo. The boulder and the spring are still a very holy icon. No photographs. Treat it with respect, even if you see Japanese tourists breaking the rules or acting frivolous. As a foreigner you are more visible.

Pilgrims pay a small admission, remove their shoes, receive blessings and then walk through the water, symbolically bathing their pilgrims' feet. Watch the more serious visitors and copy their actions.

Where to Stay

In the small community of Tōge, near Haguro-san, there are many pilgrims' lodgings (*shukubō*), which are easy enough to arrange on arrival in the off-season. **Shukubō** provide basic accommodations, but they aren't cheap. Expect to pay at least ¥7,000 per night.

If you call ahead and reserve space you can stay in the shrine complex right at **Dewa Sanzan Jinja** on Haguro-san (Tel. 0235-62-2357). Lodging costs ¥7,000 per night—more if you want to try the distinctive mountain cuisine. Try to have a Japanese person call ahead of time to arrange your lodgings. If not, just show up and hope for the best.

Camping: South of Dewa Sanzan Jinja, just five minutes from the top of Haguro-san, is the **Haguro Kokumin Kyūka-mura Camp-jō** (Tel. 0235-62-4270) which is open May 1–October 30. It costs ¥400 per person and ¥1,000 for a space. A six-man tent is available for rent for ¥3,100.

Southeast of Tsuruoka, on the east side of the Akagawa (river) in the town of Kushibiki, is the **Shizen-no-Ie Tozawa-sō** (Tel. 0235-57-4483), which is open from June 1 to the end of October. No charge with your own tent. Staying in the shelters costs ¥510 per person. If you are backtracking from Haguro-san and are headed to Yudono-san, this makes a good place to stop.

Escaping

If you want to complete the loop by returning to Sendai, don't return to Tsuruoka, but continue east on Highway 112 after you visit Yudono-san, which will take you into Sagae. Ask to be dropped off at the Sagae IC and you can take the Yamagata Expressway across to the Murata Junction and then north into Sendai. Once you get on the expressways it becomes a fast hitch. Otherwise, return to Tsuruoka and continue down the coast toward Niigata. After Murakami, stick with Highway 7 inland all the way to Niigata. Highway 113 between Murakami and Niigata is empty and the hitching is terrible.

NIIGATA

Niigata (population 480,000) is a large industrial city. It is the capital of Niigata Prefecture, an area also known as Snow Country. The mountains of the interior—and farther north as well—experience some of the heaviest snowfalls in the world. Villages are buried under two stories of snow and people tunnel their way through the streets.

The Snow Country is also a source of melancholy and romance to the Japanese. It was in Niigata Prefecture that Yasunari Kawabata set his acclaimed novel *Yuki-guni* (known in English as *Snow Country*). Though you have already passed through much of Japan's Snow Country by the time you reach Niigata, the city is still closely associated with the image.

Although the citizens of Niigata have a reputation for being boisterous and outspoken, there is little to recommend this city to the casual visitor. Just as Tsuruoka is known primarily as a gateway to Dewa Sanzan, for travelers, Niigata is primarily a gateway to Sado Island.

Where to Obtain Information

The **Tourist Information Center** inside the JR Niigata-eki is open until 7:00 P.M. every night and has English materials, maps, schedules, and information on Sado Island as well.

For English books and materials, dictionaries, and the atlas, there are two bookstores that have English selections. This may be a good time to read Kawabata's *Snow Country*, as you bid farewell to the Deep North. The **Kinokuniya** bookstore is an eight-minute walk from the station and has English books on the second floor. The **Banshōdō Shoten** bookstore is in the Furumachi area, near the Mitsukoshi and Daiwa department stores (about a 20-minute walk from Niigata-eki). It is open until 8:00 P.M. and has some English books, including the atlas, on the first floor.

Where to Stay

Niigata has the usual love hotels and station-side business hotels, but the best thing about Niigata is the ferry to Sado. If you do get stuck in Niigata, the **Niigata Hotel** near Niigata-eki (Tel. 025-246-0301) has singles that start at ¥5,200. No doubles.

Escaping

Hitchhiking *into* Niigata is easy. Getting out is tough. Fortunately, you can use Sado Island like a stepping stone. The trick is to take a ferry from Niigata to the Ryōtsu-kō on the east side of Sado Island. Hitchhike across the island and then take a different ferry back, from Ogi to Naoetsu, south of Niigata. This puts you well down the road and allows you to skip the worst of the urban sprawl around Niigata.

It is a 15-minute bus ride from the Niigata-eki area to the

Niigata Nishi-kō ferry port (also known by the ferry company's name, Sado Kisen). Buses leave from Gate 6, cost ¥160 one way, and are timed to connect with ferries leaving for Sado.

Ferries run from the Niigata Nishi-kō ferry port to Ryōtsu six times a day. The last one leaves at 9:40 P.M. The ride takes two hours and 20 minutes, and costs ¥1,780 one way.

An ultra-smooth, high-speed jet foil makes the trip in one hour flat, but it costs ¥5,460 one way. Reservations are required ahead of time for the jet foil.

Ferries run from Ogi on Sado Island to Naoetsu on the main-land about six times a day. The last ferry leaves Ogi at 5:00 P.M. It takes two hours and 30 minutes and costs ¥1,960 one way.

SADO ISLAND

Although most people will understand you if you simply say, "Sado," its full name is usually given as Sado-ga-shima. Sado is Japan's Island of Exile, where poets, pretenders, and ex-emperors were banished. Later, the gold mines of distant Sado would fund the Tokugawa shoguns. For much of the year, Sado is a windy, cold, miserable place. If possible, visit Sado between May and September.

Sado is shaped like two mountainous whales joined in the middle by a low, flat plain. On the east side of the plain is the main town and ferry port of Ryōtsu (population 20,000). On the west side is the town of Sawata. Hitchhiking between these two towns is straightforward, and the traffic flow is light but steady. Hitching the other areas can be painfully slow during the week. I was lucky to be picked up by a car filled with young ski instructors from Niigata who were on an end-of-season celebratory get-away and we drove all around the island together.

Sado's *taiko* drummers—the world-renowned Kodō Drums of Heaven—perform off-island, but during Sado's many festivals, *taiko* drums play a central role.

Where to Obtain Information

It is best to get English materials and pamphlets *before* you arrive in Sado. Make sure you pick up Sado information at Sendai-eki. The **Sado Kisen ferry company** provides an excellent color booklet that contains a map of Sado and full ferry schedules, all in English. Pick one up at the ferry port, or—if you can speak a little Japanese—call 025-245-1234 and ask them to send you a copy. If you get a nice clerk on the line they may send it to you without asking for postage. You can fax Sado Kisen as well at 0255-44-6313.

In Sawata, there is a volunteer English service (Tel. 0259-52-3163) but first you should contact the **Sado Kankō Kyōkai Tourist Office** (Tel. 0259-74-3318) in Aikawa. The office is in the Gōdō Chōsha Prefectural Building and is open 8:30 A.M.–5:00 P.M., Monday to Friday. All it really offers is an English map.

What to See and Do

In central Sado, during the **Niibo Sannō Matsuri** (April 15) and the **Hamochi-Ichinomiya Matsuri** (April 23), horseback archery events (*yabusame*) are held in medieval samurai costumes.

Sado is also a center of Noh drama in Japan, largely the legacy of the great Zeami (1364–1443), who helped codify classical Japanese dramatic aesthetics. Though exiled to Sado, where he died in obscurity, his art lives on.

Short of renting your own car, hitchhiking is probably the best way to see Sado unless you want to pay a small fortune for a package tour. The island is still worth a visit; just decrease your mileage expectations because hitching is slow. (The Shobunsha map of Sado is not very good. Other than Highway 350, the roads are not numbered and the smaller villages are not shown.) Fortunately, Sado is not a difficult place to figure out. Don't underestimate Sado's size, though. It is a big island, and there is no point trying to see it all. For hitchhikers, a Sado Island tour might run from Ryōtsu to Sawata, and then up along the coast through Aikawa to the hostel near Senkaku-wan (bay), and then back south to Sawata and down to Ogi. If you are on a limited schedule, you might want to skip the gold mines and hitchhike across from Ryōtsu to Sawata and then down to Ogi. From Ogi take a ferry back to the mainland.

No matter where you hitch in Sado, stay on the main roads as much as possible. And be patient. Relax and enjoy the scenery, and remember the mantra: *eventually somebody will stop.*

RYŌTSU

Ryōtsu is a ramshackle town built around the edge of Kamoko (lake). Some people find it depressing, but I thought it had a great atmosphere to it. Between April and October there are nightly presentations of **Okesa Odori,** a folk dance that originated in Ryōtsu. Admission is ¥600; performances begin at 8:00 P.M. Dances are held in the Okesa Kaikan (hall), about 600 meters north of the Ryōtsu-kō ferry port.

To hitchhike out of Ryōtsu, you can walk through downtown and then hitch south on Highway 354, the only national highway on Sado. Or you can take Prefectural Highway 65 which runs parallel to 354, and cross the island into Mano instead.

Where to Stay

The **Sado Seaside Hotel** (Tel. 0259-27-7211) in Ryōtsu is a member of the Japanese Inn Group and offers Japanese-style rooms without private bath for ¥5,500 per night for a single and ¥10,000 for a double, meals not included. Western-style rooms are ¥6,000 and ¥11,000 per night. This hotel is out of town, so you will probably want the breakfast as well, which costs an additional ¥800. There is a ¥150 charge for the hot-spring baths tagged on, as well as the usual consumption tax. They take American Express and VISA. This hotel is actually located in the Sumiyoshi Onsen hot-spring area, which is marked in the atlas.

It is a 20-minute walk from the Ryōtsu-kō. If you call from Niigata and tell them when you will be arriving, they will send someone to meet you at the port. Look for the green "Seaside Hotel" flag.

The **Kisaki Camp-jō** in Ryōtsu is free and not far from Sado-kūkō and near the shore of Kamoko. This basic site provides the essential toilets, water, and space, and is open May–October. If you are trying to explain to someone where it is, tell them you are heading for the Kyōdo Hakubutsukan (museum), which is not far from the campsite.

Halfway down the northwest coast at Cape Senbo is **Nyūzaki Camp-jō** (Tel. 0259-78-2153). It is open all year, but do not be tempted to camp between October and the beginning of April, because Sado can be bitterly cold. This campsite costs ¥500 per person with your own tent. Tents and blankets are also available for rent. A six-man tent costs ¥1,000 to rent.

Try one of the following hostels:

The **Sotokaifu Hostel** (Tel. 0259-78-2911) is on the northwest of the island, near Sabuto-zaki. They are closed December 26–January 4. No bicycle rentals, but it costs only ¥2,300 per night.

The **Senkaku-sō Hostel** (Tel. 0259-75-2011) is on the west coast, just south of scenic Senkaku-wan, and costs ¥2,600 per night. If you arrive during the day, this hostel makes a good place to aim for. The next day you can hitch down to Ogi and stay at the hostel there.

The **Sado Hakusan Hostel** (Tel. 0259-52-4422) is in a small farming village near Sawata. If you call from Kubota *teiryūjo* (bus stop), someone will come to fetch you. It costs ¥2,400 per night.

The **Green Village Hostel** (Tel. 0259-22-2719) is in Nibo-mura (village) in the middle of the island. They charge ¥2,800 per night.

The **Kazashima-kan** (Tel. 0259-29-2003) is way out on the east coast, south of Hime-zaki and near Benten-zaki. Closed January 1–4. No bicycle rentals. It costs ¥2,400.

MANO

From the ferry port at Ryōtsu, turn left and walk south about a kilometer to the Shiizaki Onsen area. Prefectural Highway 65 runs down the east side of Kamoko and then crosses the middle of Sado, parallel to Highway 350.

Note: This highway is shown in green but not numbered on the atlas. Prefectural Highway 65 meets Highway 350 at Mano. This route puts you closer to Ogi if you are planning to hitch farther south. It also takes you near Myōsen-ji and Kokubun-ji in a quiet, forested area.

Kokubun-ji was the official temple of Sado back when the island was an independent state. **Myōsen-ji** has a 250-year-old pagoda. Among Sado's many illustrious exiles was the young ex-Emperor Juntoku, who led a rebellion in 1222 against the ruling Kamakura shoguns (military leaders who ruled "on behalf of" the emperor). His attempt to return power to the emperor failed, and the shogun system remained intact for the next 600 years. Executing an emperor—even an enemy of the shogun—was unheard of, and so Juntoku was sent to Sado instead, where he died in lonely exile. His quiet, understated mausoleum, Mano Goryō, is in Mano.

AIKAWA

This was once a boomtown filled with gold miners, overlords, prostitutes, wine merchants, mountebanks, and slave laborers. It was a major, albeit makeshift, city. Today, the quiet Aikawa area is best known for the jagged coastline of Senkaku-wan (bay) and the Sōdayū-kō gold mines of Kinzan. A hostel and campsite make Aikawa a good place to spend the night. The **Senkaku-wan Cruises** take you through the odd formations and liquid blue of Sado's most picturesque bay. They leave from Tassha, which is a quick 20-minute ride north of Aikawa. The cruise takes 40 minutes and costs ¥650. Similar cruises also leave from Ageshima, a little farther north, and cost ¥700.

Prefectural Highway 45 (shown in green but not numbered in the atlas) runs up the west coast of Sado. If you hitchhike into Aikawa and mention that you are going to the Old Gold Mines, the odds are very good that your driver will make the detour and take you right to the mine entrance. Otherwise, you can walk from the highway up to the **Old Gold Mines** in about 40 minutes. The infamous mines of Aikawa are now a museum with miniature displays and mannequins. Admission is ¥600.

As you approach the Old Gold Mines, you will see two small twin peaks called Dōyū-no-Wareto, said to have been formed by a greedy, enraged gold miner who struck the mountain so hard with his hammer and spike that he ruptured the peak in two. Whether by one worker or thousands of gold miners, gold was mined until 1990.

From the Old Gold Mines you can continue east on the O-Sado Skyline, which follows the mountain heights back to Ryōtsu. This gives you a high vista of the island. Hitchhiking is the only really affordable way to go; there are no public buses, and the package tours are incredibly expensive. On weekends and holidays, many young couples and sightseers take this road. If you are traveling during the week or in the off-season, give it an hour and if you haven't got a ride, return to Aikawa instead. Walking back from the Old Gold Mines to Aikawa is easier because it is downhill. Many people find the gold mines only mildly interesting, or even disappointing. Go with modest expectations and you'll enjoy it more. Or else skip it and spend more time in the Senkaku-wan area instead.

OGI

This area is best known as a place where women in traditional costumes demonstrate the **tarai-bune** (barrel-boats) that are linked with a legend of a maid who paddled all the way from the mainland in a washing barrel to be with her exiled lover. Until recently, these tubs were used regularly to gather seaweed, but today they are used mainly to entertain tourists.

During Golden Week, the town is reportedly swamped with tourists, so choose your times carefully. You can try your hand at steering one of these round-tub *tarai-bune* for ¥450.

Boat cruises run down the Ogi coast to the lighthouse at Sawasaki-bana, the southernmost tip of Sado, and cost ¥1,400. On the shore, west of Ogi, is a picturesque little shrine on an islet and beyond that, small fishing villages nestled in coves along the shore.

Near Ogi are two small islands—islets really—connected by a small vermilion bridge. The name of these small tufts of land are **Ya-jima** (Arrow Island) and **Kyō-jima** (Sutra Island). The first name is derived from the bamboo that grows on the island and which is said to make arrows capable of piercing the hole in the center of a ¥5 coin from 100 paces. Examine a ¥5 coin for yourself and ask yourself if maybe the claims aren't a wee bit exaggerated.

The second island gets its name in a more dramatic fashion. Among those exiled to Sado was the priest Nichiren (1222–82) who—legend has it—was spared the executioner's blade when a lightening bolt split it in two just as it was about to decapitate him. The ruling shogun took this as a warning and, instead of having Nichiren executed, sent him into exile. When, after many years, news came of Nichiren's release, one of his disciples hurried to Sado to tell him. A storm shipwrecked the poor man on the tiny island and he kept his courage up by chanting the

Buddhist sutras through the night. (The island isn't very far from shore, so just how much danger the disciple was in is debatable.)

Nichiren, meanwhile, went on to call forth the *kamikaze* (divine winds) that would sink Kublai Khan's invasion force. Today a small temple marks the spot where the Nichiren sutra was chanted, and the two tiny islands make an attractive place to visit. If you take a cruise to the Sawasaki lighthouse, you will pass the islands on the way.

The **Ogi Sakuma-sō Hostel** (Tel. 0259-86-2565) is in a farmhouse just outside of Ogi. It is a pleasant 1.3-km walk up the hill behind the port. Make sure you ask for directions before setting off. If you are hitching into Ogi, your driver will be able to help you find it. Open March 1–November 30. They charge ¥2,400 per night. No bicycle rentals.

Across the peninsula from Ogi-machi, on a road rarely even marked on road maps, is the **Moto-hama Camp** (Tel. 0259-86-2363), which is open July 1–August 31; they charge ¥1,000 for a spot plus ¥300 per person. Tent and blanket rentals are available.

SHUKUNEGI

Four kilometers west of Ogi is the beautiful, weathered old fishing village of Shukunegi, not shown in the atlas. This cluster of old fishing homes—many over 200 years old—is also one of the few places where the *tarai-bune* are still used as working boats for gathering seaweed, shells, and abalone.

If you are staying in the Ogi hostel ask about buses to Shukunegi. The best way to go would be by bicycle, but the hostel doesn't rent them. You can walk it in about one hour and 50 minutes, and it's a nice way to spend the morning. You can try to hitch it as well, but there isn't much traffic except for the occasional fisherman. If you do get a ride, ask to be let off at the path leading to the **Shiawase Jizō,** a giant stone carving of the Buddhist protector of children.

From the stone Jizō, a path leads to **Iwaya-san,** a caveside temple featuring stone carvings of Buddha in a secluded grove. After Iwaya-san continue along the path for another 400 meters and you will be back on the road to Shukunegi. Iwaya-san can be tricky to find, but it is worth the effort.

Escaping

From Ogi take a ferry to Naoetsu which will put you south of Niigata and spare you having to escape the big city. Naoetsu is still very urban, however, and it will take some aggravation before you clear the cityscape entirely. Highway 8 runs about 2 km inland from the port. It is a long hike. The Jōetsu IC of the Hokuriku Expressway is even farther along. To get to the IC is a 15-minute bus ride to the Rījon Jōetsu *teiryūjo,* and then a 10-minute walk to the IC itself.

You can hitch it as well, from the ferry port. But be quick—try to catch traffic as it comes off the ferry, otherwise you are in for a long walk or a ¥900 taxi ride out to the Jōetsu IC. When hitching, use a sign that simply says "IC."

From Naoetsu to Kanazawa (population 430,000), the so-called Northern Kyoto, is full day of hitching. Kanazawa is a big city, despite its image as a rustic, traditional place. Like Kyoto, there is an abundance of tourist information in English.

After Kanazawa, you can enter Kyoto through the back door by hitching in on the Hokuriku Expressway down to Tsugaru. From there, follow Highway 161 along the west coast of Biwako (lake). Biwako, for all its fame, is not a particularly attractive place—especially after traveling through rural Tohoku—so you might want to stay on the Hokuriku Expressway all the way down the east side of Biwa instead, to Hikone. Hikone is home of one of Japan's oldest and most treasured castles, Hikone-jō.

Once you have entered the Hikone/Kyoto area, you have left

the realm of the hitchhiker. The cities are too close together for highway hitching and the distances too small to bother with expressways. From now on you are a tourist—take the train. Stay in overpriced hotels. Spend lots of money. And why not? You earned it.

AMA-NO-HASHIDATE

Having started your hitchhiking journey with the islands of Matsushima Bay, you may want to end your trip with a visit to another of Japan's Three Famous Sites—the pine-covered sandbar of Ama-no-Hashidate, the Bridge of Heaven. Instead of turning inland toward Kyoto, at Tsuruga get off the IC and hitchhike *around* Tsuruga on the Kanayama Bypass. This puts you on Highway 27, which follows the coast south all the way to Ama-no-Hashidate. If you leave Kanazawa in the morning you should be in Ama-no-Hashidate by late evening.

Where to Stay

Both hostels are on the north side of the Ama-no-Hashidate bridge.

The **Ama-no-Hashidate Hostel** (Tel. 0772-27-0121) is up the hill near Kago Jinja. The hostel rents bicycles, which puts everything within easy reach, and the owner speaks some English. It is closed on the third Wednesday and Thursday of the month, September–June. It costs ¥2,450 per night.

The **Ama-no-Hashidate Kankō Kaikan Youth Hostel** (Tel. 0772-7-0046) is two minutes from the Ichinomiya Sanbashi ferry port at the north side of the Ama-no-Hashidate bridge. It is closed December 31 and January 1. It costs ¥2,350 in the peak season.

Timing: A Sendai–Aomori loop will take 12–16 days. Count on two nights in the Matsushima area, a night and two days at

Kinkasan. Add another three days to go up the Miyagi–Iwate coast—longer if possible—and two or three days in the Osore-zan–Yagen Valley area. One night and a day in Hirosaki. Two days in the Towadako–Oirase Valley area, a night and two days in Hiraizumi before heading back to Sendai. If you also visit Sado Island and the Dewa Sanzan area, add at least four days. A grand tour of Tohoku and the Niigata Coast would thus take three weeks.

Shikoku and the Inland Sea

Of Japan's four main islands, Shikoku is the most overlooked and least visited by Western travelers. But Shikoku's back-road interiors and open highways compensate for what it lacks in fame. Much of Shikoku's Inland Sea coast is heavily industrialized, but the central mountains and southeastern coast are perfect for the adventurous traveler who wants to be far off the beaten track. Shikoku can easily be combined with a visit to the busier, visitor-drawing areas of Hiroshima and Kyoto. It can also be connected with a trip through Kyushu by taking a ferry across from the west side of Shikoku.

You will start and end your journey by crossing the Inland Sea (Seto Naikai). Smog-choked factories and polluted ports mar much of it, but there are still islands and small fishing villages that dot the coasts and operate on gentler rhythms.

Shikoku is best known for its 88 Temple Pilgrimage, a route that circles the island. It was first laid out by the mendicant priest Kūkai (774–835), who was born in Shikoku and known posthumously as Kōbō Daishi. (You will hear him referred to as both Kūkai and Kōbō Daishi, so you should be familiar with both names.)

Kūkai founded the esoteric Shingon sect, which marked the beginning of Japanese Buddhism. Prior to Kūkai, Buddhism in Japan was still very much an "imported" faith.

Throughout Shikoku, you will see "pilgrim tours" of retired men and women in white vests, carrying pilgrim staffs. Tour buses whisk them from temple to temple. They may call themselves *henro* (pilgrims) and they may carry the staff and wear the white pilgrim's vest and straw hat, but their journey is more of a "theme holiday" than a pilgrimage. Still, there are solitary wandering pilgrims as well, and you may see them in their straw sandals walking along the roadside. The full circuit covers more than 1,200 km and takes four months to complete. By bus it takes just a week or so. The island of Shodo-shima in the Inland Sea has a mini-pilgrimage of 88 temples as well, which can be covered in just a couple of days by people in a hurry, or in several weeks by foot. You will be visiting Shōdo-shima on this itinerary; the island makes an excellent stepping stone across the Inland Sea to Shikoku.

OSAKA TO HIMEJI

Getting There

Travelers planning on a trip through Shikoku should arrive at the Kansai Kokusai-kūkō (international airport), south of Osaka. Osaka (population 2.5 million) is a gritty, unattractive industrial metropolis. Granted, Osaka has a certain money-grubbing charm about it, but other than its towering concrete castle and high concentration of neon bars and noodle shops, there is no overriding reason to venture into downtown Osaka.

You can go from the Kansai airport directly to Shikoku via ferries. For this itinerary, take an airport train into Osaka then transfer to a JR train bound for Himeji.

Where to Obtain Information

To pick up the atlas, or any of the other books mentioned earlier, go to the **Osaka Kinokuniya** bookstore, which is in the Hankyu Umeda subway station complex near the JR Osaka station. Buy the atlas, a Japanese-English dictionary, a language guide and any other books you need before you get to Shikoku. There are English bookstores along the way in several cities in Shikoku, but the selection is not dependable.

Where to Stay

Pass through Osaka as quickly as possible. Stop in at Kinokuniya and catch the next train out—the less time spent in Osaka, the more money you will save. But if you get stuck overnight in Osaka, the **Hattori Ryokuchi Hostel** (Tel. 06-862-0600) is just ¥1,700 per night. No smoking. Some English spoken. Unfortunately, this hostel is located far from the city center. Take a subway on the Midōsuji Line to Ryokuchi Kōen-eki. From there it is another 15-minute walk north along the east side of the park. The hostel is closed December 29–January 3.

─────────────── KEY TO MAP ───────────────

1. Osaka	12. Ōtoyo	24. Oki-no-shima
2. Himeji	13. Nankoku	25. Sukumo
3A. Shōdo-shima	14. Ryūgadō	26. Uwajima
3. Uchinomi	15. Kōchi	27. Yawatahama
4. Kankakei Valley	16. Katsurahama Beach	28. Misaki
5. Takamatsu	17. Ino	29. Sada-misaki
6. Yashima	18A. Yokonami	30. Ōzu
7. Kotohira	18. Uranouchi-wan	31. Uchiko
8. Miyoshi	19. Susaki	32. Ikazaki
9. Ōboke-Koboke	20. Nakamura	33. Matsuyama
Gorge	21. Tosa-Shimizu	34. Hiroshima
10. Iya-no-Kazurabashi	22. Ashizuri-misaki	35. Miyajima
11. Oku-Iya	23. Ōdō Kaigan	36. Iwakuni

SHIKOKU and the INLAND SEA

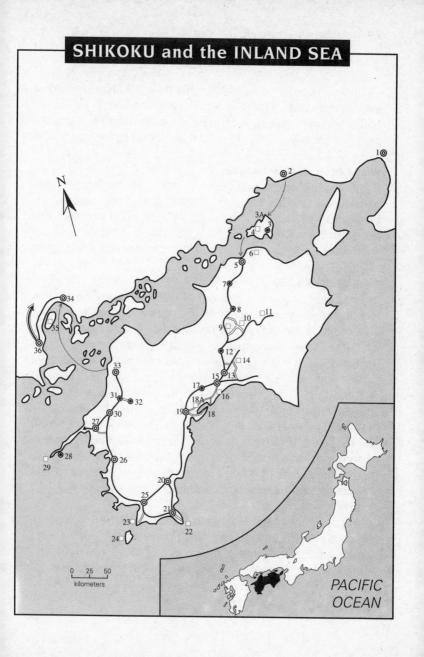

HIMEJI

Himeji (population 495,000) is the home of Japan's grandest extant castle. Take a train west from Osaka to Himeji-eki, a one-hour 35-minute ride by local train. From the station it is a 20-minute walk down the wide central boulevard to Himeji-jō.

Where to Obtain Information

The **Tourist Information Center** in front of Himeji station tries to have an English speaker on staff during the day, usually between 10:00 A.M. and 3:00 P.M. The office is open 9:00 A.M.–5:00 P.M. daily. They can help you find cheap accommodations in the station area, and can also provide English pamphlets and maps.

What to See and Do

The castle, known as *Shirasagi-jō* (White Heron), dominates the cityscape and is visible from the station. Statues line either side of the boulevard, so the usual advice is to walk down one side of the street and return on the other. There are coin lockers in Himeji-eki, if you want to leave your bags while you visit the castle.

Himeji-jō is the largest castle in Japan. It was built by Toyotomi Hideyoshi, "the monkey-faced general," in 1580, a time of warlords, samurai armies, and ninja assassins. During World War II, the castle became a defiant symbol of Japanese survival; when the city was firebombed, the castle miraculously survived. It was later learned that American pilots were using the castle as a reference point when flying bombing missions, which is why they didn't destroy it.

You can buy a detailed English booklet that explains both the castle's architecture and the many legends and ghosts associated with it. Note the mournful tale of a servant girl who was tossed to her death down the well as punishment for breaking a plate. At night you can hear her counting, end counting, her master's plates. More recently, Himeji-jō is familiar to Western audiences as the castle used in the se ..es *Shogun*.

You will need a full afternoon to see Himeji-jō properly. It is open daily 9:00 A.M.–5:00 P.M. (Until 4:00 P.M. during winter.) Admission is ¥500.

Where to Stay

In addition to the listings here, the TIC office in front of Himeji-eki can arrange inexpensive accommodations and provide maps on how to get there.

There is no longer a hostel in Himeji, but a five-minute walk from the station, along the walking mall, takes you to **Capsule Hawaii** (Tel. 0792-23-8800). It is near the Ginbiro Store, not far from the Sanyo department store. It costs ¥3,300.

The **Business Hotel Kisshin** (Tel.0792-22-4655) is a five-minute walk from Himeji-eki, with singles that start at ¥5,100.

Escaping

A bus runs from in front of Himeji-eki to Himeji-kō ferry port. Take Bus 37 from Gate 37—ask for "Himeji-kō no basu." It is a 25-minute, ¥240 bus ride to the port.

SHŌDO-SHIMA

With roughly the same proportion of mountains, plains, agriculture, city, and coastline as the Japanese nation, Shōdo-shima is a miniature Japan. As the second largest island in the Inland Sea, it offers high mountain views, wild monkeys, a rugged coast, a canyon ropeway, a giant Goddess of Mercy, and a unique syncretic Greek temple/Shinto shrine. Why Greek? Because Shōdo-shima is Japan's only major olive-producing center.

Getting There

The ferry from Himeji to Shōdo-shima runs eight times a day (11 times during peak seasons). The one-hour 40-minute ride costs ¥1,300 and takes you to Fukuda-kō (port) on the northeast side of the island.

Note: The quarry town of Fukuda is not shown in the atlas. In the atlas, the town and the port are located where the Kansai-kyūkō ferry line from Himeji arrives.

Hitchhike south along coastal Highway 436 all the way down and around to Uchinomi-wan (bay). On the way you will pass the *zannen ishi* (that's-too-bad stones), boulders originally cut for Osaka Castle in the 1600s, but rejected for imperfections. These rough-cut boulders are beside the road, in among the forest, and a few still bear faded Chinese characters cut by the original stonecutters. Beneath one such boulder lie the ghosts of several workers who were crushed when the huge stone slipped and rolled over them.

What to See and Do

To reach **Hoshigajo-yama** (816 meters), hitchhike inland from Uchinomi. Set off early in the day and aim for the ropeway. The ropeway costs ¥1,150 round trip, and takes you up past the craggy valley of **Kankakei**. Buy a one-way (*kata-michi*) ticket instead and you can then hitchhike down from the other side of the peak. The ropeway doesn't take you to the summit; to hitchhike down, you will have to hike up and over the summit to the highway, a pleasant and easy hike. From the end of the ropeway, a path leads to the summit. Follow the footpath down the other side to reach the Shōdo-shima Skyline, officially labeled Prefectural Highway 27. The highway is hard to miss; it's the only road up there.

If you hitchhike west, toward Tonoshō, you will pass through the **wild-monkey zone**. If you hitchhike east—to your right—you will come back down the mountain and pass the Greek/Shinto shrine on the way. The traffic is sparse along the skyline until you get to the shrine, so start walking. If it is a weekday, you may end up walking most of the way to the Greek shrine. Fortunately, this stretch of skyline is so remote that the first car by will probably stop for you.

Many guides mock the the **Greek/Shinto shrine** as kitsch; nonetheless, it is an actual Shinto shrine, and although small, its unique blend of Greek architecture and Shinto is striking.

After the shrine, traffic picks up considerably since most sightseers drive up the mountain only as far as the shrine and then turn around and come back.

Shōdo-shima's newly built **Dai-Kannon,** the Goddess of Mercy, towers 70 meters high and is said to be the largest in Japan, though the height and the claim have been disputed. For an admission fee of ¥300, you can enter and take the elevator or stairs up and look out from Dai-Kannon's eyes and see the world through the eyes of enlightenment.

The Dai-Kannon is north of Tonoshō town in Koumagoe pass. It was built by the head priest of Bushi-ji temple, and not without raising some controversy about whether such an attraction was appropriate for an island as holy as Shōdo-shima.

It is often compared (in fits of bravado) to the Statue of Liberty, so you may want to know the Japanese term for New York's Big Lady. In Japan they call her Jiyū no Megami, the Goddess of Liberty.

En Route

As you hitchhike around Shōdo-shima you will pass many of the pilgrim spots. Some are simple roadside altars, others are 600-year-old family temples. Like mainland Shikoku, Shōdo-shima attracts many white-vested pilgrims in air-conditioned pilgrim buses. You could easily spend a week or more on Shōdo-shima if you wanted to explore its more remote temples and altars.

Where to Stay

Shōdo-shima Olive Youth Hostel (Tel. 0879-82-6161) is in Uchinomi town, beside beautiful Uchinomi-wan (bay) on the island's south shore. ¥3,100 per night. Closed January 26–30, and June 5–9. This well-kept, comfortable hostel is strategically located for hitchhiking along the island's coast or into the interior. Highway 436 runs along the coast, right in front of the hostel. The road that leads into the Kankakei canyon begins at the port east of the hostel.

The hostel has bicycles for rent: ¥500 for four hours and ¥1,000 for a day. Mountain bikes are more expensive: ¥1,200 for four hours, and ¥1,500 for a day. Don't let Shōdo-shima's size fool you. It is too large and too steep to bike all the way around. To get to the top of the mountain you will have to hitch. If you are lucky I suppose you might get a ride with someone in a truck who will take you and your bicycle. Scooter rentals from the hostel are ¥2,000 for four hours and ¥2,900 for a day. There are some restrictions on which roads you can ride; check with the hostel before heading out.

South of Highway 436 and Ikeda town is the **Furusato Mura Auto Camping Village** (Tel. 0879-75-2266), which is open all year and requires a reservation. It costs ¥2,000 for a space and ¥250 per person.

On the less-visited northern shore, near Obe-kō, is the **Taihama Camp-jō** (Tel. 0879-67-2174), which is open all year and costs ¥1,000 per person. This campsite is roughly in the Dai-Kannon area.

Note: Obe-ko port is not shown in the atlas. It is the end point of the Olive Line ferry from Hinase.

Escaping

You will be using Shōdo-shima as a stepping stone across the Inland Sea. Getting from Shōdo-shima to mainland Shikoku is easy; many ferries go directly to Takamatsu from Uchinomi,

Ikeda, and Tonoshō. The Shōdo-shima Hostel will have complete schedules and prices, as will most coffee shops and public offices.

TAKAMATSU

Takamatsu (population 350,000) is best known for its wide **Ritsurin Kōen,** 2 km south of the ferry port and station area. The park is open daily till dusk. Admission is ¥310.

Where to Obtain Information

The **Tourist Information Center** (Tel. 0878-51-2009) is in front of JR Takamatsu-eki, and is open 9:00 A.M.–5:00 P.M. daily. They usually try to have an English speaker on staff and were very helpful when I went through.

For English books, the **Miyawaki Shoten** bookstore (Tel. 0878-51-3733) is located near the Takamatsu Bijitsu Museum Gallery. The English books are on the third floor. They didn't have the atlas in stock when I went. You can call and check to see if they have it—and reserve a copy for your arrival. But try to get the atlas *before* you arrive in Shikoku.

What to See and Do

If you are planning to visit the garden, rent a bicycle rather than making the hike. Bicycles can be rented in front of JR Takamatsu-eki at ¥400 for three hours. Or you can take the private Kotoden Rail Line to the Kotoden Ritsurin Kōen-eki and walk west. Alternatively, you can take a bus from Platform Number 2 in front of the Grand Hotel, across from the JR Takamatsu-eki. The 20-minute bus ride costs ¥210.

Ritsurin Kōen appeals to the Japanese largely because of its size, which is a luxury in Japan. But the park doesn't seem to stir the blood of many Western travelers. Unless you have a refined taste in gardens, you may want to give it a miss.

The Takamatsu-kō ferry port is right in front of the ruins of **Tamamo-jō,** which makes a nice stroll if you have time to spare while waiting for a train or ferry. The original castle was built in 1588, but today only the walls, some of the moat, and a couple of turrets remain.

As noted, the ferry port is beside the JR Takamatsu-eki, which makes escaping the city very easy. If you arrive during the day, you can jump off the ferry and onto the next train out of town.

The Takamatsu specialty is *udon* (noodles), an inexpensive and filling food. At the **Udon Ichiba restaurant,** you get a basic bowl of noodles for ¥130, to which you add your chosen toppings. Pick from 20—at ¥80 per topping, it's a bargain. The restaurant is closed Sundays and holidays and is straight down the main street (Highway 30) about 600 meters from the station. It will be on your left. If you pass the Tokyu Inn, you've gone too far. There are many other such *udon* shops in Takamatsu as well, including several around the station.

Where to Stay

Unless you are planning a side trip to Yashima (see below), the Yashima Youth Hostel is not a convenient place to stay. A variety of inexpensive accommodations near JR Takamatsu-eki will cost at least double what the hostel would, but this keeps you near the station—and without hostel rules and early curfews.

The **Pearl Hotel** (Tel. 0878-22-3382) across from JR Takamatsu-eki has rooms for ¥5,350 for a single and ¥10,000 for a double.

Beside the Pearl is the **Urban Hotel** (Tel. 0878-23-3001), which has rooms that start at ¥6,000 for a single and ¥11,000 for a twin.

If you want to stay in a capsule, try the **Sauna Goldon Time,** a 20-minute walk south of the station, toward Ritsurin Koen. It costs ¥3,500 a night.

Another capsule, the **First Inn Takamatsu** (Tel. 0878-22-1919), is a 20-minute walk east of the station, about 15 minutes past the Mitsukoshi department store. When asking directions, make sure you pronounce it "fasto inn capseru." Prices begin at ¥3,500 and range to a deluxe ¥5,300, though "deluxe capsule" seems an oxymoron.

YASHIMA

Before entering the heart of your hitchhiking journey, consider a side trip to the Yashima Plateau, west of Takamatsu. The epic clash between the Minamoto and Taira clans, a Japanese version of the War of the Roses, took place on this site in the twelfth century. The white flag of the Minamoto eventually triumphed, and the red-bannered Taira were scattered to the four winds.

Getting There

There are two Yashima stations: JR Yashima-eki and the private Kotoden Yashima-eki. The private trains run more often, and the station is closer to the Yashima cable car. From Kotoden Yashima-eki, it is a ten-minute walk north to the cable car.

From the Takamatsu-kō port area, take a train from Kotoden Chikko-eki. It is a 17-minute, ¥260 ride to Kotoden Yashima-eki. If you are coming from the gardens, first take the Kotoden train one stop north from Ritsurin Kōen-eki to Kawaramachi-eki, where you will have to change for a train heading east.

Note: Kotoden Yashima-eki is shown but not labeled in the atlas; it is north of JR Yashima-eki.

What to See and Do

Yashima-san offers an expansive view of the Inland Sea and can be reached by hitching up the Yashima Driveway, a skyline road that starts east of Kotoden Yashima-eki. Although the area is initially quite cluttered, it is still an acceptable hitchhiking route. A cable car also goes up Yashima-san as well; it operates daily until 7:00 P.M.; a round-trip ticket costs ¥1,200.

The Yashima Plateau is wide enough that you may want to rent a bicycle. Bicycles are available at the upper cable-car station for ¥300, plus a deposit.

On your way to the cable car, you will pass near the Shikoku Mura (village) to your right a bit. You can visit this **open-air museum** daily until 5:00 P.M. (4:30 during winter) for ¥500. The museum grounds house a collection of traditional farmhouses, shops, and inns that have been gathered from around Shikoku and the islands of the Inland Sea. This fascinating folk village is worth the short detour on your way to the cable car.

Where to Stay

The **Yashima-Sansō Hostel** (Tel. 0878-41-2318, 6010) is a five-minute walk northeast of Kotoden Yashima-eki and costs ¥2,600 a night. The owner is a table-tennis fanatic, and if you can beat him (doubtful) he will give you a prize.

MARUGAME CASTLE

If you want to see all four of Shikoku's extant castles, you can take a train out from Takamatsu or Yashima to Marugame. The castle dates back to 1660, the walls to 1597. The castle is about a kilometer south of Marugame-eki. If you do decide to go to Marugame, you don't need to backtrack to Takamatsu. Just continue south by train to Kotohira and then start hitching from there.

Escaping

If you want to skip Marugame, take a train directly from Takamatsu to Kotohira on the private Takamatsu Kotohira Line, also called the Kotohira Dentetsu. Like Yashima, Kotohira has two stations downtown: JR Kotohira-eki, and the private Kotoden Kotohira-eki. The trip from Takamatsu to Kotoden Kotohira-eki takes one hour and costs ¥560.

You can hitchhike to Kotohira as well, but this takes you through a fairly populated area. If you are new to hitchhiking, you might want to wait until you get into the open country south of Kotohira before you stick out a thumb. If you do hitch in, it can be helpful because you can ask to be dropped off right at the grand shrine of Kotohira-gu or at the youth hostel. To hitchhike into Kotohira take the train to Hayuka-eki. Highway 37 runs beside it, to the west. Hitchhike on 37 and you will catch a ride right into Kotohira.

Note: Hayuka-eki is not shown on the atlas. It is just before the intersection of Highways 32 and 377, west of Ryōnan.

KOTOHIRA

This town is the site of the **Kotohira-gū,** one of the most famous shrines in Shikoku. Kotohira-gū was once a Buddhist temple, but the Meiji Restoration of 1868 established Shinto as the state religion. "Imported" Buddhism came under attack and the temple was converted into an imperial grand shrine (*jingū*).

What to See and Do

It is a steep, 500-meter climb up Zozu-san to reach Kotohira-gū, also known as **Kompira-san.** There are 785 steps to the main shrine, which is dedicated to the God of the Sea and Protector of Seafarers, making it particularly popular with the people of the Inland Sea. If you are feeling decadent and don't want to make the long walk up, men will carry you in a palanquin for the outrageous price of ¥6,500.

The main shrine area is usually crowded, but if you continue 583 steps higher you will be rewarded with the quieter, natural surroundings of the Okusha inner shrine.

Kotohira also has a venerable Kabuki theater, the **Kana-maruza**. Built in 1835, it is the oldest Kabuki theater standing in Japan, and still houses performances every April. The theater is open to the public 9:00 A.M.–4:00 P.M. daily, except Tuesdays. Admission is ¥500.

If you are from New Zealand and are feeling homesick for the sight of sheep, you can visit the **New Zealand Village** (New Zealand Mura) located near Kotohira. For ¥500, you can see such traditional New Zealand pastimes as miniature golf, the Super Slider amusement ride, and the battery car. They also have sheep dogs, horse rides, a restaurant called **Auckland,** and lots of sheep.

Where to Stay

The **Seinen-no-le Hostel** (Tel.0877-73-3836) is near the entrance to the Kotohira-gū grand shrine, about 200 meters from Kanamaruza. At ¥2,200 per night, it is the only real budget accommodation available in the area. If you are hitching into Kotohira, ask to be dropped off at the Kabuki theater, which is better known than the hostel.

If you were planning to spend one night in an expensive, traditional Japanese inn you could do worse than the **Shikishima-kan** (Tel.0877-75-5111), a ryokan that dates to the Edo period (1600–1868). Only the entrance and main hall are old. You will probably end up staying in the newer annex. Prices start at ¥15,000 per person with two meals.

Escaping

To escape Kotohira, you can hitchhike from inside the town. Highway 32 runs through Kotohira east of the JR Kotohira-eki. Or take a train south to Kurokawa-eki and walk east to Highway 32. Highway 32, also known as the Awabetsu-kaidō (road), runs south from Kotohira and takes you deep into the Shikoku interior. South of Miyoshi town, the highway follows the Yoshino-gawa (river) as it cuts through the rugged Ōboke Gorge.

En Route

Just east of Miyoshi is the **Mino Tanofuchi Camp-jō,** a free site which is open all year. No tent rentals available. Call the Miyoshi town office (Tel. 0883-79-3111) for more information. This campsite is on the north side of the Yoshino-gawa, a few kilometers east of Miyoshi along Prefectural Highway 12.

Note: Prefectural Highway 12 runs along the north side of the river, parallel to Highway 192 along the south side. Prefectural Highway 12 is not numbered, but it is shown in green and is labeled "Muya kaido" in the atlas. You may want to spend the night at this campsite so that you can make an early start toward Koboke Gorge.

ŌBOKE-KOBOKE GORGE

Highway 32 runs south, beside the Yoshino-gawa and through a canyon-like gorge named for two narrows at either end: Koboke in the north and Ōboke in the south. These two names translate, respectively, as "with small steps, it is dangerous" and "with big steps, it is also dangerous." The dark humor of these names reflects the very real danger that this canyon posed to travelers in the pre-highway days.

Getting There

From the campsite, cross the bridge to Highway 192, and then hitch along the south shore of the Yoshino River to where Highway 192 meets Highway 32. On Highway 32, turn south. This will save you having to backtrack through Miyoshi town.

What to See and Do

You will be hitchhiking south along the gorge, but the river flows northward. At the **Manaka restaurant** near Ōboke-eki you can arrange a 30-minute boat ride for ¥1,000 (Tel. 0883-84-1211) down the mildly exciting "rapids," to **Senjōjiki**. The boat then takes you back upstream to the Manaka restaurant, so you don't have to re-hitch the same stretch of road. Tame, but fun. Whitewater rafting is also available from just above Kōmori Iwa, the Bat Rock.

KAZURA-BASHI

From Ōboke, turn east on the Iyakei Dōro toll road, a route that will take you across to the Iyadani-kei gorge. Go south on Prefectural Highway 32 (shown in green but not numbered in the atlas) and you will come to the 45-meter-long, swaying **Kazura-bashi** (vine bridge) which spans the rocks and river below. It is—and I quote—one of the "Three Most Unusual Bridges in Japan." It's quite safe since the bridge is rebuilt every three years. The toll for crossing it is ¥410, which helps to cover the cost of rebuilding it so often.

By now you will be hungry. If you want to try a local specialty go to the **Takini Shokudō** restaurant near the vine bridge, where they serve fish and potatoes and miso-tofu skewered on sticks and cooked in traditional ash firepits. At ¥300 per stick, it isn't filling, but you can pick and choose.

OKUIYA KAZURA-BASHI

There were once 13 vine bridges crisscrossing the vertigo heights of central Shikoku, but today only two remain—the Kazura-bashi you have just visited and another, lesser-known and rarely visited bridge farther east on Highway 439. These two remaining bridges are known as the Husband-and-Wife Bridges, because they both span the Iya-gawa (river), 30 km apart.

Highway 439 along the Iya-gawa runs through the very heart of mountainous Shikoku. This remote stretch of road is one of the few mountain passes in the area; there should be enough traffic going between the two bridges for hitchhiking, but don't head out late in the day, and brace yourself for a long wait.

After the second vine bridge, hitchhike back along Highway 439 until it rejoins Highway 32 south of the Ōboke Gorge, a route that will take you through the hairpin turns of the Kyōbashira Pass. Tell people that you are headed for Jōfuku-ji temple, which has a youth hostel in it. If you are apprehensive about hitchhiking through such a remote area, stay on the tourist route instead; hitch in to the Kazura-bashi and then out again. The traffic flow is steady back and forth between the Ōboke Gorge and the first vine bridge, so catching rides either way with Japanese sightseers is not a problem.

Where to Stay

About 10 km east of Higashi-Iyayama-son (village), on the south side of Highway 439, is the **Seishōnen Ryokō Mura camp-site** (Tel. 0883-88-2975, 2211) in the vicinity of the second vine bridge. It's open April1–November 30 and costs ¥400 for a tent space, regardless of the number of people in it. The campsite rents blankets and tents, and has all the amenities: public kitchens, toilets, telephones, a small shop, and even a restaurant. Five-man bungalows are ¥3,500. Tent rentals are ¥500. If the rides are slow, you may have to spend a night here, either before or after visiting the second vine bridge.

Near the intersection of Highway 439 and Highway 32 is Jofuku-ji temple, part of 88 Temple Circuit. The main hall dates to 1151. **Jōfuku-ji** (temple) is marked in the atlas and has a **youth hostel** (Tel. 0887-74-0301) located in the temple grounds. The hostel manager speaks English. Bicycle rentals are available. The hostel is closed from Monday to Wednesday during January, February, May, June, October, November, and December, and

November 8–18 as well. At ¥3,100 per night, this hostel is well worth the price if you're there on the right day.

Timing: If you leave Kotohira early in the morning, you should be able to visit the gorge, take a boat ride, scramble across the first vine bridge, and still make it to the Jōfuku-ji hostel in time for supper. Even better: Leave Kotohira after lunch and camp at Miyoshi's free campsite and then take your time going through the gorge and on to the Jōfuku-ji temple hostel. If you want to see the second vine bridge as well, add a night at the Seishōnnen Ryokō Mura campsite to be safe.

Escaping

From Jōfuku-ji hostel, it's a short trip to Japan's largest *sugi* (cedar) tree at Yasaka Jinja (shrine). This 3,000-year-old tree is divided in two, towering more than 60 meters in height. A *shimenawa* (rope) marks it as being a *kami* (divine). A stop at the shrine is on your way out as you hitch west from Jōfuku-ji Youth Hostel along Highway 32. Tell your driver that you are going to Yasaka Jinja, and if they don't know where that is, say "Ōsugi-eki." After Yasaka Jinja, return to Highway 32 and hitchhike south. The tree is near the Ōtoyo IC, just a 15-minute walk from Ōsugi-eki.

RYŪGADO

East of Nankoku are Shikoku's most famous caves, the 4-km-long **Ryūgadō Stalactite Caves**. It takes about an hour to walk through the narrow, dank section open to the public. It's a bit expensive at ¥850, but well worth the side trip.

If you have an archaeological bent you will be interested in the stone rings of houses dating to the Yayoi period (ca. 300 B.C. to A.D. 300), evidence that a community of ancient Japanese dwelled within these caves.

Getting There

You will be coming south on Highway 32. You need to get over to Highway 195 above Nankoku. From there, hitchhike north on Highway 195 until you come to Prefectural Highway 22. Hitchhike east on Prefectural Highway 22 and you will come to the start of the Ryūgadō Skyline, which will take you to the caves.

This sounds complicated but it isn't. Prefectural Highway 22 isn't numbered in the atlas, but it is easy to find. In maps, it is marked in green and runs from the Yumeno Onsen area on Highway 195 to the Ryūgadō Skyline. The only tricky part is the first step: getting from Highway 32 over to Highway 195. As you hitch south toward Nankoku city on Highway 32, tell your driver that you are going toward Ryūgadō and that anywhere along Highway 195 is fine. Or, you can simply say "Please take me in the direction of Ryūgadō cave." (*Ryūgadō no hō.*) The problem with this is that drivers may feel awkward because they won't be going to the caves, or—even worse—if they know you are going to the caves they may simply drive you into downtown Kōchi and show you where to catch the bus. On the other hand, if it is a Sunday afternoon, they may decide to take you all the way to Ryūgadō and save you the trouble.

Escaping

After the caves, hitchhike south on the Ryūgadō Skyline. You will probably be traveling with other sightseers, so you won't be expected to pay the ¥600 toll.

The Ryūgadō Skyline meets Highway 55 at Noichi town. Hitchhike west on Highway 55 and it will take you into Kōchi. The traffic along 55 is steady and the rides are good. By visiting the caves *first*, on your way in, you have avoided having to backtrack. Congratulations! If you can thread your way across from Highway 32 to the caves and then into Kōchi, you are now a seasoned hitchhiker.

NANKOKU

If you decide *not* to visit the caves on your way in, Highway 32 will take you past Nankoku (population 48,000), which is more or less a suburb of Kōchi.

What to See and Do

There is no pressing reason to go into Nankoku, unless you want a glimpse of the bizarre, long-tailed *onaga-dori*. Although ostensibly fighting birds, these coddled roosters have been carefully bred over the years to produce limp, languid tail feathers that are regularly five meters in length, and sometimes even longer. If you have some extra time, a visit here is worth it. In that case, ask to be taken to the Chōbikei Center (near the Holiday Inn), also known as the **Nankoku Onaga-dori Center.** It costs ¥500 to enter. Open until 5:00 P.M. daily except Thursdays. To get to the center, take a Ryūgadō bus (the same bus you would take to get to the caves) from the Seibu department store at Harimaya-bashi downtown. The Onaga-dori Center is about halfway to the caves, or roughly a ¥500, 25–30-minute ride.

For hungry horticulturists, near the Chobikei Onaga-dori Long-Tailed Bird Center, is the **Nishijima Engei Danchi Tourist Gardens** with more than 300 kinds of flowers and tropical plants. It is open all year and costs ¥720. The admission includes a small fruit snack.

KŌCHI

Kōchi (population 315,000) is on the warm Pacific side of Shikoku. As you cross the mountains of the interior and come down into Kōchi, the temperature and humidity quickly reach balmy subtropical levels.

Where to Obtain Information

Kōchi-eki is fairly inconvenient since it's north of downtown and across the river. When you hitchhike in, ask to be taken to the Washington Hotel, which puts you on Phoenix Boulevard, down from the castle, and just one block up from the shopping arcades and nightlife district.

If, however, you need English maps and information on Kōchi, ask to be dropped off at Kōchi-eki instead, where the **Tourist Information Center** (Tel. 0888-82-7777) is located. The Kōchi TIC keeps odd office hours, 9:00 A.M.–9:40 P.M., though it's best to visit when an English speaker is on staff usually during the day.

There is a selection of English books and magazines at the **Kinkodō Honten** bookstore (Tel. 0888-82-0161). Walk five minutes south of the Washington Hotel; the bookstore is near Daiei department store south of the walking arcade.

What to See and Do

Kōchi is the site of Kōchi-jō, the second major extant castle on your Shikoku–Inland Sea tour. Although originally built during the civil wars of the Sengoku period, the castle was rebuilt in 1753 during the relatively stable government of the Tokugawa shoguns. As a result, the castle was converted into a manor residence rather than a fortress. **Kōchi-jō** is open 9:00 A.M.–4:30 P.M. daily. Closed December 31–January 1. Admission is ¥350.

Bicycle rentals can be arranged at **Kagiyama Cycle,** near the station, at ¥600 for two hours. The owner speaks some English and asks that you show either a passport or ID Card when you rent—to prevent the lucrative black-market trade in rental bicycles, I suppose.

Kōchi comes alive every Sunday with its **street-stall markets,** Nichiyō Ichi. The markets have a 300-year history in Kōchi. The stalls are crowded in along Phoenix Boulevard, the wide, palm-tree lined main street of Kōchi that leads to the castle gate.

I would advise going to **Kōchi-jō** (castle) *first* and then visiting the market after; I did it the other way around and ended up lugging bags filled with fruit and food all over the castle grounds.

The Beach: The main day trip from Kōchi is south to **Katsura-hama,** which has beautiful Pacific views and a pebble coast. Undertows make it too dangerous to swim, so you'll have to satisfy yourself with wading along the shore.

Kōchi's romantic hero is Sakamoto Ryōma, a young samurai rebel and reformer who led the alliance of southern lords that eventually toppled the last of the Tokugawa shoguns. He was assassinated at the age of 31 by agents of the shogun. His statue stands at Katsura-hama. Also at the beach is the **Tosa Tōken** (dogfight) center which stages dogfights (*tōken*) when numbers warrant—usually when 30 or more visitors are in attendance. It is open daily until 5:00 P.M. Admission is ¥1,000. These huge mastiff-like dogs are ranked like sumo wrestlers and accompanied by much the same pomp and pageantry. Champions even sport *yokozuna* white ropes.

There is a shell collection, an **aquarium** with a dolphin and seal show, and various other tourist traps at Katsura-hama. The residents of Kōchi consider this view to be the number one spot for moon viewing. It is also spacious enough for unofficial, surreptitious camping.

If you are in the Kōchi-eki area, a bus runs to Katsura-hama every hour. The 40-minute ride costs ¥610. If you are downtown, a bus runs every half-hour from the Minamai Harimaya-bashi bus stop beside Seibu department store. This 35-minute ride costs ¥560.

Godaisan Kōen: A quieter day-trip is to the palm trees of **Godaisan Kōen** (park), atop Godai-san which looks out across the bay to the east of the city center. The park features a **botanical garden,** a **hilltop pagoda,** and **Chikurin-ji** temple. Founded by Kōbō Daishi in 724, this temple is number 31 on the 88 Temple Circuit. The structure, which dates from the thirteenth century, maintains a collection of wooden statues—some over 800 years old—and is a popular stop for latter-day, bus-driven Japanese pilgrims.

To get to Chikurin-ji take a Godaisan bus from in front of the Seibu department store downtown at Harimaya-bashi to the last stop. The 20-minute ride costs ¥320. Buses run every one or two hours, 8:40 A.M.–4:30 P.M. If you want to have at least an hour to visit the temple grounds and still be able to catch the bus back into downtown, you have to leave downtown on the 1:30 P.M. bus at the latest.

Ryūgadō Cave

If you missed the caves on the way in, take a **Ryūgadō bus** from in front of the Seibu department store at Harimaya-bashi downtown. The bus to Ryūgadō costs ¥1,010 and the ride takes about one hour. Buses run every one or two hours from 8:50 A.M. (from 9:00 A.M. on Sundays). The last bus back leaves Ryūgadō at 5:10 P.M., so if you want to take a bus back as well, make sure you leave downtown Kōchi on the 2:40 P.M. bus at the latest. This will give you about an hour and a half at the caves. There is no reason to take a bus back. The traffic from the caves will largely be other sightseers returning to Kōchi, so hitching a ride back won't be hard at all.

Where to Stay

The **Kōchi Eki-Mae Hostel** (Tel. 0888-83-5086) is a ten-minute walk east of Kōchi-eki; walk left when you exit. It costs ¥2,800 a night. The owner speaks some English, which can be helpful in finding your way around or recommending cheap restaurants. No alcohol allowed.

Two blocks south and three blocks east of the central Harimaya-bashi tram stop is the **Kōchi Business Hotel Honkan** (Tel. 0888-83-0221) which has simple lodgings for ¥3,800–¥4,000, and doubles for ¥7,400. The **Tosa Business Hotel** (Tel. 0888-25-3332) downtown has singles from ¥4,500–¥5,000 per night. It is a five-minute walk south of the Horizume tram stop. Walk three blocks down and the hotel will be just off the road to your right.

Capsule Hotel Kōchi (Tel. 0888-24-7117) is a 15-minute walk from Kōchi-eki and costs ¥3,090.

Escaping

There are two ways to leave Kōchi: Taking the train out to Ino is probably the simplest. From Ino, hitchhike west on Highway 33 to Sakawa and then south on Highway 494 to Susaki. If you don't plan on visiting the paper center listed below, stay on the train until you clear Ino and then get off at a more rural station, such as Okabana-eki, farther west.

West of Kōchi, in the quiet town of Ino, is a traditional paper-making craft center, the **Ino Machi Kami no Hakubutsukan** (Tel. 0888-923-0886). Admission is ¥300 and another ¥300 if you want to try making your own. It is closed Mondays. If Monday is a holiday, it closes on Tuesday instead. If you are planning to leave Kōchi via Ino, don't bother hitching out of the city. Take a train—it's only four stops. The paper-making center is a ten-minute walk from Ino-eki.

En Route

Northwest of Ino, along Highway 194 and on the bank of the Niyodo-gawa (river), is the **Kada Camp-jō,** which is open May 1–November 30. There's no phone number, but it is easy to find; just keep your eyes toward the river as you travel west along Highway 194 and you will see the campsite. Once you spot the campsite, the entrance is a few kilometers farther along. It costs ¥100 per person.

URANOUCHI-WAN

You can also escape Kōchi along the coast from Katsura-hama, a more scenic route. Hitchhike west across the Urado-ōhashi toll bridge (¥260) and then along the pine-tree coast. This will take you to another toll bridge, the Niyodogawa-kakō-ōhashi (¥510), which crosses the mouth of the Niyodo-gawa.

If you follow the southern shore of Shikoku, you will pass through the inland fjord of Uranouchi-wan (bay), six kilometers after you cross Niyodogawa-kakō-ōhashi. Few Westerners visit this secluded, hidden corner where the water is so calm the bay has earned the nickname *yokonami* ("where the waves are flat"). Several ancient temples and shrines—**Kiyotaki-ji**, **Seiryū-ji**, **Otanashi Jinja**—are tucked up in the wooded hills along the bay, making it a historical as well as scenic route.

You can hitch along Uranouchi-wan on two roads, either north on Prefectural Highway 23 or south along the coast on Prefectural Road 47. Both roads are shown in green but not numbered in the atlas. The southern route, along Prefectural Highway 47, is slightly more scenic. You'll have to cross yet another toll bridge, the Usa-ōhashi (¥260). From the bridge, the highway follows the rugged coast of the Yokonami Kuroshio line, a beautiful, unspoiled, 19-km stretch of highway. I hitched this on the weekend and the rides were excellent, but weekdays may not be as reliable. There are fog warnings along this road in spring, and in the late summer–early autumn typhoons from Okinawa sometimes reach this far north.

SUSAKI

At the end of Uranouchi-wan you will come into Susaki (population 30,000), a pleasant place to stop for lunch and a stroll. Between Highway 56 and the city center is a wide, newly land-scaped main street with roadside canals and an "eyeglass bridge" which, when the reflection is right, mirrors its double arches like a pair of spectacles. It is modeled on a similar bridge in Nagasaki. On this street every Thursday is a fresh-food morning market from 6:00 A.M. to noon; at night the street is invitingly illuminated.

Where to Stay

Located 35 km south of Susaki on Highway 56 in Kubokawa, is the **Iwamoto-ji Hostel** (Tel. 08802-2-0376) in the grounds of Iwamoto-ji (temple), which is marked in the atlas. Look for the famous ceiling painting in the temple hall. The temple is not far from Kubokawa-eki; ask your driver to take you to Iwamoto-ji and you will be dropped off right at the door. The hostel costs ¥2,800 per night.

NAKAMURA

From Kubokawa town, hitch south on Highway 56, a splendid drive that skirts a cape and passes near several beaches before curving in toward the riverside city of Nakamura (population 36,000).

The **Shimanto-gawa** flowing through Nakamura is said to have the cleanest water in Japan, an impressive claim in a land of hot springs and natural mineral water. A bicycle path runs along its shore, past wooden waterwheels and old canals.

Boatmen offer rides to visitors as well. North of the city is **Tombo Ōkoku**, a dragonfly park where over 70 species live.

Where to Obtain Information

The **Nakamura Tourist Office** (Tel. 0880-34-111) has maps of the trails, but because almost no Western visitors ever make it to this small city, there are no English materials available. **Bicycle rentals** are available in front of the station, but call for information first (Tel. 0880-35-4171). Bicycles cost ¥500 for four hours and ¥100 for each additional hour. You really need a bike to explore Nakamura's canal-side paths.

Where to Stay

South from Nakamura, and just north of Tosa-Shimizu, is a campsite located on the Ōki Kaigan (shore). If it is late in the day, you may want to stay here and then push on to the Ashizuri peninsula the following morning.

If you are running out of time and want to skip the Ashizuri-hantō, ask your driver to drop you off to the west of Nakamura on Highway 56. The traffic between Nakamura and Sukumo is steady, and hitching is steady. Note that if you take this short-cut, you will miss out on some of Shikoku's grandest, most rugged scenery.

ASHIZURI-MISAKI

This entire cape is magnificent. Sheer dropping cliffs, ocean views, wildflowers, and a lonely lighthouse: Shikoku at its best. From the cape lighthouse a long set of stairs leads down to Hakuzandō-mon, a dramatic, naturally formed stone gate that looks out onto the Pacific. It is also a favorite spot for love suicides, so if you are hitchhiking as a couple and you are in the middle of an upheaval, you may want to skip this area.

Getting There

There are two ways to hitchhike to the cape. Prefectural Highway 27 (shown in green but not numbered in the atlas) loops down the east side of the peninsula and then back up the west. Otherwise, the Ashizuri Skyline (¥510) runs down the middle through the center of Tosa-Shimizu (population 25,000), whose main claim to fame is as the birthplace of Nakahama "John" Manjirō.

In 1841, young Manjirō was shipwrecked off the coast of

Shikoku and was rescued by American whalers, who took him to the United States—the first Japanese person ever to visit America. This was during Japan's harsh Era of Seclusion (*sakoku*) under the oppressive Tokugawa shoguns. Manjirō returned ten years later on money he made during the California gold rush. A few years later, Commodore Perry sailed his black ships into Tokyo Bay and demanded that Japan open its ports to international trade. The startled shogunate called on Manjirō to interpret.

Manjirō's English ability and international *savoir faire* made him a much-needed but highly resented figure—a fate that still awaits Japanese nationals who live abroad too long and are deemed to have "gone native." Manjirō later became a university professor and was a leading voice in the call for reform.

Where to Stay

Ashizuri-misaki's unique hostels offer lodging in both a Buddhist temple and a Shinto shrine. Neither is a particularly grand structure, but they are a nice change of pace.

Kongōfukuji Hostel (Tel. 08808-8-0038) is in a Shingon temple—number 38 on the Temple Circuit—at the tip of the cape and costs ¥2,600 per night. No alcohol allowed. This temple appears on most road maps, including the atlas. The hostel is closed January 1–4.

If you want to try a Shinto shrine instead of a Buddhist temple, the smaller **Ashizuri Hostel** (Tel. 08808-8-0324) is just 300 meters west of Kongōfuku-ji and costs ¥2,600 per night as well. Check out both before deciding.

TATSUKUSHI KAIGAN

The coast between Ashizuri-misaki and Sukumo, a favorite for swimmers and scuba divers, has been declared a national park. This rocky coral coast also offers a chance to take a glass-bottom boat. Near the Tatsukushi *teiryūjo* is the **Kankō Kisen Garasu Bōto** (Glass Boat) departure point. Boats leave every 15 or 20 minutes, and for ¥700 they take you to the unspoiled Minokoshi-hama with its unusually striated coast. The boat bobs around for half an hour looking at tropical fish before dropping you off on the beach. Try to go when the morning sun is shining—the water depths seem clearer.

Where to Stay

In Tatsukushi near the beach is the **Fujii-dera Hostel** (Tel. 08808-5-0120), a *very* basic hostel associated with a temple. It costs ¥2,400 per night. No smoking.

ODO KAIGAN

From Tatsukushi, Highway 321 narrows and twists through several tunnels on a hell-raising stretch of road called the Ashizuri Sunny Road. If you want to go more off the beaten track, ask your driver to let you off at the road that runs southwest from Highway 321, down the Odo Kaigan (coast). This road, marked in green in the atlas, winds its way 16 km to the sea.

Just south of the **Odo tenbōdai** (lookout) is the Nozaru Kōen monkey preserve, where wild monkeys congregate looking for handouts. Beware—sometimes they can be found in the parking lot and along the highway.

Have someone point you in the right direction to follow the walking path out to a view of a standing rock pillar called **Kannon Iwa,** after its resemblance to Kannon, the Goddess of Mercy. The walk takes about an hour; there is an occasional bus, but your feet are more reliable.

SUKUMO

Sukumo (population 26,000) is a port city built inside a deep natural harbor. From Sukumo port, ferries run four or five times per day to Saiki on Kyushu. The two-and-a-half-hour ferry costs ¥1,640. Near the port are a couple of low-priced *minshuku*.

What to See and Do

Ferries from Sukumo go to distant Oki-no-shima (island). The village walls that protect Oki-no-shima from bad spirits and typhoons suggest Okinawan influences. The island's history is murky and lost in myth and legend. Some suggest it was settled by Okinawan slave laborers who escaped the heavy hand of the Kagoshima lords of Kyushu who controlled Okinawa.

If you want to make a day-trip to visit **Oki-no-shima,** the **Sukumo Youth Hostel** can arrange day-trips to the island, but only if you are staying at least two nights at the hostel. The ferry to Oki-no-shima costs ¥2,400 round trip. The ferry goes once a day and gives you seven hours to swim, stroll, and explore before catching the return ferry. Check for departure and return times at the hostel.

Where to Stay

The **Sukumo Youth Hostel** (Tel. 0880-64-0233) is inland, near the bus center and beside the Matsuda-gawa (river), where night swimming is popular. In summer, take part in the firefly hunts. The hostel is closed September 25–October 5, December 31, and May 1–20. It costs ¥2,800 per night with no meal; for ¥1,000 extra, though, enjoy a meal of homemade tofu, homegrown rice, and other delicacies. Up to 30 people can stay in this hostel, but only 20 meals are provided. Call to reserve a spot at the table.

Escaping

For much of the way, the road between Sukumo and Uwajima is beautiful, with villages in small bays and high views of peninsulas and the sea. Hitchhiking from Sukumo to Uwajima will take less than two hours; most of the traffic flows from city to city, so you may want to make a sign reading "Uwajima." However, the highway does not have enough lanes to handle the amount of traffic that flows between Sukumo and Uwajima, so it can get congested. In that case, expect to spend three hours or more getting to Uwajima.

UWAJIMA

Uwajima (population 70,000) is one of my favorite undiscovered cities in Japan. It is said to be a City of Good Fortune, and they may be right. It escaped nuclear destruction by a hair's-breadth; a test run was made over Uwajima in preparation for a second nuclear attack. The target was later changed to Kokura in northern Kyushu, but cloudy weather prevented the pilot from finding his target and he flew instead to the third choice—Nagasaki.

Where to Obtain Information

The **Kankō Jōhō Information Center** (Tel. 0895-22-3934) is across the street from Uwajima-eki, and though their English is limited, the staff is very helpful. They have some English maps and materials available, and they can arrange accommodations. They also rent bicycles at ¥100 per hour. Unfortunately, the office is open only 8:30 A.M.–5:00 P.M. so you have to return the bicycles before closing time. Even with this time limit, bicycles are by far the best way to see Uwajima.

What to See and Do

The main attractions in Uwajima give a nice mix of the somber and the sublime, the primal and the ridiculous.

Bullfights: The key to enjoying Uwajima is to make sure you arrive in time for the bullfights and festivals at **Tōgyū-jō**. Call the Kankō Jōhō Information Center (see above) to double-check before making your travel plans. Bullfights are called *tōgyū* in Japanese, though everyone seemed to understand when I said *ushi no sumō* (bull sumō).

Similar bullfights are held in Okinawa, in Niigata, on Hachijō-jima south of Tokyo, on the Okishotō islands of Shimane, and on Tokuno-shima south of Kagoshima. But with the exception of Okinawa, nowhere else in Japan has taken to the cult of the bull as strongly or as deeply as has Uwajima. The city's main shrine and festival are both dedicated to Oni-ushi, the Demon Bull. The dates for bouts may change from year to year, but generally they are as follows: January 2, the first Sunday of March, April 3, the third Sunday of May, July 24, August 14, and the third Sunday of November.

Tickets are on sale at the Togyū-jō the day of the tournament, and they are expensive: ¥2,500. Go early, and line up. Seat numbers aren't assigned and you don't want to get stuck somewhere in the back. Sit near the edge if possible.

Bullfights have all the pageantry of real sumo, with ranks, banners, and white-roped champions. The bouts begin when two bulls are brought into the ring. As with human sumo, the fights do not involve injury or violence but are tests of strength and willpower. Bulls weighing up to 800 kg or more lock horns, twisting and shoving until one loses his fighting spirit and backs down.

On the day of the tournament, a free bus takes you up the hill from Uwajima-eki to the arena, but you can easily walk it if you have the time. Take the scenic route around the back, past the graveyards and white Kannon Goddess of Mercy statue. The arena is farther up the hill, behind the Kannon.

Demon-Bull Festival: Uwajima's largest festival is the **Oni Ushi Matsuri,** a festival sponsored by the Warei Jinja (shrine), which is dedicated to the spirit of the Demon Bull. Giant bull-shaped floats with heads of demons, bodies of bulls, and tails of swords are paraded throughout the city. They finally meet at the riverside and engage in battle. The festival is held on July 23 and 24.

Fertility Shrine: The Taga Jinja fertility shrine has a giant wooden phallus as an object of veneration, and beside it is a **Sex Museum** stuffed to the rafters with—well—see for yourself. It costs ¥800 to enter the museum. The shrine, with its impressive phallic icon, is free.

Castle: Uwajima-jō sits high above the city on a forested hill. This ţiny castle—more of a samurai cottage—was first built in 1595. Originally this castle guarded the coast, but the shoreline has been pushed back and much of the downtown core of Uwajima now sits on reclaimed land.

Where to Stay

Uwajima Hostel (Tel. 0895-22-7177) is a 30-minute walk southeast from the station, up a hill and near Uwazu Hiko Jinja (shrine). Although they rent bicycles, this is still not a very strategic location. It costs ¥3,100 per night and is closed June 18–24.

The **Business Hotel Shōchiku** (Tel. 0895-22-1166) is near the station and has singles that start at ¥3,700. For almost the same price as the hostel, you can have a private room in a more convenient location.

The **Uwajima Dai-Ichi Hotel** (Tel. 0895-25-0001) is about 500 meters from the station, south along the canal and then toward the castle. Ask for directions as you go—it's easy to miss. Rooms start at ¥4,500 per night.

The **Uwajima Terminal Hotel** (Tel. 0895-22-2280) is near the station and has rooms that begin at ¥5,400. The **Uwajima Grand Hotel** (Tel. 0895-24-3911), also near the station, has rooms that begin at ¥5,500.

Escaping

You can hitchhike north out of Uwajima without taking a local train. Visit Warei Jinja in the morning and then hike north along Highway 56, which runs by the shrine to the east. The road is narrow and busy, but hang in there because most of the traffic is heading all the way to Ōzu and beyond. Just make sure you avoid rush hour. Hitchhike either very early in the morning—before 7:30 A.M.—or after 10:00 A.M. I hitched in front of a gas station and got a ride in about 30 minutes. If you want to clear Uwajima first, simply take a train two stops north to Takamitsu-eki. Highway 56 runs beside it, to the west.

YAWATAHAMA

If you stay on Highway 56 north from Uwajima, it will take you right into Ōzu. Unfortunately, this bypasses the dramatic spear of land called **Sada-misaki,** which juts out to the west. If you want to visit the Spear of Shikoku, don't hitchhike all the way into Ōzu. Instead, turn west when you get to Prefectural Highway 25.

Note: Prefectural Highway 25 is shown in green but not numbered in the atlas; it runs from the Uwajima-Higashi-Tada intersection on Highway 56 to Yawatahama.

You can pass right through Yawatahama (population 39,000), but if you want to make a detour, south of the city is Suwasaki, a small hook of land beside the sea. Its cherry-blossom path in the spring, wildflowers, and clean sea air make it a popular place for Sunday drivers. There is a campsite nearby.

What to See and Do

Ferries run from **Yawatahama to Beppu** in Kyushu five times a day and cost ¥1,740. The ride takes two and a half hours. If you want to cross over to Kyushu, a cheaper, quicker ferry runs to Beppu from Misaki at the end of the spearlike Sada-misaki peninsula.

Where to Stay

Call the city office's **Kankō Kyōkai Department** (Tel. 0894-22-3111) to arrange a stay at the **Suwasaki campsite**. The campsite is open all year. No charge, but you have to mail in a reservation ahead of time. That's the official rule. If you just show up, however, or call that day, you should be able to squeeze in.

SADA-MISAKI

Sada-misaki (also written Sata-misaki) is the Spear of Shikoku. This narrow peninsula stretches for nearly 50 km—the longest and narrowest in Japan. Even if you aren't heading for Kyushu, a trip down Sada-misaki is a terrific hitchhiker's course.

Getting There

Hitchhike north from Yawatahama on Highway 197. When you get to Ikata you have a choice to make: either stick with 197 and follow the sharp knifelike corners along the coast, or a take the Melody Line highway that runs down the center of the peninsula and offers higher panoramic views. Both routes will take you to the town of Misaki. The Melody Line is actually a branch of Highway 197.

Rides are sparse along Sada-misaki, but almost the first car by will give you a ride *because* the place seems so far-flung and remote. I recommend this route strongly. Make sure you have food and water for the trip; you will be far from the crowds. There is a restaurant near the cape, but you should have your own store of supplies as well.

From the town of Misaki, it is a 30-minute ride farther down the peninsula and then a 20-minute walk out to the very tip of the cape. Climb the steps inside the lighthouse, out on the last outcrop of rock, and you will get a near-360-degree view of blue ocean.

What to See and Do

You can use Sada-misaki as a departure point for a trip through Kyushu. Ferries run from **Misaki** to **Beppu** four times a day and cost ¥1,120 one way and take just over two hours. Other ferries run to **Saganoseki,** on the cape east of Beppu, seven times a day. The ride costs ¥600 for the cheapest seats and takes a little over an hour. When you get to the Saganoseki ferry port, you can hitch into Ōita and Beppu on Highway 197 in about 40 minutes.

Where to Stay

At the very tip of the spear, at the end of Sada-misaki, is the **Satamisaki Camp-jō.** Call the town office in Misaki for more information (Tel. 0894-54-1111.) This free campsite is officially open only during July and August. Rent a three-man tent for ¥1,000. Four-man bungalows are available for ¥3,000. If you come here on the off-season the bungalows won't be open, but you will still be able to pitch a tent.

Inland at Ikata town, the gateway to Sada-misaki, is the **Muro-bana Kōen Camp-jō** (Tel. 0894-38-1460), which is open July 1–31 only. It costs ¥200 for a space, with no per-person charge. No tent rentals.

ŌZU

Ōzu (population 40,000) has a wide river, an open park, and many well-preserved old homes. It is called with unabashed overstatement "the Little Kyoto of Ehime Prefecture." It's a pleasant city, easy to hitchhike into, and it makes a nice place to spend the night.

Getting There

Backtrack to Yawatahama, and then hitchhike east to Ōzu on Highway 197. The traffic flow is fairly steady between Yawatahama and Ōzu, and hitching it should only take about half an hour. The road cuts under a mountain range via a surprisingly long tunnel.

What to See and Do

The city of Ōzu lies between the river to the north and the hills to the south. There are a half-dozen temples spaced out among the hills, and they make a popular, all-day ambling hike. Ask at the hostel for directions.

Walk for 1 km along the river bank from the castle grounds and you will come to the thatched-roof house **Garyū-sansō**, with its picturesque landscape and moss garden. To return to the hostel, cut back through the city's old quarter. Across the street from the thatched-roof house is **Ōzu Jinja** (shrine). From here, walk north and then west a block and you will come to **Ohana-han Dōri** (street) with its row of houses from the Meiji era (1868–1912).

Along the river 6:30 P.M.–9:00 P.M. you can see fishermen using cormorant seabirds to catch fish. This form of fishing, famous also in the Gifu region, is called *ukai* and is performed nightly June 1–September 20. Rope or metal rings are tied around the birds' necks to stop them from swallowing the fish. This is a mean trick, but the birds are not very smart and they never seem to catch on. Ōzu is—and I quote—one of the "Three Biggest Cormorant Fishing Areas in Japan."

Near the *kokumin-shukusha* listed below, you can take a short ride in an old-style boat down the river to the gardens beside the thatched-roof house. It is a simple ride, costs just ¥100, and operates every Sunday and national holiday from April to October, 10:00 A.M.–4:00 P.M.

Where to Stay

The **Ōzu Kyōdokan Hostel** (Tel. 0893-24-2258) is across the Hiji-kawa (river) from Iyo-Ōzu-eki and beside the castle ruins.

(Iyo-Ōzu-eki is shown but not labeled in the atlas.) Ask your driver to help you find the hostel rather than asking to be dropped off at the station—it's a long walk. The hostel costs ¥3,000 a night. The manager speaks English and has maps of the city. Bicycle rentals are available.

At the other end of the river walk, past the thatched-roof house and near Suiten-gū shrine is the **Ōzu Kokumin-shukusha Garyū-en** (Tel. 0893-24-3133), which costs ¥6,600 and includes two meals. (In comparison, the youth hostel, with two meals, would cost ¥4,500.)

UCHIKO

Ōzu and Uchiko make a good pair; they are both attractive places easily visited en route to Matsuyama. Uchiko (population 12,000) is 10 km northeast of Ōzu and is the quieter and more attractive of the two.

Uchiko is a wooded town that has a **well-preserved row of old houses**—an entire neighborhood, really—that date back to the late Edo period of the Tokugawa shoguns (1600–1868). Unfortunately, there is no youth hostel in Uchiko and the hotels listed are expensive. Don't arrive on a Monday, because most of the sites will be closed.

Although Ōzu and Uchiko are very close and a train ride will cost only a couple of hundred yen, you may want to hitch it anyway so that you can arrive with an ally to help you get to the old streets and sites of Uchiko. The Uchiko train station is a long walk from the old part of town, so there is really no need to be dropped off there. Highway 56 passes within a block of the Old Town.

Where to Obtain Information

Uchiko has a pamphlet and an *accurate* English map available—after endless cartoon maps, this was greatly appreciated.

The **Uchiko Sightseeing Association** can be reached at 0893-44-2111. Highway 56 takes you into Uchiko and near the Uchiko Yakuba town hall, which holds the office of the Old Town Preservation Society.

What to See and Do

Ask your driver to drop you off at the **Uchiko-za** Kabuki Theater, built in 1916 and recently restored. Its elaborate stage is still used for plays and concerts. When it's not in use, you may visit for ¥200. Closed Mondays. From the Kabuki Theater, it is a short walk to the Old Town area. To ask directions, say *Furui machi-nami*? (Old Town?)

If you are not interested in Kabuki theaters, ask your driver to take you to the **Machiya Shiryōkan Museum** instead, at the start of the old lane. They have English maps of Uchiko. From here the street is lined with museums, shops, teahouses, and old homes. A few places to look for: The **Nagaike Mingei-ten** shop specializes in traditional Shikoku folk crafts. They make umbrellas, straw raincoats (*mino*), and sandals.

The **Kami Haga-tei** house, the old residence of a wax merchant, was built in 1894 and has a courtyard garden and a tea room. It costs ¥200 to enter. Closed Mondays. The ceiling beams are cut from the giant *yakusugi* trees of Yakushima, south of the Kyushu mainland.

At the end of the lane, past the stone lantern, is the sixth-generation **Ōmori Wa-rōsoku** Japanese candle maker where *rōsoku* (vegetable oil wax) candles are still made by hand using traditional Japanese methods. Watch them make candles and buy a few as light, easy-to-pack souvenirs. Closed Mondays. West of the candle maker is Kōshō-ji temple.

I would recommend hitchhiking to Uchiko from Ōzu in the morning. Spend the day walking through the old section of Uchiko and then continue on to Matsuyama in the early evening. It will take only about an hour to hitchhike from Uchiko to

Matsuyama. Remember the rule: It is always easy to hitchhike *into* a large city.

Escaping

From the Ōmori candle makers, it is a short walk east to Highway 56. From there hitchhiking is easy. Matsuyama is 40 km away and much of the traffic will be headed all the way in. You may want to make a sign, though I didn't bother.

IKAZAKI

Just a few kilometers south of Uchiko on Prefectural Highway 32 is the small town of Ikazaki (population 6,000), which has been designated a "craft heritage community." It is just a five-minute drive south of Uchiko, and is worth the detour.

Note: Prefectural Highway 32 from Uchiko to Ikazaki is shown in green but not numbered in the atlas.

What to See and Do

Most craft centers in Ikazaki close early, so try to arrive well before 5:00 P.M. The **Tourist Association** is run through the town office. They have an English booklet available, but the staff does not speak English. The phone number is 0893-44-2121.

Ikazaki is a center for the Japanese art of kite fighting, celebrated locally on May 5 during the **Tako Matsuri**. This festival has a 300-year history and features giant kites that do battle in the skies above the Odo-gawa. Kites are equipped with *gagari*, "kite knives," which they use to cut their opponents' strings.

Ikazaki also has a kite museum, the **Ikazaki Tako Hakubutsu-kan**, which has 1,300 different Japanese kites on display and 400 kites from other nations, including an elaborate multi-level Chinese kite. Admission is ¥300. Closed Mondays and days following national holidays. You can try your hand at making your own kites as well, a bulky and breakable—but light—souvenir.

If you are getting good at making Japanese crafts, Ikazaki also has a traditional, handmade-paper factory, the **Tenjin Sanshi Kōjō,** where you can buy Japanese stationery and paper (*washi*). It is free to enter but ¥500 to make your own *washi*. You need to call ahead before coming (Tel. 0893-44-2002). Closed Mondays.

If your feet are sore by this point, you may want to buy a pair of Japanese wooden raised clogs (geta) at the **Miyabe Mokuri Kōjō.** If you call ahead, you can arrange to watch a demonstration of geta making (Tel. 0893-44-2426). Closed Sundays and national holidays.

MATSUYAMA

Your arrival in Matsuyama (population 448,000), the largest city in Shikoku, marks the end of your hitchhiking itinerary in Shikoku. Unless you use the expressway, the northern coast of Shikoku should be avoided. The area is heavily industrialized, there are few attractions, and the hitchhiking is painfully slow and erratic.

Matsuyama, however, is worth a visit. Because it is the main urban center of Shikoku, it is an easy place to hitchhike into, but a hard city to escape. The best strategy? I recommend hitchhiking into Matsuyama and then taking a ferry out. You can take ferries from Matsuyama back to Osaka and complete the loop, but a better choice is to take one across the Inland Sea to Hiroshima. If you have already been to Hiroshima, you could take a ferry over to Beppu instead and connect with the Kyushu itinerary (see Chapter 14).

Where to Obtain Information

The main **Matsuyama Tourist Information Center** is in the JR Matsuyama-eki (Tel. 0899-31-3914), which is open 8:30 A.M.–5:15 P.M. and has all the English information and maps you need.

Note: There are two Matsuyama stations. One is the main JR

Matsuyama-eki and the other is Matsuyama-shi-eki, which is part of the private Iyo Yokokawara Line. The latter station is closer to the downtown entertainment area.

If you have reversed this itinerary and are beginning your Shikoku journey in Matsuyama, you can buy the atlas and English-Japanese Pocket Dictionary and other recommended books on the fourth floor of the **Kinokuniya Bookstore,** near Matsuyama-shi-eki. The bookstore also has English travel material on Shikoku and Matsuyama. Trams in Matsuyama, like those in Nagasaki and Hiroshima, charge a flat rate. In this case: ¥170 (¥90 for children).

What to See and Do

Matsuyama has two main attractions: **Matsuyama Castle** (downtown) and the **Dōgo Onsen area** (east of the city center).

Matsuyama Castle: High on its hill in the middle of the city, **Matsuyama-jō** is regarded by many as Japan's most beautiful castle. After the grandeur of Himeji and the tiny perfection of Uwajima, you will better appreciate the elevated aesthetics of Matsuyama's "Black Crane" castle. In Japan, castles are said to have their own personalities. Where Himeji Castle is graceful, and Kōchi Castle friendly and down-to-earth, Matsuyama Castle is haughty and aristocratic. Its black presence contrasts sharply with the soft white of Himeji earlier in your journey. Matsuyama-jō is also the youngest of Japan's 12 authentic castles. Originally built in 1602, it burned down twice and the present structure was finished only in 1854.

It is open daily 9:00 A.M.–5:00 P.M. (until 4:00 P.M. in winter). Admission is ¥260. It is only 130 meters up the "mountain," but if you don't feel like making the hike, a ropeway will take you up for ¥160 one way. You can then walk back down.

Haiku: Matsuyama's literary reputation lies in its rich haiku traditions. The best known of Matsuyama's poets is **Shiki**

Masaoka (1867–1902). Shiki almost single-handedly revived the art of haiku in the nineteenth century and is considered by some to be second only to Bashō (1644–94) in importance. Indeed, it was Shiki who coined the term "haiku."

There are 36 different "haiku posts" around Matsuyama where the public can write and read haiku. There are several haiku monuments as well; among them is a reconstruction of Shiki's home, the **Shiki-dō,** located just south of Matsuyama-shi-eki. If you have an interest in Japanese poetry, or feel a sudden haiku coming on, stop in. It is a short stroll from the main shopping arcade area of Matsuyama. The **Shiki Memorial Museum,** or Shiki Kinen Hakubutsukan, is located in the Dōgo Park area.

Dōgo Onsen: With a legendary history dating back 3,000 years, Dōgo Onsen is the oldest and most venerable hot-spring area in Japan. The celebrated novelist **Natsume Sōseki** (1867–1916) taught English in Matsuyama briefly, and often soaked in Dōgo. His novel *Botchan* is set in the Dōgo–Matsuyama area. Japanese regard Botchan, the title character, with a certain nostalgic affection similar to the way that Americans consider Huckleberry Finn or Tom Sawyer. Sōseki's portrait graces the ¥1,000 note.

The main complex in Dōgo is the **Dōgo Onsen Honkan,** which has a "Botchan Room" in honor of Sōseki's hero. Sōseki and the poet Shiki were friends, and Shiki in turn is indirectly honored with a haiku post near the entrance, where bathers who are taken with sudden inspiration while soaking in the waters can pen their work. Feel free to add your own haiku in English.

The main building dates from 1894, and its weathered wooden façade is justly famous in Japan. On the first floor are the crowded *kami-no-yu* baths with their granite pools. The second floor houses the *tama-no-yu*, a luxury bath and lounge area. On the third floor are the drum tower and several private rooms—including the Botchan Room. The higher up you go, the more expensive the baths. They are around ¥280 for the basic baths on the lower floor, and ¥1,240 for the upper-level luxury bath and lounge with complimentary tea. Dōgo also has an Imperial Suite, the *yūshinden*, which is reserved for members of Japan's imperial family. They don't drop by much, however, and the suite is now preserved as cultural property.

Where to Stay

Matsuyama Youth Hostel (Tel. 0899-33-6366) has been awarded the prize as the most popular youth hostel in Japan. It carries a four-star rating and a ¥3,100-per-night charge. This hostel is the best location and cheapest place to stay while in Dōgo. Bicycle rentals are available, and the hostel has ferry schedules and maps as well. It is closed November 24–December 8, January 22–February 3, May 8–9, and June 18–30.

In front of JR Matsuyama-eki is the **Central Hotel** (Tel. 0899-41-4358) with singles that start at ¥4,120 without a private bath or private toilet. (The hotel has a public bath and public toilets.) Single rooms *with* a private bath and toilet are ¥4,840 per night. Doubles with a private bath and toilet begin at ¥7,720 per night. This is fairly economical, but keep in mind that the JR Matsuyama-eki is not in the heart of things. If you are looking for excitement, go instead to the Matsuyama-shi-eki area, which is closer to the shopping arcades and love hotel zone of Chifune-machi.

The **New Grand Capsule**—pronounced "nyū gurando"— (Tel. 0899-45-7089) costs ¥2,600 per night and is right in front of the Matsuyama-shi-eki.

Escaping

Matsuyama is a tough city to get out of. No less than five national highways come together at Matsuyama, and the misnamed Matsuyama Expressway begins far to the east of town. Construction is slowly inching toward the city but it is still a long ride out of town to the expressway.

Ferries: Take a ferry from Matsuyama across or along the Inland Sea. Unless you plan on taking time out to do some island hopping, I recommend the ferry from Matsuyama to Hiroshima, which will take you through a cluster of islands and give you a sense both of the beauty of the Inland Sea and the heavy industrialization that has spoiled so much of it. There are three ferry ports servicing Matsuyama: Mitsuhama-kō, Takahama-kō, and Matsuyama Kankō—this is the main one.

Ferries to Hiroshima run from both Mitsuhama-kō and Matsuyama Kankō, but Matsuyama Kankō is easier to get to and the ferries are more frequent. To get to **Matsuyama Kankō,** take a bus in front of the JR Matsuyama-eki. The 30-minute ride costs ¥440. Buses leave every hour.

Ferries to Hiroshima run 12 times a day. The ride costs ¥2,130 and takes two hours 50 minutes. A more expensive hydrofoil also makes the trip in one hour eight minutes but costs ¥5,700. There are 14 hydrofoils a day, but they do not have an observation deck and the price is just not worth it.

HIROSHIMA

Hiroshima (population 1.07 million) is on the itinerary of almost every Western visitor to Japan. This is part of the main tourist path, and while it is not really well suited for hitchhiking, I have included it because of its historical significance.

Getting There

From Matsuyama you will arrive at Hiroshima port, called Ujina-kō. From Ujina-kō, several tram lines run into town; take a Number 1 or Number 3. (Number 5 will take you to Hiroshima-eki, which is far from the Peace Park area.) Trams in Hiroshima charge a flat rate of ¥130 (¥250 on the longer Miyajima Line). Hiroshima also has a new, state-of-the-art monorail.

Note: When you take the tram in from Ujina-kō, be careful

when the tram comes to the Minami-machi 6-chome stop. Here, the tram lines split. Make sure you are on a tram going left toward Hondōri.

If you want to go immediately to the Peace Park or Green Hotel, get off at the Hondōri tram stop and walk west—to the left from the tram line. This will take you down the covered arcade, and then—dramatically—to the A-bomb Dome and into the Peace Park. If you want to go to the English bookstore first, get off one stop later at the Kamiya-chō tram stop. The Sogo department store is across and to your left. Kinokuniya is on the sixth floor.

Where to Obtain Information

After hitching along the back roads of Shikoku, you may find the presence of so many non-Japanese people in Hiroshima startling. Hiroshima is a city geared for foreign visitors, and there is an abundance of English materials, maps, and books available.

There are two **Tourist Information Centers,** both with English staff and similar English materials. One office is in **Hiroshima-eki** (Tel. 082-261-1877) and is open 9:00 A.M.–5:30 P.M.

The second **Tourist Information Office** (the official JNTO one) is in the **Peace Park** itself, across the river from the A-bomb Dome. Call 082-247-6738 or just drop in. You will pass right by it when you enter the park. Look for the "i" symbol. It is open 9:30 A.M.–6:00 P.M.

Both tourist offices can help you find accommodations, but the office in Hiroshima-eki is out of your way. You will be arriving by ferry, and there is no pressing reason for you to go into the station area at all.

The Hiroshima International Exchange Lounge is on the first floor of the **International Conference Center** and is open 9:00 A.M.–7:00 P.M. Japanese residents and foreign visitors gather here and it is a good place to find English speakers and advice.

For more information, call 082-242-8007. The center is closed December 29–January 3.

English books are in the **Kinokuniya Bookstore,** on the sixth floor of the Sogo department store on Aioi-dōri (street), not far from the Peace Park. Kinokuniya is open until 7:30 P.M. daily. The downtown **Maruzen Bookstore** also has a selection of English books. The **Peace Park Museum** has many English books dealing with the Hiroshima tragedy.

What to See and Do

The **Genbaku Dōmu**, called the A-bomb Dome in English, is across the river from the Peace Park. This building, originally the Hiroshima Industrial Promotion Hall, was left a skeletal wreck by the bomb and has become a symbol of both the A-bomb and the city. Just south of the Dome is a small tower-monument marking the actual epicenter of the atomic explosion. Although it was practically at ground zero, the Dome survived because of the pulsing wave nature of an atomic explosion, which leaves small rings of lesser destruction.

Just north of the Dome, and at the tip of the Peace Park, is an odd T-shaped bridge, the **Aioi-bashi**, which was used as a reference point for the pilots flying the mission to aim the bomb.

Across the river from the A-bomb Dome is the spacious green **Heiwa Kinen Kōen** (Peace Park). Like Nagasaki's, Hiroshima's Peace Park is bursting with collections of origami cranes. A young girl, dying of leukemia in the aftereffects of the attack, was told by her desperate mother that if she could fold 1,000 paper cranes she would recover. She died before she could finish, and to this day, schoolchildren across Japan finish her task for her and present it in the spirit of all those who perished.

In the center of the park is Japan's most-visited museum. The **Peace Park Museum** documents the suffering and devastation of the August 6, 1945, atomic bomb. Three days later, the second bomb fell on Nagasaki. The Japanese government estimates that almost 300,000 people have died from the two attacks and their aftereffects. With the bombings of Hiroshima and Nagasaki, the end of the world became a distinct possibility, as the arms race and the Cold War began. The museum is open daily 9:00 A.M.– 6:00 P.M. and until 5:00 P.M. between December and April. Please enter at least half an hour before closing. Admission is only ¥50. Closed December 31–January 1.

Among the monuments in Hiroshima's Peace Park—to Japanese women, children, students, workers—there is no government-funded monument to the 20,000 or so Korean slave-laborers who died in the blast. A privately funded monument that stands across the Honkawa-bashi (bridge) was erected in 1970. The city refused to allow the **Korean monument** to be placed within the park. In 1995, on the 50th anniversary of the attack, a request was made to the city to move the Korean monument into the Peace Park. The city refused.

Hiroshima Castle: Having seen four or five of Japan's 12 extant castles, you may want to see a modern reconstruction to compare. **Hiroshima-jō** was destroyed in the firestorm that followed the nuclear attack, but was rebuilt in 1958. The castle is a 10–15-minute walk from the Peace Park, and it is open 9:00 A.M.– 5:00 P.M. (until 4:30 P.M. in the winter). Admission is ¥300.

Where to Stay

Hiroshima Youth Hostel (Tel. 082-221-5343) is a haven for foreign travelers. It is 4 km from the Peace Park, north of Hiroshima-jō, and costs ¥2,260 per night. They can provide all the information you need about visiting the Peace Park and Miyajima, but unless you are either broke, or in need of foreign company, there is no need to stay in this hostel. It is not very conveniently located.

The **Hiroshima Green Hotel** (Tel. 082-248-3939) is conveniently located at the end of the Hondōri Arcade behind the A-bomb Dome and has singles starting at ¥5,500 per night. If you can afford it, this is a good place to stay because of its location. This puts you just around the corner from the Peace Park and the A-bomb Dome and not too far from Hiroshima's bustling "new paradise" of the Shintenchi night-life district. The A-bomb Dome is all the more poignant at night lit up and reflected in the river.

There are two establishments in Hiroshima that belong to the Japanese Inn Group. You should call ahead well in advance to arrange a reservation.

The **Mikawa Ryokan** (Tel. 082-261-2719) has Japanese-style rooms that cost ¥3,500–¥3,800 without a private bath. Couples pay ¥6,000. This ryokan is not in a traditional Japanese-style building and it is far from the Peace Park. It is a seven-minute walk from Hiroshima-eki. Visa and American Express are accepted.

The **Minshuku Ikedaya** (Tel. 082-231-3329) is near the Peace Park and not far from the Korean monument. Japanese-style rooms are ¥4,000 per night without a private bath. Couples pay ¥7,000 per night. There is an English pamphlet about the Minshuku Ikedaya available at Hiroshima-eki. If you are coming from the station, take a tram to the Dobashi tram stop; from there, the *minshuku* is a two-minute walk. Visa, American Express, and MasterCard are accepted.

With the constant influx of Western visitors to Hiroshima, the two capsule hotels in Hiroshima have become reluctant to rent to non-Japanese. Don't try to get into them unless you can speak *some* Japanese, otherwise expect to be told "we're all full." Both capsule hotels are in the Yagenbori night-life district. Ask at a police box for directions. **Capsule Inn Hiroshima** (Tel. 082-242-2021) costs ¥2,300 per night. **New Japan Capsule** (Tel. 082-243-0227) costs ¥3,600 per night.

MIYAJIMA

Just west of Hiroshima is one of Japan's Most Famous Sites, the vermilion "floating" torii gate of Miyajima, also known as the island shrine of Itsukushima Jinja. This is one of the most photographic views in Japan.

You need a day and a night to fully appreciate all that Miyajima has to offer. Though crowded with tour groups during the day, when the last ferry leaves and dusk falls, Miyajima becomes sublime. So make sure you arrange overnight accommodations—Miyajima is not a day-trip. If you have to, see Hiroshima as a day-trip instead and then hurry over to Miyajima.

Getting There

Note the following names: Miyajima is the island. Miyajima-guchi-eki is the train station. Miyajimaguchi-sanbashi is the mainland port across from the island; ferries depart from here to the island. Miyajima-kō is the port on the island where the ferry arrives.

From **Miyajimaguchi-sanbashi,** ferries run to the island every ten minutes 9:00 A.M.–6:00 P.M. The 15-minute ride costs ¥170. There are three ways to get from Hiroshima to Miyajima:

- Take a tram from Hiroshima headed west on Line 3 or 5. At Nishi-Hiroshima-Koi, change to the Miyajima Surburban Line. Go to Hiroden-Miyajima, the end of the line. Both the tram stop and the Miyajimaguchi train station are near the port. Trams run more frequently but they take longer and are only marginally cheaper than the train.
- Take a train from either Nishi-Hiroshima-eki or Hiroshima-eki (Nishi-Hiroshima-eki is closer to Miyajima.) The train to Miyajimaguchi-eki takes 20–30 minutes and costs ¥310. It is a short, six-minute walk from the station to the Miyajima-guchi-sanbashi port.
- Take a tram south to Ujina-kō ferry port. From there, a high-speed boat whisks you to Miyajima-kō. The ride takes just 22 minutes and costs ¥1,440 one way. Boats run every hour

(more during peak times) 8:30 A.M.–4:45 P.M. (5:10 P.M. on the weekends).

If you are coming from Matsuyama you will arrive at Ujina-kō. Here, you can change boats and go directly to Miyajima without going into Hiroshima at all, saving it for your way back.

Where to Obtain Information

English maps and pamphlets are readily available and there is no lack of information. You can pick up maps and materials in Hiroshima as well.

What to See and Do

Miyajima is larger than it seems and is best seen with a bicycle rented at the port. The main shrine is to the right along the shore from the port. Beware! The island is populated with fearless deer who will all but pick your pocket in their quest for snacks. High in the mountains are colonies of wild monkeys.

Pagoda and Hall: As you walk down the shore, admiring the view and fending off deer, you will pass the **Senjōkaku Hall** and **Pagoda** on your left, high on a wooded bluff and almost out of view. The hall dates back to 1587, and like many structures on Miyajima, it has an open, airy feel. The name itself means "1,000 tatami mats." The pagoda beside it dates to 1407 and is a syncretic blend of Japanese and Chinese influences.

Itsukushima Jinja: The torii gate of Itsukushima is in front of the main shrine on the island. The shrine is built out over the water on piers. The torii of Itsukushima Shrine is rebuilt when it begins to decay. The present torii—the largest in Japan—was constructed in 1875. At low tide you can walk out to it, and you will notice just how weather-beaten it is. Coins are wedged into the cracks of the wood as offerings to the shrine. Shrine hours are 6:30 A.M.–6:00 P.M. (until 5:00 P.M. in winter). Admission is ¥300. Try to go at dawn when it is most beautiful. Unfortunately, there are no English tide tables posted anywhere on the island, so it is important to spend the day here to see the shrine in both high and low tide.

Miyajima Festivals: On March 3, the **Kiyomori Matsuri** honors the memory of the hero of the fallen Heike clan with a historical procession of costumes and music.

The **Kangensai Matsuri,** the island's main festival, is held in mid-June (the date changes slightly according to the phase of the moon). Illuminated boats ply the waters to the sounds of ancient shrine music. Every August 14, a **fireworks spectacular** is held out on the water in front of the shrine, illuminating the torii in bursts of light.

Note: Accommodations will be almost impossible to arrange on Miyajima during either festival, unless you make arrangements at least several months in advance.

Monkey Mountain: After visiting the main shrine and pavilions of Miyajima, you may want to go up the mountain for a wider view. You can either climb the 530 meters to the summit of **Misen** in about an hour, or take the ropeways instead. From the top of the second ropeway, a trail leads to the summit, past a temple with a smoldering fire and a large cauldron that has been brewing since the days of Kōbō Daishi. The fire was first set by the wandering priest over 1,100 years ago, and it has been kept alive by faithful monks ever since. There certainly appears to be about 1,000 years' worth of soot on the rafters and ceiling. Watch out for monkeys. Just as the lowlands of the island are infested with deer, the top of the mountain is infested with monkeys. Thieves by any other name, these monkeys are good at their work—one of them stole my lens cap.

Where to Stay

The **Miyajimaguchi Hostel** (Tel. 0829-56-1444) is *not* on the island, but is a two-minute walk from the Miyajimaguchi-sanbashi ferry port. The manager speaks some English, and it costs

¥2,300 per night. Although friendly, it is not in a very quiet spot and I don't recommend it unless you arrive too late to get to the island.

Instead, spend the money and stay overnight on Miyajima. By spending a night on the island you can enjoy the full tidal view of the shrine and torii gate in the moonlight. You can rent bicycles overnight as well.

I stayed at the **Pension Miyajima** (Tel. 0829-44-0039), which is back inland from the ferry port. Walk through the tunnel and turn right—a five-minute walk. The pension is in front of Zonkō-ji, so when asking for directions, head for the temple. The rooms are twin beds and cost ¥7,000–¥7,500. Make sure you call at least a couple of days ahead to make a reservation. I called from Matsu-yama the day before I caught the ferry across to Hiroshima.

Great news for the budget traveler is the **Tsutsumi-ga-ura Camp-jō** (Tel. 0892-44-2903) on Miyajima which costs just ¥360 per person and is open all year round. Four-man tent rentals are available for ¥2,060. To get to this campsite you must follow the coast to the northeast—away from the main tourist zone; it takes 40 minutes by foot. A bus runs to Tsutsumi-ga-ura as well and takes just ten minutes.

Hitchhiking out is a little tricky, but hitchhiking in, *from* the campsite, is easy because most of the traffic at the start will be other campers returning to the ferry port. There is a spacious beach across from the campsite and a view of the Inland Sea.

Note: On the English tourist maps, the camping area is labeled "Tsutsumigaura Natural Park."

Escaping

After you visit Miyajima, you can hitchhike back into Hiroshima along the coast on Highway 2, but there really is no need since the San-yō Expressway is nearby. From the Hatsu-kaichi IC you can hitchhike along the expressway all the way to Himeji, where your journey began.

IWAKUNI

Before you rush back to Himeji and Osaka, try to make a short side trip south from Miyajima to Iwakuni (population 111,000), a city is best known for its famous and very photogenic Brocade Sash Bridge, the **Kintai-kyō**.

Getting There

Iwakuni is close enough to Miyajimaguchi that you may want to forgo hitching and take a train to Iwakuni-eki. From there regular buses run out to the bridge. Nishi-Iwakuni-eki is actually closer to the bridge, but fewer trains stop at Nishi-Iwakuni-eki.

There is a constant stream of sightseers driving between Miyajima and Iwakuni, so catching a ride south on Highway 2 all the way to Kintai-kyō bridge is very easy. Highway 2 takes you within walking distance of the bridge area. It should be noted that a large U.S. naval base is located in Iwakuni, so you may be offered a ride by American servicemen. If you are wary or uncomfortable about this, take the train from Miyajima instead.

Where to Obtain Information

Iwakuni doesn't have a TIC office (yet) but the **Iwakuni Kankō Kyōkai Visitors' Office** (Tel. 0827-41-2037) is located near the start of the bridge. English is not spoken; you're better off just showing up. The office is open Monday to Friday, 9:00 A.M.–5:00 P.M. The bridge area is not hard to figure out, so you don't really have to stop at the visitors' center first.

Kintai-kyō: This bridge is a beautiful structure, built more for aesthetics than function. The rounded spans make it a dizzying up-and-down walk to get across it, with your gaze first down toward the sea and then up toward the sky. The present bridge is actually the third to be built. The original, built around 1670, washed away the following year.

According to local legend, two young maidens offered their lives in sacrifice to the river so that the second bridge would not suffer a similar fate. Apparently it worked, because the second bridge, built in 1673, stood for almost 300 years before succumbing to a typhoon and flood in 1950. The bridge was rebuilt to the exact specifications of the original—although hidden steel reinforcements were added.

The Kintai-kyō bridge was originally reserved for samurai. Merchants and other commoners had to take boats across. But today anyone with ¥210 is allowed to cross the bridge and back. The cable car up the hill is another ¥520 (round trip) and entrance to the castle is another ¥260. Buy a combination ticket (*setto-ken*) for the bridge, the cable car, and the castle for ¥820. The merchant spirit, it would seem, has triumphed.

At the other end of the bridge is **Kikkō Kōen** containing the usual museums as well as several old samurai residences. Behind the park, atop the forested hill of Shiro-yama (Castle Mountain), is **Iwakuni-jō** (castle), reconstructed in 1962. This is the seventh—and last—castle of your trip, so enjoy it.

White Snakes and Dumb Birds: Although the bridge is the main reason to go to Iwakuni, there are other attractions as well. Near Iwakuni-eki is the **Shiro-hebi Jinja,** the White Snake Shrine, where dozens of albino snakes are venerated as messengers of the Goddess Benten. Benten is one of the Seven Lucky Gods. She is also a notoriously jealous deity, so couples should approach her shrine separately to avoid her wrath—though this superstition is rarely observed today.

Near Kintai-kyō bridge, in June and July you can see **cormorant fishing** similar to that in Ōzu. Fishermen go out at night and light fires to attract fish.

Where to Stay

The **Iwakuni Youth Hostel** (Tel. 0827-43-1092) is conveniently located near the footpath leading to the castle. The manager speaks English and the hostel's wooded location makes it a good place to stop and recharge your batteries before hitchhiking back to Osaka. It costs ¥2,300 and is closed December 30–January 3. If your driver drops you off at Iwakuni-eki, take a bus to Kintai-kyō bridge. The hostel is a five-minute walk from the Kintai-kyō *teiryūjo* (bus stop).

Escaping

From the Kintai-kyō bridge and Kikkō Kōen area, cross to the east side of the river and then walk toward Highway 2. This highway runs alongside the river, on the opposite side from the park, and goes right to the Iwakuni IC.

From the Iwakuni IC, the San-yō Expressway runs all the way to the east of Himeji. From there you have to hitchhike north on Highway 372 to the Takino-Yashiro IC on the Chūgoku Expressway. The Chūgoku Expressway will take you all the way back to Osaka or even on to Kyoto.

KYOTO

If you haven't visited Kyoto yet, this is your chance. Stay on the expressway until you get to the Suita Junction. This is a tangled knot of expressway entrances and exits—just make sure you get past it and onto the Meishin Expressway headed for Kyoto. Get off at the Kyoto-Minami IC. Downtown Kyoto is a short hitch north from there on Highway 1.

Timing: A grand tour of Shikoku and the Inland Sea will take 19–23 days. Of course, you can do it much faster, but it is better to take your time and if necessary, do only part of the itinerary.

You will probably have to spend the night in Himeji and catch the ferry to Shōdo-shima the following morning. Count on two nights on Shōdo-shima, then down to Kotohira the following day. Two days to go through the Koboke-Ōboke Gorge, and one or two days in the Kōchi area. One day to get to Ashizuri-misaki, and a night and a day on the cape. Include another two nights in Sukumo, including a day-trip to Oki-no-shima. Spend a day in Uwajima, two days and a night on the Spear of Shikoku. Add another night in Ōzu, and a full day to get to Matsuyama, including a stop in Uchiko. (Add a day if you are planning to visit Ikazaki.) Two nights in Matsuyama and then across the Inland Sea to Hiroshima the next morning. Spend a day and a night in Hiroshima, then head down to Miyajima the following morning. A night on Miyajima—two if you have the time—then head to Iwakuni the next day. Spend the night in Iwakuni, and be prepared to spend one full day of hitching to get back to Osaka.

Kyushu

The southern island of Kyushu is a superb travel destination for hitchhikers in Japan. Kyushu has a bit of everything: hot springs, high plateaus, active volcanoes, mountain hikes, traditional fishing villages, beautiful coastlines, wind-swept capes, and friendly, boisterous residents.

Youth hostels in Kyushu are generally bland places, unlike those in Hokkaido's far reaches. Fortunately in Kyushu, quiet business hotels and rural *minshuku* are not much more expensive than youth hostels.

Kyushu is hot, humid, and unbearable July through the first half of September, especially for a hitchhiker standing by the road. It stays pleasantly warm well into November, and spring in Kyushu is lush and green. The best time to come to Kyushu is at the beginning of April to catch the cherry blossoms, just after Golden Week, or in October or November.

Some of the campsites listed in this itinerary are open only during the hot sticky summer months of July and August, but generally, if you go during the off-season you can stay anyway, often for free, but with limited services.

This itinerary is divided into two loops, one in the north and one in the south. If you are beginning your journey to Japan with a hitchhiking tour of Kyushu, fly into Fukuoka for the north loop or into Kagoshima for the south.

THE NORTHERN KYUSHU LOOP

FUKUOKA

Fukuoka (population 1.7 million) is *the* best point of entry for visitors coming to Japan. The uncrowded airport is easy to figure out, and it connects to downtown by subway. The subway itself turns into a local train leading out of the city, which means that you can go directly from the airport to the highway and be hitch-hiking within an hour of your arrival.

Note: The eastern part of Fukuoka is known by its old name, Hakata. The airport is Fukuoka-kūkō. The main train station is Hakata-eki. The Hakata subway stop will put you right at Hakata-eki, which can be a confusing place. It's larger than the airport and seems more like a glittery shopping center than a train station. Inside the station, follow signs to the **Information Desk,** which is open 9:00 A.M.–7:00 P.M. daily. They can provide city maps and some English materials. If you need to cash traveler's checks or change money, go to the main post office near Hakata-eki.

Where to Obtain Information

If you need to pick up the road atlas, dictionary, or any other reading material, get off the subway at Tenjin when you come from the airport. **Kinokuniya Bookstore** (Tel. 092-721-7755) has a wide selection of English books on the sixth floor of the Tenjin-Core Building and is open 10:00 A.M.–8:00 P.M. daily, though it closes on the occasional Wednesday.

If you arrive in Fukuoka in the morning, make a short stop at

Tenjin to pick up the atlas and then return to the subway and catch a train headed for Karatsu. Get off at Shimoyamato-eki and hitchhike west on Highway 202. Fukuoka is a lively, modern city, but you will be returning at the end of your loop, so save Fukuoka for your return.

What to See and Do

If you arrive in the afternoon or evening, you will have to save your hitchhiking for the morning. There are a number of interesting sights around Fukuoka, which should give you a taste of the area.

Downtown Shrines and Temples: From Hakata-eki, there are two sites nearby worth visiting. **Sumiyoshi Jinja** is said to be the oldest surviving Shinto shrine in Kyushu; the present structure dates from 1623. **Shōfuku-ji** is the oldest Zen temple in Japan,

─────────────── KEY TO MAP ───────────────

1. Fukuoka	18. Ushibuka	35. Kobayashi
2. Dazaifu	19. Minamata	36. Golden Python and
3. Niji-no-matsubara	20. Amakusa Five	Two-Headed
Beach	Bridges	Snake Shrine
4. Karatsu	21. Misumi	37. Miyazaki
5. Higashi-Matsura-	22. Uto	38. Aoshima
hantō	23. Kumamoto	39. Udo Jingū
6. Imari	24. Mt. Aso and Caldera	40. Nangō
7. Arita	25. Kujū-san	41. Kōjima Wild
8. Nagasaki	26. Kurokawa Onsen	Monkey Island
9. Mogi	27. Yamanami Highway	42. Toi-misaki
10. Obama	28. Yufuin	43. Kushima
11. Fugen-dake and	29. Beppu	44. Kanoya
Unzen Onsen	30. Ōita	45. Nejime
12. Shimabara	30A. Usuki Stone	46. Sata-misaki
13. Tomioka	Buddhas	47. Ibusuki
14. Takahama	31. Kagoshima	48. Kaimon-dake and
15. Ōe	32. Ebino Kōgen	Ikedako
16. Kawaura	33. Five Volcano Hike	49. Chiran
17. Hondo	34. Takachiho-no-mine	50. Sakurajima

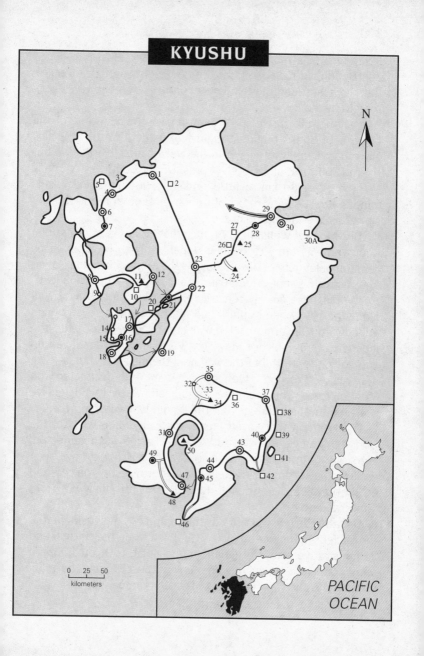

KYUSHU

N

PACIFIC
OCEAN

0 25 50
kilometers

founded by the monk Eisai in the year 1195. Eisai introduced Zen Buddhism to Japan from China. He also brought over the first tea seeds, and the temple—appropriately—has several tea rows in his honor.

A short walk east of the Tenjin area is **Nakasu,** one of the biggest, brashest, brightest night-life districts south of Osaka. Nakasu is actually an island in the Naka-gawa (river) delta, but the fun spills out along both shores. On the southwestern bank of the river are the smoky little food stalls (*yatai*) that Fukuoka is famous for. A steamy bowl of ramen by the neon backdrop of Nakasu makes an excellent meal.

Anti-Mongol Walls: In 1274, the great Mongol warlord Kublai Khan sent his army to conquer Japan, only to be stopped by samurai defenders at Hakata Bay. As the Mongol invaders sailed away a storm swept through and many of their ships were lost.

The Japanese quickly constructed a 20-km Anti-Mongol Wall along the bay. When Kublai Khan returned with an even bigger armada and an army of 140,000 men, seven years later, the Japanese were ready for him. For two months battles raged up and down the coast, but the wall held them back and then—like a miracle—a second typhoon blew in and decimated the Mongol force. The Japanese lords maintained the defensive walls for another 20 years, but the Mongols never returned.

The typhoon that saved Japan was called "the Wind of the Gods," or kamikaze. In World War II the name was resurrected. Parts of the Anti-Mongol Walls, called *genkō no bōheki*, have been excavated and can be viewed in Imazu, northwest of the city, and at Iki-no-Matsubara beach just across the highway from Shimoyamato-eki.

Dazaifu Shrine: Dazaifu was the capital city of Kyushu during the ancient Kofun period (300–710). Even when the cultural and administrative center of Japan shifted north to Kyoto, Dazaifu remained a prestigious government outpost. Today, the main attraction is the Grand Shrine of **Dazaifu Tenmangū.**

This isn't really a hitchhiking destination. Dazaifu is a 30-minute train ride south of Fukuoka, on the private Nishitesu Line. Take the train from the Nishitesu Fukuoka-eki, across the street from the Tenjin-Core Building. The trip to Dazaifu is only ¥360, and it isn't practical to hitchhike. The information desk at the Nishitetsu Dazaifu-eki near Dazaifu Shrine has an English map of the area. The shrine is a short walk from the station.

The Grand Shrine of Dazaifu Tenmangū is dedicated to Suga-wara no Michizane, the deified patron of scholars and students. It is odd how much his memory is revered here, because the man hated Kyushu. He was sent south in exile from the Kyoto courts as punishment following some court intrigue, and he died broken-hearted. His angry spirit terrorized Kyoto after his death and had to be placated by building shrines in his honor. He even got a posthumous government promotion. Better late than never, I suppose.

On the first Sunday of March, the **Kyokusui-no-en** floating poetry contest is held in Dazaifu, a tradition that originated in Korea (although this is rarely acknowledged in Japan). During the contest, costumed participants have to write lines of verse before floating cups of saké reach them.

Beside busy Dazaifu Tenmangū shrine is the quiet Zen landscape garden of **Kōmyō Zenji**. By visiting both the shrine and the temple you can see in plain counterpoint the differences between Shinto and Buddhist aesthetics. A short day-trip from Fukuoka is manageable; you shouldn't have to stay in Dazaifu.

Where to Stay

There are many business hotels around Hakata-eki. The area is not a very interesting place to spend the night. If you are a couple, stay in a love hotel either in the Nakasu area or across from Shimoyamato-eki.

The **Hakata Park Hotel** (Tel. 092-451-1151) is a five-minute walk from the Hakata-guchi exit. Singles range ¥5,000–¥6,000 per night; doubles are ¥8,000.

The **Green Hotel I** (Tel. 092-451-4111) and **Green Hotel II** (Tel. 092-473-7112) are near each other, have singles for ¥6,400 per night, and doubles for ¥8,600. To get to the Green Hotels, leave Hakata-eki from the Chikushi-guchi (exit) and walk left down the first side street.

The **Sun Life II** (Tel. 092-473-7112) is a short walk straight out of the Chikushi-guchi of Hakata-eki, across the main street, and then to your left. It has singles for ¥7,500 per night and doubles for ¥12,360.

South of Nakasu Island you will see the unmistakable purple and pink neon signs of Fukuoka's love hotels. There are also two capsule hotels in the Nakasu area.

Walk to the south of Nakasu island and then turn east (to your left) on Kokutai-dōro (street). Turn right on the next street, which meets Kokutai-dōro at an angle, and you will come to the **Well-Be Capsule and Sauna** (Tel. 092-291-1009). It costs ¥3,800. Look for an English sign reading "Daiwa Club."

To get to the other capsule, stay on Kokutai-dōro. You will soon come to the **Capsule Inn Hakata** (Tel. 092-281-2244), which costs ¥3,000 per night. The two places are not far apart.

If you are planning to start hitchhiking the next morning, don't spend the night in Nakasu. Instead, take a Karatsu-bound train to Shimoyamato-eki; beside the highway is a beautiful purple love hotel better suited for hitchhikers—look for the castle turrets. (The hotel is called the "**Hilton**," but the name is not written in English.) To get to the love hotel, you need to walk back alongside the tracks and then go under a small overpass which will put you near the back of the drive-in love hotel. Walk in the back door and quickly go up the stairs into the first available room—making sure you turn on the red light. Rooms start at ¥7,000 for an overnight stay (10:00 P.M.–10:00 A.M.). For a couple, this is far cheaper than staying at a business hotel or even a hostel, and the rooms are much more interesting.

Escaping

The key station is Shimoyamato-eki, west of Fukuoka on the Chikuhi Line, one stop after Meinohama. Take a subway headed for Karatsu. The subway turns into a local train headed west.

Note: Shimoyamato-eki is not labeled in the atlas. If you can escape in the evening for a stay at the Hilton love hotel, you can walk out the front door the next morning and you will be on Highway 202 pointed toward Karatsu.

If you cross the highway to the beach at Iki-no-Matsubara, you can view the remnants of the Anti-Mongol Walls. If you are discreet, you could even pitch a tent along this beach after dark. They may be opening a camping area at Iki-no-Matsubara soon, which will be a boon for travelers.

KARATSU

From Shimoyamato-eki, you can hitchhike to Karatsu (population 80,000) in about an hour and a half. Karatsu is a pleasant place with a beautiful pine forest, a long beach, and a reconstructed castle perched on a hill.

Where to Obtain Information

North of Karatsu-eki is the **Karatsu Tourist Information Center** (Tel. 0955-74-3355), located just across the street from the Karatsu Kōtsū Sentā bus station and just south of the Hiki-yama Tenjijō display center. If you are interested in pottery, the tourist center can give directions and hours for visiting a kiln.

What to See and Do

The white sand beach and black pine forest of **Niji-no-Matsubara** is labeled in the atlas. It is—according to the JNTO—

one of the "Three Most Beautiful Forests in Japan." Much of it is virgin stands of trees, never cut and over 300 years old. Walk or ride a bicycle through the forest path and you will eventually come to the bridge at the river's mouth, which leads across to **Karatsu-jō** perched on a hill overlooking the ocean.

The castle has earned the nickname **Maizuru-jō**, the Flying Crane Castle; the main keep is open daily 9:00 A.M.–5:00 P.M. Admission is ¥300. At night, the castle is lit and the grounds are free to enter.

Between November 2 and 4, you can see the giant ceremonial floats called *dashi* in action during the lively **Karatsu Okunchi** festival. If you miss the festival, you can see the floats on display at the **Hikiyama Tenjijō** display center, which is located downtown, not far from the Tourist Information Center.

Where to Stay

There are many *minshuku* and ryokan ouside of Karatsu among the pine forests and beach of Niji-no-matsubara. Ask your driver to help you find one. Most are in the ¥8,000–¥10,000 per-person per-night price range.

The **Niji-no-Matsubara Kokumin-shukusha** (Tel. 0955-73-9111) is also called the **Niji-no-Matsubara Hotel**. It costs ¥6,000 for a single and ¥10,000 for a double, without meals. Breakfast is ¥930. There are three very expensive set meals available for supper, ¥3,000–¥5,000. From the Kokumin-shukusha, it is a five-minute hitch or a long but pleasant walk along the beach or through the forest to the castle.

The **Niji-no-Matsubara Camp-jō** (Tel. 096-354-2251; this a long-distance Kumamoto phone number, so dial all the numbers and have lots of change handy) is near the Kokumin-shukusha and costs just ¥500 per person. Rent a six-man tent for ¥1,800. This campsite is open only from the first Saturday of July to the last Saturday of August. During the rest of the year it is empty, unsupervised, and inviting. Unofficial camping elsewhere along the beach is possible, as long as you pitch your tent at dusk and leave at dawn.

Staying on or near Niji-no-Matsubara is best, but you can also stay downtown. Just behind Karatsu-eki is the **Karatsu Hotel** (Tel. 0955-72-1100) with singles for ¥6,800 per night and doubles for ¥12,000 per night.

HIGASHI-MATSURA-HANTŌ

The Higashi-Matsura-hantō (peninsula), north of Karatsu, has an attractive coastline and several small fishing villages tucked into coves along the way. It is an easy side trip for hitch-hikers. Follow the coast around through the town of Yobuko and then continue south toward Imari.

If you are staying on Niji-no-Matsubara, hitchhike along the highway, past the castle, and you will follow the coast north, avoiding central Karatsu. If you are downtown already, take a local train to the end of the line at Nishi-Karatsu-eki. Highway 204 is west of the station. Hitch north on Highway 204.

En Route

You should be able to follow Highway 204 all the way around and south into Imari in a single day, but should you get stuck, stay in Yobuko along Highway 204. The houses and *minshuku* of this **tumble-down fishing village** all but fall into the harbor as they crowd in along the shore. Yobuko has a lively morning market and also a *kokumin-shukusha* (Tel. 0955-82-3006), which costs ¥6,500 per night, including Japanese breakfast and supper.

Camping: At the tip of Hado-no-misaki (cape), north of Chin-zei, is the **Hado-no-misaki Camp-jō.** Call the town office (Tel. 0955-82-2111) for information. It is open all year, but a custodi-an is on the grounds only during the summer holidays. It costs ¥200 per person.

If you are coming south on Highway 204 to Imari, you will pass near the bridge connecting the mainland to the island town of Fukushima. If it is late in the day, you may want to cross over to the island. About 3 km inland, after the Fukushima Ōhashi (bridge), is the **Tsubaki Marina Camp-jō** (Tel. 0955-47-2137), which is open all year and costs ¥700 per person.

IMARI

If you like pottery, this is your chance to buy an expensive, fragile souvenir to worry about during the rest of your trip. Imari (population 63,000) and smaller Arita are Japan's oldest pottery centers. Japanese ceramic arts began in 1598, when the kidnapped Korean artisan Ri Sanpei built Japan's first kiln. After that, all it took was the capture and forcible deportation of some more Korean artists and the "Japanese" art of ceramics was born.

Note: It is considered bad manners to dwell on the outstanding, and largely unacknowledged, contribution that Korea has made to Japanese culture. Among other things, the tumulus tombs of Nara, the Grand Shrine of Izumo, and the Japanese imperial family itself, can, some historians argue, be traced back to Korean origins.

Where to Obtain Information

The **Tourist Information Center** in JR Imari-eki is open 9:00–6:00 P.M. daily. They offer day-use bikes at no charge.

What to See and Do

The most accessible and interesting kiln-town to visit is **Okawachiyama**, once the canyon-like prison village of Korean artisans. This secluded pottery village is surrounded by mountains on three sides and is located about 6 km southeast of Imari.

Note: Okawachiyama is not marked on the atlas.

A bus runs every hour between the Imari Kōtsū Sentā and

Okawachiyama. It takes 15 minutes and costs ¥200–¥300 depending where you get off. You *could* try to bike it on one of the free, day-use bikes, but there is a large mountain you have to cross. Take a bus instead.

NAGASAKI PREFECTURE

The western coast of Nagasaki is a journey all in itself. Nagasaki must be the most thoroughly attractive prefecture in all of Japan, and nowhere is this more evident than along the coast and islands of Saikai National Park.

Getting There

You can either follow the coast north from Imari to Hirado, or you can cut across to Shikamachi town, the gateway to the 99 Island Chain. Shikamachi has access to campgrounds in Nagushi-yama Park.

If you want to hitchhike directly from Karatsu to Nagasaki, without a side trip around the Higashi-Matsura-hantō, take the local train south from Karatsu-eki to Onizuka-eki. Highway 202 is parallel to Onizuka-eki on the west.

You can hitch south on Highway 202 to where it meets Highway 205 near Huis Ten Bosch, a theme park that faithfully re-creates an entire, old-fashioned Dutch city—if old-fashioned Dutch cities were peopled by Japanese tourists. Huis Ten Bosch is hyper-reality at its worst, but it is not as incongruous a choice as you may think. During the 250 years of seclusion during the Tokugawa period, the Dutch still managed to maintain a presence in Nagasaki.

From Huis Ten Bosch hitchhike south on Highway 205, along the traffic-heavy east coast of Ōmura-wan, one of the few unattractive stretches in Nagasaki Prefecture. Highway 205 will take you all the way into Nagasaki. (It changes into Highway 34 along the way.) This is the quickest, surest way to get to Nagasaki, but there are other, more scenic routes available, as outlined in the following.

Instead of changing highways north of Huis Ten Bosch, stay on Highway 202 and you will cross over to the less hectic western peninsula of Nagasaki. Highway 202 will take you out along the outer coast, past small fishing villages and offshore islands. If you show an interest in visiting the Nanatsugama Cave your driver will probably make the detour for you. As well, there is shrine in Ōseto town that I missed, but which is reportedly quite beautiful. You will be traveling through quiet scenic surroundings most of the way. But be warned: This is not a very busy route.

Alternatively, follow the inside coast of the Nishi-Sonogi Peninsula, down Highway 206 past Oranda Mura (Holland Village), the smaller prototype of the Dutch theme park. Traffic is steady on this inside route, so you will get you into Nagasaki sooner. This is the route I recommend.

NAGASAKI CITY

Nagasaki (population 444,000) is one of Japan's most fascinating cities. Although it is best known as the site of the second atomic bomb, which obliterated the north end of the city on August 9, 1945, there is much more to Nagasaki. The city has long been a contact point between East and West, even during the centuries of isolation under the Tokugawa shoguns.

Nagasaki reminds me slightly of Hakodate in Hokkaido. Both are older, slightly jaded, cosmopolitan blends of West and East. To explore Nagasaki properly you need at least two or three days.

Where to Obtain Information

When you hitchhike into Nagasaki, ask to be taken to Nagasaki-eki. Inside the station is the **Nagasaki Information Center**

(Tel. 0958-23-3631), open 8:30 A.M.–7:00 P.M. daily. They can make reservations at hotels and provide a few discount coupons, but the better office is across the street.

The **Nagasaki Prefectural Tourist Information Center** (Tel. 0958-26-9407) is across the street from the station, on the second floor of the Kōtsū Bus Center. Walk across on the pedestrian overpass and enter the second floor directly. This office has an English staff and lots of material on both the prefecture and the city. Pick up maps and materials on the Unzen/Shimabara area as well. This office is open 9:00 A.M.–5:30 P.M. Monday–Friday, and until 5:00 P.M. on Saturdays.

What to See and Do

Peace Park and Urakami Church: The **Heiwa Kōen** (Peace Park) is north of downtown, a short walk east of the Matsuyama tram stop. The symbol of the Nagasaki Peace Park is a muscular man pointing skyward, a sculpture that strikes many as somehow inappropriate. The sculptor, Seibo Kitamura, chose his portrayal carefully, refusing to render the victims of the atomic bomb as either weak or frail. The finger pointing skyward seems both a warning and an accusation.

To the east of the Peace Park are the statues of **Urakami Tenshudō Catholic Church,** scarred by the blast. The choice of Nagasaki as a target for an atomic attack is ironic. No city in Japan had embraced Western culture and international relations more than Nagasaki. Long a prime trading port, it was also the center of Japanese Catholicism. Urakami Church was the focal point of Christian faith in Japan and the largest Catholic church in Asia.

The Americans had originally intended their nuclear attack for the industrial city of Kokura, now part of Kita-Kyushu. But Kokura was obscured by clouds, and so the pilot flew instead to Nagasaki where a break in the clouds sealed the city's fate. The bomb exploded almost on top of Urakami Church, the bastion of

Western influence in Japan. The church was rebuilt in 1959, but the scarred and headless statues of the saints were incorporated into the present approach to the site.

A-bomb Museum and Ground Zero: The main A-bomb Museum is the **Kokusai Bunka Kaikan** (International Culture Hall), located just south of the Peace Park, near the epicenter. Hours are 9:00 A.M.–6:00 P.M. (until 5:00 P.M. from November to March), and admission is ¥50. Like the museum in Hiroshima, it vividly displays the horrors of nuclear weaponry. Kimono patterns burned into skin, bodies reduced to shadows in a single blinding flash, unborn children condemned to mutations and sickness—it is a deeply moving and disturbing place to visit.

While in the museum, you should also note the copies of pamphlets dropped on the city by the U.S. Air Force. They warn of a nuclear attack and tell the citizens to leave the city. Few took heed. Oddly enough, critics of the American decision to drop the bomb have stated categorically that "there is no evidence that such pamphlets were ever dropped," yet the Nagasaki Museum has original copies on display.

Across from the museum is the **Chūshinchi Kōen** (Epicenter Park), where a black pillar marks ground zero above which the bomb exploded. A section of Urakami Church has been moved to the site as well. A 15-minute walk farther south is the One-Legged Torii, known as the *kata-ashi-torii* in Japanese. Once the gateway to **Sannō Shintō-gū** shrine, it was blasted in half by the bomb and remains a stark reminder of the attack.

It is estimated that of Nagasaki's population of 240,000 people, 150,000 were killed by the blast and it aftereffects. Almost a third of the city was destroyed by the blast and the firestorm that followed. As in Hiroshima, throughout Nagasaki you will see thousands of origami paper cranes draped over monuments.

Temple Row: **Teramachi** Temple Row, to the east of downtown, was spared destruction because the bomb was dropped north of its intended target (the Mitsubishi shipyards) and a row of hills diverted the impact of the blast. Take a tram to the end of the line at Shōkakuji-shita and then walk east to **Sōfuku-ji**, a Chinese Zen temple founded in 1629. From there, wander the narrow street past the various temples until you get to **Kōfuku-ji**, another Chinese temple founded in 1620.

Suwa Jinja was established in 1625 to help counter the growing influence of Christianity and is one of the most fascinating shrines in Kyushu. A detailed English pamphlet explains the variety of odd attractions, such as the stone lions, yin-yang stones, and two *kappa*-style guard dogs that are routinely doused with water by worshippers. The shrine even has English fortune slips written in suitably cryptic English with headings such as "chance, wishes, illness, marriage, things lost," and "direction." The steep stone steps of Suwa Jinja are the focus of a crowded, raucous dragon dance during the city's Okunchi Matsuri October 7–9. To reach Suwa Jinja, from the station take streetcar No. 3 to Suwa Jinja-mae.

Glover Park: Thomas Glover (1838–1911) was a Scotsman who helped to industrialize Japan. He was also an arms runner and a master of intrigue. He even had a hand in the downfall of the last of the Tokugawa shoguns. Glover settled in Nagasaki and married a local geisha. During World War II, his son was wrongly accused of espionage by the Japanese government and was hounded into committing suicide. (Jack Seward based his saga *The MacNeils of Nagasaki* partly on that of the Glovers.)

Thomas Glover was also responsible for the introduction of beer to Japan, and his company, Kirin, is still producing lager today. The *kirin* is a mythological creature; here you can see the original pair of stone *kirin* that inspired the beer logo. The face of the beer-label *kirin* was drawn to resemble Glover himself.

Glover Park (pronounced "gurabā") offers some of the best examples of syncretic architecture in Japan. The park also boasts an incongruous outdoor escalator and a statue of Madame Butterfly—though the connection between the opera and Glover is more tenuous. The opera is set in Nagasaki, and it is only coincidence that the Glover family crest is a butterfly. Glover was married to a Japanese woman, he didn't abandon her, and the only suicide in the family was Glover's son, who killed himself in the incident mentioned above. Glover Park is open daily 8:30 A.M.–5:00 P.M. Admission is ¥600.

Nagasaki has great night life, especially in and around the Chinatown district. You could spend several nights wandering through the maze of side streets in Maruyama and still find new nooks to explore.

The night view from **Inasa-yama** (332 meters) is—and I quote—one of the "Three Best Night Views in Japan." The ropeway costs ¥1,280 round trip, and runs until 10:00 P.M. (5:00 P.M. in winter). Take bus No. 3 or 4 from in front of Nagasaki-eki and get off at Inasayama-mae *teiryūjo*. To get back, take bus No. 30 or 40.

Where to Stay

Across the street from the Nagasaki-eki, and beside the Prefectural Information Center, is the **Capsule Inn Lucky** (Tel. 0958-22-4466), which costs ¥3,100 per night. If you are female, this is your chance to try a capsule; the **Nagasaki Kenkō Center** (Tel. 0958-28-1126) in front of the station reserves one floor for women. It costs ¥3,500 a night; make sure to try the sauna.

The area behind the bus center (the same building that has the Prefecture Information Center) and up along the base of the hill has several **love hotels** in among the back streets. They are in the ¥6,500–¥7,500 range per night (10:00 P.M.–10:00 A.M.) There is also a cluster of love hotels in the Peace Park area, across from the Epicenter Park.

From the bus center, follow the street that curves around the base of the hill to the right and in about 15 minutes you will come to the **Nagasaki Youth Hostel** (Tel. 0958-23-5032) on your left. Some English is spoken here, and it costs ¥2,800 a night. If you stay two nights or more, they will give you a 20-percent discount ticket for the ropeway up Inasa-yama. The hostel is closed December 29–January 3. (If you continue east, around the hill from the hostel, you will come to Suwa Jinja.)

The **Oranda-zaka Youth Hostel** (Tel. 0958-22-2730) located south of the downtown area, near Glover Park, is open during New Year's. It doesn't supply any meals, but with all the restaurants to choose from in Nagasaki, there is no reason to eat at a hostel. They charge ¥2,400 per night.

The **Minshuku Tanpopo** (Tel. 0958-61-6230) across the river from the Peace Park area, near Urakami-eki, is a member of the Japanese Inn Group. A Japanese-style room for one person costs ¥4,000 per night without a private bath. Doubles cost ¥7,000 per night. They accept American Express. To get to Tanpopo, take a tram to the Matsuyama stop. Cross the river and turn left. Follow the river until you come to a gas station. Ask for the final directions there.

UNZEN-DAKE AND THE SHIMABARA-HANTŌ

To the east of Nagasaki is the Shimabara-hantō, site of the Unzen-dake volcano group. At the center of it all is **Fugen-dake** (1,359 meters), the notoriously active volcano that erupted in the spring of 1991, spewing a lava-and-mud flow down the east side, wiping out villages and killing dozens of people.

The Fugen-dake blast was equal to half the explosive energy of the atomic bomb that was exploded over Nagasaki. From across the bay, on the Amakusa islands, crowds watched the fiery red lava flow at night. I was among them, and the night fires of the volcano were as beautiful as the imminent threat of a tidal wave was frightening. Today, alas, the impressive lava flow that has hardened looks more like cold congealed porridge.

Historically, the Shimabara-hantō (peninsula), together with the Amakusa islands, was the site of the great Christian revolts led in 1637 by the mystical, 14-year-old boy, Amakusa Shirō, the

Child of God. At the abandoned castle of Hara-jō on the south-eastern side of the peninsula, the Christian insurgents—mainly farmers and fishermen—made their bloody last stand against the armies of the Shōgun Ieyasu Tokugawa. **Shimabara-jō,** another castle involved in the rebellion, has been reconstructed in Shimabara.

The cluttered hot-spring town of **Unzen Onsen** lies roughly in the center of the peninsula. There is a three-hour walk you can make from the top of the ropeway, around Fugen-dake, past a small pond and a shrine. If you are energetic, you can skip the ropeway fee and walk all the way up. The volcano rumbles now and then, but it probably won't erupt when you are there.

Less developed, and more attractive than Unzen Onsen, is the seaside resort of **Obama,** with waters that purportedly cure everything from rheumatism to hangovers, though I can vouch only for the latter.

Getting There

Hitchhiking from Nagasaki to Shimabara-hantō can be frustrating. Most of the traffic will be headed north to the airport instead. To save yourself the aggravation, take a local train to Nishi-Isahaya-eki beside Highway 57, which runs east to Shimabara-hantō. Don't begin hitching immediately, however, because Highway 57 soon meets Highway 34, and Highway 34 runs to the north toward the airport. A lot of the traffic will be turning off. To eliminate traffic heading to the airport, walk east along Highway 57 past the intersection before you start hitchhiking.

The numbering of highways on the Shimabara-hantō is confusing. At Aino, Highways 57 and 251 meet and cross over; stay with Highway 57 the entire way. It will turn south at Aino and take you to Obama, and then across Unzen-dake and into Shimabara-shi (city). If you hug the coast instead, you will circle the peninsula and come down around to Shimabara-shi; you will have to backtrack up the mountain to visit the Unzen-dake area.

Where to Obtain Information

There is a Tourist Information Office near the ferry port in Shimabara-shi (population 45,000). If you are planning to hitch-hike all the way in on Highway 57, make sure you pick up Shimabara–Unzen maps and guides in Nagasaki before you set out, because you won't be visiting Shimabara-shi until the very end of your trip.

The **Unzen Visitors' Center** (Tel. 0957-73-2642) is in the heart of the Unzen Onsen area. They have an English slide presenta-tion on the Unzen area and a sketchy but adequate English-Japanese map for the Fugen-dake walk. The map also shows the *jigoku* (boiling hells), thermal springs once used to boil alive those Christians who refused to apostatize. Try not to fall into one of those hells.

Not far from the Unzen Visitors' Center is **Mammyō-ji,** site of the Golden Buddha, one of Japan's three largest Buddhas.

Where to Stay

The **Shimabara Hostel** (Tel. 0957-62-4451) in Shimabara-shi is near the Shimabara-kō (port), beside Shimabara-Gaikō-eki. It costs ¥2,300 per night.

Camping: On the south side of the Shimabara-hantō, in Kazusa, are the Iwato-Kannon and Ana-Kannon temples dedi-cated to the Goddess of Mercy, not a bad deity to placate when you live in the shadow of an active volcano. Nearby is the **Bungalow Mura** (Tel. 0957-87-2573), which is open July 10–August 31. This isn't exactly a campsite, but it does have pre-standing six-man tents that you can rent for ¥5,000 a night. No smaller sizes are available. Cabins for three rent for ¥10,000 per night.

In the atlas, south of Obama, a prefectural highway marked in green runs inland from the shore. Just below where this road meets Highway 389 is a small lake named Suwa-ike (shown but not labeled in the atlas). Beside this lake is the **Kokumin Kyūka-mura** campsite (Tel. 0957-74-9131), which is open all year and costs ¥300 per person and ¥1,000 for tent space. Tent rentals are available in summer holidays only; a four-man tent is ¥3,000. You can also get to this campsite by hitching south from Unzen Onsen on Highway 389. The lake is well known, so when people stop just ask, "Suwa-ike?" You will need an advance reservation if you want to stay at the campsite during the peak summer months.

There is also a campground in the Unzen Onsen area, beside Shirakumo Pond and near the Unzen Park Hotel. Ask at the Unzen Visitors' Center for more information and directions.

THE AMAKUSA ISLANDS

Few Western travelers ever make their way to this chain of over 120 islands. It is the most traditional, remote area in Kyushu that is readily accessible to hitchhikers. Amakusa shares with Shimabara a long history of resistance by Japanese Catholics against the oppressive rule of the shogunate, and offers glimpses of an older Japan mingled with Christian influences: small fishing villages lost in time, a Spanish church, the rugged Myōken-ga-ura coastline, and the high-spanning vistas of the Amakusa Five Bridges. Coming from Nagasaki, the best Amakusa trip begins at Tomioka and then runs down the west coast of the island to Ōe and then east, through Sakitsu and Kawaura, and then either up to Hondo and across the five bridges of Amakusa or south to Ushibuka and then over to Minamata by ferry.

Most of the towns covered on this hitchhiker's tour of Amakusa are not covered in any depth by the usual general guides to Japan. Many of them do not even appear in the atlas. The villages of Takahama, Ōe, and Sakitsu, are not shown in the atlas because they are technically part of larger towns. Thus, even though Takahama and Ōe are separated by deep forests and high mountains, they are considered part of Amakusa-machi. The village of Sakitsu is technically a part of Kawaura-machi, some 13 km to the east. Before you start out, you should write in some missing towns in the atlas. Takahama is located where "Amakusa-machi" is marked. Ōe is south of Takahama, where the highway nears the sea again, before turning east along the bay. Sakitsu is on the coast halfway between Ōe and Kawaura.

Note: The west coast of the island is part of the rugged Myōken-ga-ura coast. The best way to see this coast would be to hitch north along coastal Highway 389. The Japanese drive on the left side of the road, so if you are heading north, the passenger side of the car will be nearest the coast, giving you impressive views. Unfortunately, in order to make a loop from Fukuoka, the itinerary I have outlined runs *south* along the coast of Amakusa, meaning that you will be looking across the driver at the scenery. I apologize.

Getting There

Take a ferry from Kuchinotsu on the Shimbara Peninsula to the ferry port **Oni-ike-kō** (port) in **Itsuwa**. This ferry runs 17 times per day; the last ferry is around 6:00 P.M. The 30-minute ride costs ¥320.

What to See and Do

North of the Oni-ike port are the **Itsuwa-machi Dolphin Cruises** called *iruka kenbutsu* (or *iruka* watching). Call 0969-33-0881 for more information. The boats leave just east of tiny Tsūji-jima, which is shown in the atlas. The one-hour ride costs ¥3,000; call at least several days in advance.

Where to Stay

If you take the ferry from Kuchinotsu-kō on the south tip of

Shimabara Peninsula, you will arrive at Oni-ike port north of the town of Itsuwa. A ten-minute walk south of the port and near Wakamiya beach is the **Wakamiya Kōen Camp-jō**. (You can see the campsite from the port.) The campsite is open all year and is free, but water is not usually available during the off-season. If you have any questions, you can call the town office (Tel. 0969-32-1111.) No tent rentals. Farther south from Oni-ike port, along Highway 324, is the **Kurosaki Camp-jō**, which is handled through the same town office number listed above and is open during the same season.

TOMIOKA

The ferries arrive at Tomioka-kō on a hook of land north of Reihoku. Also near the ferry port is a **Marine Park** and the ruins of **Tomioka Castle**. There are plans to rebuild Tomioka Castle, so don't be surprised if you see a real castle beginning to take shape above the ruins.

Getting There

If you are planning an extensive trip through Amakusa and don't mind either skipping Unzen or backtracking to Nagasaki, this is the ferry to take. **Mogi Port** is south of Nagasaki, an 8-km bus ride from the Nagasaki Kōtsū Sentā bus station. The station is across from Nagasaki-eki, on the ground floor, under the Prefectural Information Office. The bus ride to Mogi costs ¥210 and takes about 25 minutes. There are 20 buses a day.

Note: The ferry line from Mogi is shown in the atlas, but the port of Mogi itself is not labeled.

Seven ferries a day run from Mogi to Tomioka; four are express ferries that cost ¥1,720 and take 40 minutes. The other three are slow ferries that cost ¥1,200 and take one hour ten minutes. The last ferry is an express that leaves at 5:00 P.M.

Where to Stay

A short walk west from the Tomioka-kō ferry port takes you to a **muncipal campground,** so if you arrive in the evening you can pitch a tent and start hitching the next day. For information you can call the **Reihoku town office Shōkō Kankōka** tourist section at 0969-35-1111. The campsite is a 20-minute walk from where Nagasaki ferry arrives, and is open June 20–August 31. It costs ¥300 per person. Rent a six-man tent for ¥800.

SHIMODA

Hitchhike south from Tomioka/Reihoku on Highway 389 to Shimoda Onsen, a hot-spring town that has a reputation for seediness and risqué entertainment. Unfortunately, as a Western traveler, you probably won't encounter much of this.

To the east of Shimoda along Prefectural Highway 24 is **Todoroki-no-Taki Kōen** (park) which features a large wooden water wheel, once the largest in Japan. The water wheel is well known; tell your driver you are headed for the *suisha*. Beside the water wheel is a summertime *sōmen* (noodle) shop where the noodles swirl around in counter-top moats to be picked out, dipped, and eaten with deft chopsticks. The water wheel, though interesting, is not a must-see. If you are pressed for time, skip it in good conscience.

Where to Stay

On the way to the water wheel, across the river and back into the woods, is the **Todoroki Mantarō Mura Camp-jō** (Tel. 0969-42-3424). It costs ¥200 per person and has spacious six-man, tent-style bungalows that cost ¥2,000 per night. The site is open May–September. It is too far to walk in from the highway, so make sure you tell people where you are going. If they know you are headed to the campsite, they will probably drive you in. You can arrange a ride back out to the highway with one of the other campers.

TAKAHAMA

From the water wheel, hitch back into Shimoda and then continue south along Highway 389. This will take you down the high coast of Myōken-ga-ura and into the beach town of Takahama. If you are still in Nagasaki, there is a high-speed ferry that makes the run from Nagasaki-kō to Takahama, halfway down the Amakusa coast, in one hour, for ¥2,500. There is a campsite in Takahama. Take your time along this coast. If you are interested in scuba diving, there are several good coves along the way, but you will have to arrange equipment ahead of time.

Takahama's **Shiratsuru-hama** (beach) has excellent swimming. If you leave Tomioka in the morning, you should be able to arrive in Takahama early enough to pitch your tent and go for a swim. But be advised that in mid-August the jellyfish float in, and though not life-threatening, their stings smart.

Where to Stay

There is a campsite ideally located right beside the beach at Takahama. The **Ai-no-Misaki Camp Mura** charges ¥500 per person and ¥800 for a space. Rent a four-man tent for ¥1,200. The site is open from the beginning of July to the end of August. If you come through in May, June, or September, it will be warm enough to swim, there will be no crowds, and the camping will be free. The campsite itself is little more than a fringe of trees and grass along the beach. There are shelters on the south end of the beach in case of rain.

Escaping

After Takahama, the hitching becomes a little slower. The number of sightseers thins out, and the waits become longer.

Hang in there. Highway 389 will take you through the mountains and into the cove-side town of Ōe. (You will pass the Ōe church on your right on the way.) Older Highway 389 is the scenic route to take.

A new superhighway from Takahama to Ōe is near completion, however, and with it should come more traffic and easier rides. This new highway runs inland, back from the beach, and right past Amakusa Nishi Kōkō high school, where I taught English for several years. You will probably notice how excellent the young people's English is in this area because of my efforts. (Note my use of bitter sarcasm.) You can walk to Amakusa Nishi Kōkō high school from the beach. From there, turn south on the new superhighway—you can't miss it, it's the big, wide inexplicable highway cutting through the rice fields.

ŌE

The persecution of Japanese Christians by the early Tokugawa shoguns was brutally effective in most areas, but here in the farthest west coast of Amakusa, the Catholic faith has hung on tenaciously.

What to See and Do
The lofty white Romanesque **Ōe Tenshudō Catholic Church** is atop a steep hill and well worth a visit. At the base is the **Rosario-kan Catholic Museum,** which charges ¥300 for admission. No English explanations. It's not really worth it. Behind it is the **Omocha no Shiryōkan** toy museum, which has a collection of traditional Japanese folk toys on display. The toy museum costs ¥210 but there is not a lot to see unless you have an interest in folk crafts. No hands-on demonstrations or souvenirs for sale—just a bunch of toys in a big room. If you want to see both the Catholic museum and the toy museum, a combination ticket is ¥460 plus tax.

Near Ōe harbor is a boggy, duck-teeming marshland created several centuries ago by a massive tidal wave that swept over the area. The pond is called **Oman-ga-ike** after the ghost of a ship-builder's daughter said to inhabit its waters. The pond is also said to be haunted by a dragon that lives in its murky depths. And in August 1995, over a dozen well-defined sasquatch-type footprints were found around the edge of the pond. The apelike footprints were over 41 cm long and 20 cm across. The story was covered by several newspapers, but the mystery remains. Not surprisingly, the people of Ōe shun the pond and avoid it completely after dark. It is very spooky at night, especially when the fireflies are out. Near the marshland and pond is a beautiful, secluded little sea cove with a distant view of **Shark-fin Island**. Do not be tempted to swim here. There is a dangerous undertow that will pull you under. More than one seasoned fisherman has mysteriously died in this cove.

Where to Stay

Minshuku Umekawa (Tel. 0969-42-5302) is not far from Oman-ga-ike (pond). It costs ¥5,000 a night with two meals, and ¥3,000 without meals. There are three other *minshuku* lodgings in Ōe, all with prices that start at ¥6,000 a night with two meals, and around ¥4,000 without: **Ryokan Takasagoya** (Tel. 0969-42-5135), **Ryokan Hiranoya** (Tel. 0969-42-5106), and **Minshuku Isoya** (Tel. 0969-42-5139).

If you have a tent, surreptitious camping is easy in Ōe. Just find a quiet nook and pitch your tent. Haunted Oman-ga-ike pond has lots of space—if you have the nerve.

SAKITSU

From Ōe you will take Highway 389 up, up, up and over the mountain with impressive vistas of jagged, distant islands. You will then wind your way in and down. If you are ever going to get carsick, this is the road to do it on. The views back across Ōe are magnificent and are definitely worth the risk of nausea.

After crossing the mountain, the road winds along the coast and into the fishing cove of Sakitsu. Set amid this traditional Japanese village is the steeple of an old **Gothic church**. The church's interior, with its tatami floor and Catholic altar, illustrates best the joining of Japanese culture and Western religion. On display in the museum in front of the church is a wooden block *fumie* with a much-battered image of Christ in the middle. It was customary to round up villagers and force them to stomp on the image of Christ in order to root out any secret believers. Those who refused were often boiled alive. The *fumie*-stomping ritual became such a part of Japanese culture that it was a recognized seasonal referent in haiku. There is also a bust of Amakusa Shirō, the God Child who led the ill-fated Christian rebellion against the shogunate.

What to See and Do

Sakitsu is compact, which makes exploring it easy. Take some time to wander through the narrow streets of this ramshackle little village. A steep footpath, beginning near the Nazareth Cafe, takes you up **Chapel Hill** to the high wooden cross that overlooks the village, giving a full view of Sakitsu. It also gives you an idea of how the Christians of Sakitsu managed to escape detection for two centuries—the village is obviously in a very secluded spot.

It is interesting to note as well that the path leading to the wooden cross atop Chapel Hill passes through a Shinto shrine and torii gate. At the top of the mountain, near the cross itself, is a small Shinto monument, demonstrating once again the Japanese flexibility in adapting divergent faiths. The bell in the wooden hillside cross rings at 10:00 A.M., noon, 3:00 P.M., and 5:00 P.M. Try to climb the hill in time to hear the bell from the top.

Where to Stay

Try to spend the night in Sakitsu. The **Ryokan Minatoya** (Tel. 09697-9-0380), near the bay, has a good view of the church across the water. If you rise early, you will have a misty morning view of Sakitsu at dawn. Unforgettable. The ryokan costs ¥7,000 with two meals.

The scenic lookout point at Chapel Hill has a shelter and lots of space if you want to pitch a tent at dusk. The cross is usually lit up, giving you illumination, but bring a flashlight just in case. If you spend a night on Chapel Hill, you will wake to a dawn view of Sakitsu from above, but the eye-level view across the bay from the Ryokan Minatoya is better.

Escaping

A huge tunnel has recently been blasted through the mountains east of Sakitsu. If at all possible, avoid this shortcut. It is very fast, but it cuts off the best part of the coast, where the bay narrows into a fjord and small wind-bent pines cling to rocks. If it is the weekend, you should be able to hitch along the old coastal highway with fishermen and Sunday drivers. At the very least, you should walk out to the lighthouse across the bay. The view from here shows Sakitsu at its best. You will be able to see Maria on the far side of the bay. Outgoing fishermen still reflexively make the sign of the cross as they pass her.

KAWAURA

The town of Kawaura is spread out and isn't easily explored by foot. Kawaura's newly built **Colegio-kan Museum** has a rare Gutenberg-period Bible from the days of the first Jesuit missionaries to the area. It also has a replica of a press. Unfortunately, this museum has no English explanations.

Sōen-ji, near the river, dates from the time of the shogun's counteroffensive against Christianity, when large Buddhist centers were built to entice followers back to the established faith. This temple, faded now with time, is built on crumbling stone walls and the ruins of what was once Kawaura Castle.

While in Kawaura make sure you stop at the **Michi** restaurant at the edge of town, across the river from the Kawaura Yakuba town office. This restaurant has the best Korean *bibimba* this side of Seoul.

Where to Stay

The **Yamaguchi Ryokan** in Kawaura (Tel. 09697-6-1301) charges ¥5,000 a night with two meals, though this price is negotiable for sad-eyed foreign travelers. They also can provide box lunches for the road at just ¥450.

About 5 km south of Kawaura on Highway 266 is—incredibly—a love hotel. It is called **The Hotel Roppongi** and it's a bit of a landmark. At night its glitter-sign winks suggestively from a forested hill overlooking the farmlands and rice fields of rural Amakusa. You can't miss its English sign and purple turret roof. Rooms are ¥7,500–¥8,000 overnight. Unfortunately, check-in time is after 10:00 P.M. and hitching after dark is not a good idea. If you do want to stay there take a taxi. Taxis are rare in Kawaura, so your best bet is to go to a shop and ask someone to call a taxi for you. For a couple, even with the taxi fare, staying at the Roppongi love hotel will still be cheaper than staying at a ryokan. And best of all, the next morning it puts you right beside Highway 266.

Note: When asking for directions to this love hotel, make sure you say "Roppongi Ho-te-ru," because "Roppongi" is a district in Tokyo and you may get some puzzled, "Boy are *you* lost" looks.

Escaping

Note: When leaving Kawaura, do not to confuse the Prefectural Highway that runs just beside the town with the main National Highway 266 farther over. Highway 266 is too far to walk to, even from the Colegio-kan Museum. You will have to hitchhike out to the highway. Highway 266 runs down the middle of the island, tip to tip. It is a wide, easy road to hitch along. If you hitchhike north, you will arrive in Hondo (population 42,000) in about an hour. If you want to see the actual tattered war banner of the God Child Amakusa Shirō, you can stop in at the hilltop Kirishitan-kan Museum. Otherwise, try to pass through Hondo. It is not a very interesting place.

To avoid getting bogged down in Hondo, as you near the city explain to your driver that you are headed for Kumamoto and ask to be dropped off on the other side of the bridge if possible. In Japanese it would be: *Kumamoto-shi ni ikitai no desu. Ō-hashi no mukō gawa made ii desu ka?*

If you do end up in the middle of Hondo, it's a long walk across the bridge. Instead, go to the Hondo Kōtsū Bus Center and take a bus headed to Ariake-machi, which will take you across the bridge. Once you get across, get off and pay whatever fare is displayed on the sign at the front of the bus. If you can't get out of Hondo, try the **Amakusa Hostel** (Tel. 0969-22-3085); it costs ¥2,200. The **Amakusa Plaza Business Hotel** (Tel. 0969-23-5511) has singles beginning at ¥5,000.

As soon as you get across the Big Bridge of Hondo, turn left. The highway soon meets the coast. This is Highway 324 and it is the start of one of the finest hitchhiking routes in Japan. The highway changes numbers several times, but this needn't concern you. Stick with it and it will take you across the heart of the Amakusa islands and over the Five Bridges of Amakusa.

THE FIVE BRIDGES OF AMAKUSA

Amakusa is joined to the mainland at Misumi by the Five Bridges (**Amakusa Go-Kyō**) which leapfrog across smaller islands, often at vertiginous heights. The vistas and steady traffic of the Five-Bridge route makes it one of the best hitchhiking roads in

Japan. This is a scenic route with lots of traffic. Much of the traffic will be going all the way to Kumamoto, about three hours away, so it may only take one ride. You may want to make a "Kumamoto" sign to improve your odds, though I have never bothered.

After you leave the Amakusa islands and cross the peninsula, you will meet Highway 3 at **Uto**. From Uto, Highway 3 runs north into Kumamoto. If it is late and you find yourself stuck in Uto, don't panic—there are all kinds of entertaining love hotels along the highway at Uto, and you can always catch an inexpensive train into Kumamoto from Uto.

Where to Stay

Ōyano is the last town in Amakusa. It is near the Ichi-Gō-Kyō bridge that joins Amakusa to Misumi. The five bridges of Amakusa, *go-kyō* in Japanese, are numbered from 1 to 5: *ichi-gō-kyō*, *ni-gō-kyō*, *san-gō-kyō*, *yon-gō-kyō*, and *go-gō-kyō*. If you want to astonish and amaze your Japanese hosts with your ready wit, refer to the first bridge—in English—as "the strawberry bridge." (*ichigo* is Japanese for strawberry.)

Ōyano has several small campsites, some on tiny islands, but the easiest to find is the **Ōyano Seishōnen Ryokō-mura** campsite in the Iwaya area, a five-minute drive from Ichi-Gō-Kyō bridge. Ask to be dropped off at the Iwaya area and you will be able to find the campsite from there. The campsite is open July 1–August 31, and costs ¥500 per person. A five-man tent rents for ¥700. Bungalow cabins rent for ¥5,000.

USHIBUKA

If you stayed at the Hotel Roppongi in Kawaura, you are already halfway to Ushibuka (population 22,000). Hitchhike south on Highway 266 and you will be in Ushibuka in about 45 minutes. Ushibuka is a bustling fishing port hemmed in by steep mountains on three sides. This is a great blue-collar kind of town, with some of the friendliest, hard-drinking fishermen you'll run into in Japan.

There are two ferry ports in Ushibuka. The main port is for car ferries to Nagashima island (if you like potato fields, Nagashima is the place for you). The other one is the **Garuda ferry port**, where high-speed boats depart for Minamata. The Garuda ferry port is the very heart of the Ushibuka harbor, just a five-minute walk from the larger main ferry terminal. When hitchhiking in, ask to be dropped off at Garuda.

What to See and Do

If you are killing time in Ushibuka, you may want to take the **glass-bottom boat** out to look at the coral and fish off the coast. If you have never seen coral before it will be interesting, otherwise you may find it a bit tame. The boat leaves ten times a day between 8:10 A.M. and 3:40 P.M. and costs ¥1,600.

Where to Stay

Near the Garuda ferry port is the **Business Hotel Awaya** (Tel. 09697-2-2165), which has rooms for ¥4,000 per night; breakfast is an additional ¥500. They don't seem very keen on foreigners here, so make sure you arrive with your Japanese driver to help smooth things over.

If you can't get into the above hotel, walk along the street another block (away from the port) and you will pass the **Dai-ei Business Hotel** (Tel. 09697-3-3300) on your right. This hotel is easy to miss; it's on the third floor and has singles for ¥3,800 without meals. ¥5,000 with two meals.

Farther along is the tall black building of the **Business Hotel Kubota** (Tel. 09697-3-4315) with singles for ¥6,500 with two meals.

Escaping

A high-speed boat leaves from the Garuda ferry port to

Minamata on the mainland four times a day; the last ferry leaves at 4:30 P.M. The ride takes one hour 20 minutes and costs ¥2,300 one way. The Minamata-kō (ferry port) is several kilometers from the city center. When you arrive at Minamata-kō, don't dawdle; a bus connects with incoming ferries and whisks you to the bus center across from Minamata-eki for ¥130. Don't miss the bus—it's too far to walk.

MINAMATA

Minamata (population 36,000) was the site of one of the world's worst environmental disasters. Even guidebooks that claim to be hip and environmentally aware tend to dismiss Minamata in a few breezy sentences.

During the 1950s and 1960s, the Chisso Corporation dumped mercury effluent into Minamata Bay. The mercury passed through the food chain, poisoning local fishermen and their families living in villages along the coast. The painful, crippling illness became known as Minamata-byō, or Minamata disease. Mercury poisoning is passed to children through the placenta, so that apparently healthy women can give birth to diseased children. Minamata has much in common with Hiroshima and Nagasaki since one ghastly event affected future generations.

The Japanese and prefectural governments, together with the company, tried to cover up the scandal and the resulting conflict tore apart the town. The town is still deeply divided by the disaster. The American photographer Eugene Smith's haunting photographs of the victims brought it to the world's attention. For this he was beaten and almost killed by Japanese right-wing thugs. His death later may have been partly attributable to this assault. Smith's ex-wife remains in Japan and is still active in the environmental movement.

Over 13,000 people have been diagnosed with Minamata disease, but the government and Chisso only agreed to compensation for 3,000 claims in 1995. The issue is a sensitive one in a city where Chisso is still the largest employer and main economic source.

One of the first things you notice upon visiting Minamata is what a beautiful place it is. **Hachiman Jinja** and its turtles, the high coastal road with its view of the distant Amakusa islands, the hot springs and beach at **Yunoko Onsen**, make the tragedy harder to bear.

Where to Obtain Information

The **Information Center** in Minamata-eki has an English pamphlet and a very sketchy map. Make sure you get a proper Japanese map of Minamata as well, for cross-reference. You can rent a bicycle from the station 9:00 A.M.–4:00 P.M. Monday–Saturday; they cost only ¥100 a day, plus a ¥400 deposit which will be returned to you when you bring the bicycle back.

What to See and Do

There are two Minamata disease museums in Minamata, a municipal one dealing "objectively" with the toxicology of the disease, and a private museum which focuses on the personal plight of the victims.

The **Municipal Minamata Disease Museum** (Minamata-byō Shiryōkan) is across the flat land beside the ferry port. This open field is the landfill site of what was once the mouth of Minamata Bay where the mercury entered the sea. From the ferry port, the museum is a 20-minute walk along the shore to the museum, but the best way is by bicycle from Minamata-eki. The museum is open daily except Monday, 9:00 A.M.–5:00 P.M. (please enter before 4:30 P.M.) Call 0966-62-2621 for more information. No charge to enter. It has English videos and some English materials.

The smaller, private museum, the **Minamata Disease Museum** (Rekishi Kōshōkan), is harder to reach, but you won't get a full sense of the tragedy unless you visit it as well. It is up in the hills south of Minamata. A taxi from Minamata-eki will cost ¥1,030. You can hitchhike south on Highway 3, and when someone stops tell them you are headed for the museum. If you smile innocently and give them a "lost puppy look" the chances are very good that they will take you off the main highway and all the way to the museum themselves. The museum is open 9:00 A.M.–5:00 P.M. and asks for a ¥500 donation to enter.

Other attractions: A man named Kanasashi Jumpei and his wife operate a natural paper-making and craft shop in the hills south of Minamata, a few kilometers from the privately run Minamata Disease Museum. Mr. Kanasashi's cottage industry is known for using only natural products and traditional techniques. His wife uses non-chemical, natural dyes and fabrics on a traditional loom, with cotton she grows and picks herself. The dyes come from plants and flowers.

You can make your own handmade paper, with dried-flower inlays, for ¥1,050. Call **Mr. Kanasashi** at 0966-63-4140. He speaks English. Paper making is offered Monday–Saturday 9:00 A.M.–5:00 P.M. You can come on Sunday as well, but you need to call at least two days before.

Mr. Kanasashi also runs an international work camp during the last half of August. Most of the work is outdoors and hard. It is open to all ages, and costs ¥25,000 for two weeks, room and board included. About 15 to 20 people take part in the Minamata program, from countries around the world. If you are interested, contact the main office of the NICE (Nippon International Camping Exchange):

NICE
View 501
2-2-1 Shinjuku, Shinjuku-ku
Tokyo 160, Japan
Tel. 03-03352-7727
Fax. 03-03352-3635

For nighttime entertainment, turn right on the road that runs in front of Minamata-eki. As you walk down from the station you will pass **Menkichi Ramen shop** (just beside the Fantajia Video Rental shop). The owner's wife is Filipino, she speaks English, and the shop offers big, inexpensive bowls of noodles as well as some Filipino dishes.

The night life of Minamata is centered around the **Yamashita Biru I and II** buildings, which are easy to find. Everybody knows where they are. Just keep asking for directions. Across from the Yamashita Biru I is an affordable *yakitori* shop called **Tanuki**. The owner of Tanuki lived in Germany awhile, and among his other menu items is an artery-choking German potato dish. Next door to Tanuki is **Don Goros,** a Thai restaurant that also features free-form jazz and occasionally Minamata folk music on the weekends. A five-minute walk from the Yamashita Biru area is Isshin-taishō, a lively and affordable red-lantern eatery.

Where to Stay

The private **Minamata Disease Museum** offers overnight lodging for ¥1,000 a night; call ahead for a reservation (Tel. 0966-63-5800.) Be advised that the museum's lodgings are very basic and do not have air conditioning. If it is a hot or muggy day, you may find it an uncomfortable place to spend the night.

Across the street from Minamata-eki is the **Minamata Ryokan** (Tel. 0966-62-2625), which costs ¥3,000 per person without meals. Beside it is the **Katsura Business Ryokan** (Tel. 0966-63-2431), which costs ¥3,200 per person without meals. Be prepared: both of these establishments may try to pull the old "all full" ruse.

Highway 3 runs parallel to Minamata-eki, one block over; turn right on Highway 3, walk five minutes, and you will come to a purple business hotel on your right. The **Hotel Sunlight** (Tel. 0966-63-0045) has singles for ¥5,000 and doubles for ¥8,600.

South on Highway 3, several kilometers and up the hill, is the love hotel **La Pie** (pronounced *la pee-aye*). It is too far away to walk to, especially after dark. So, take a taxi from in front of the station; it will cost ¥870 after 10:00 P.M. The Hotel La Pie is a drive-in love hotel. Walk up the stairs to a room. Room charges are ¥6,800 for overnight during the week and ¥7,300 for weekends and holidays. Stay at La Pie if you are planning to see the cranes in Izumi the following day, because the hotel is located right beside Highway 3, south of Minamata.

YUNOKO

The calm Shiranui Sea, with its dotted islands and steep coast, has been called the Mediterranean of Japan. A high, coastal road runs from Minamata to the spa-town of Yunoko, offering views of the **Shiranui Sea** and the Amakusa islands. Along the way is a **free, roadside campsite** in a clearing on your left. This road is—and I quote—one of "Japan's 100 Best Cherry-Blossom Viewing Spots," so if you come through in spring, make sure you take a detour out to Yunoko.

The white sand beaches, hot springs, and outdoor *rotenburo* make a nice day-trip. Yunoko is an expensive place to stay; you could try bivouacking under the shelter at the top of the small island beside the beach, or simply backtrack along the road to the campsite.

YUNOTSURU

Go inland from Minamata, instead of down the coast, and you will come to the run-down, eclectic hot-spring town of Yunotsuru, which is much more affordable than Yunoko.

Getting There

To hitchhike to Yunotsuru you will have to follow the south shore of the Minamata-gawa inland. This river runs north of the downtown area and is a 20-minute walk from Minamata-eki. To get to the river ask someone to put you on the bicycle path that runs beside the train tracks. Say, *Nihon ichi nagai undōjō* or, if they don't understand that, *Senro zoi no jitensha michi*. Walk along the tracks on this path until you reach the river, and then turn right. Don't cross the river itself. Walk inland along the river until the town ends and the forested valley starts. It is a 30-minute ride to Yunotsuru once you get picked up.

Another strategy for getting to either Yunotsuru or Yunoko is to begin back on Highway 3, which runs parallel to the tracks, one block west of the station. Hitchhike north on Highway 3, and when a car stops tell them that you are headed toward Yunoko (or Yunotsuru, depending). The driver will take you to the start of the road that you need to be on. Or, if they are not in a hurry, they may take you all the way. Both Yunoko Onsen and Yunotsuru Onsen are marked in the atlas. The English pamphlet for Minamata lists several hot-spring ryokans in Yunotsuru; some charge less than ¥3,000.

What to See and Do

While in Yunotsuru, make sure you try the mixed bathing in the dilapidated **Jungle Onsen** of the **Kikuya Ryokan**. You don't have to be a guest at the ryokan, just pay ¥100 and walk to the top of the many rattle-bang staircases. This is a "hidden hot spring" in the truest sense of the word.

If you are an avid bird-watcher you may want to make a day trip south to **Izumi** (population 40,000). Every winter migrating cranes (*tsuru*) arrive in Izumi from Siberia. Between October and March there are as many as 10,000 cranes in the field at any one time. This is bird-watching heaven.

If you want to see them, hitchhike south on Highway 3 from Minamata. The crane-viewing area is in the fields far to the west of downtown Izumi. Drop hints to your driver—"Boy, those Izumi cranes sure sound interesting"—and he or she may take you out to see them, or at least put you on the right road. In Japanese, you would say *Izumi no tsuru ni wa kyōmi ga arimasu.*

KUMAMOTO

Hitchhike north on Highway 3 from Minamata and you will be in Kumamoto (population 618,000) in about two and a half hours. Kumamoto is the gateway to the Mount Aso area, and the home of Kumamoto-jō (castle), located in the city center.

Where to Obtain Information

The **Shimotori walking mall** is the heart of Kumamoto. The **Kinokuniya Bookstore** is at the intersection of Ginza-dōri (not *the* Ginza) and Shimotori. On the third floor is a selection of English books, including the atlas.

There is an **information desk** in the JR Kumamoto-eki, but the station is south from downtown and not in a very interesting area. To get to the station from downtown, take a Number 2 tram. Just make sure you ask *Eki made?* when you get on. The trams run often and the ride only takes about 15 minutes and costs ¥140.

The local delicacy in Kumamoto is an expensive dish called *basashi*: raw horse meat, sliced thin, and soaked in a ginger marinade. Hi ho, Silver!

What to See and Do

The JNTO has dubbed **Kumamoto-jō** one of "The Three Best Castles in Japan." Originally built in 1607, it was burned down during a full-scale siege in 1877. The castle was rebuilt to original specifications in 1960. It is huge, and, when lit at night, looks every bit like the raven to which it is often compared. But even more impressive than the castle keep are the sweeping stone walls which lead you into a maze of narrowing alleys and stairways. It costs ¥200 to enter the grounds and ¥300 to enter the main castle tower. To see the walls at their best, enter from the southwestern entrance, across from the Kumamoto-jō-mae tram stop. If you are already downtown, you don't need to take the tram, but the stop makes a handy reference point.

Suizenji Kōen (park) was first laid out by the Hosokawa lords in 1632. This family has a long, illustrious history. As recently as 1990 a Hosokawa was the governor of Kumamoto, and he went on to become prime minister of Japan. The garden re-creates the 53 stations of the old Tōkaidō highway that ran from Edo (Tokyo) to Kyoto, including a miniature Mount Fuji and Lake Biwa. To get to Suizenji Kōen, take a Number 2 or 3 tram, heading *away* from the castle and toward Ken-gun. It is a 10–20-minute ride. Get off at Suizenji Kōen-mae. Be careful; two stops before it is the similar-sounding Suizenji-dōri stop. From the tram stop, the park is to the left and not visible from the street.

You should try to go to Suizenji Kōen in the late afternoon, after the crowds have thinned. The park closes at 6:00 P.M. during the summer and at 5:00 P.M. in winter. Admission is ¥200. You can get into the park for free after 6:00 P.M. if you circle around and come in from the back entrance. A full-moon view of Suizenji's Mount Fuji makes a romantic stroll for travel-weary couples.

If you are a big **Lafcadio Hearn** fan, you may want to see the house he lived in, preserved and surrounded by the city, tucked in behind the Tsuruya department store right downtown. It is just off the Shimotori walking arcade. Lafcadio Hearn (1850–1904) was born in Greece and raised in the United States. Dissatisfied and restless, he traveled the world and ended up in Japan. He lived in Kumamoto for three years and absolutely hated the place, a fact that seems to have escaped the Kumamoto tourist board. After Kumamoto he moved to Kobe and later Tokyo.

His many books, including *Kwaidan*, *Kokoro*, and other collections of Japanese folk tales and ghost stories, are well stocked in the **Kumamoto Kinokuniya Bookstore**. In Japan he is better known by the Japanese name that he was required to adopt: Koizumi Yakumo.

Where to Stay

The main love hotel area is along the river. From the downtown area, walk away from the castle. Across the river you will see the familiar lights of love hotels. The **Hotel Dinks** is right in the heart of it. If you don't want to cross the river, look for the sparkle-sign of the **Hotel Kyushu**. There are love hotels on the hill behind JR Kumamoto-eki as well, toward the white stupa.

Kumamoto's capsule hotel is on a side street not far from Parco department store. From Parco, cross the wide Densha-dōri (where the trams run) and turn left. Turn right on the first side street and you will soon see a pair of small stone lions on your left. This marks the entrance of the Lion building. The **Capsule Inn Kumamoto** (Tel. 096-322-3933) is on the second floor. The charge is ¥3,500, with check-in after 5:00 P.M.

The **Suizenji Youth Hostel** (Tel. 096-371-9193) is located near Misotenjin-mae tram stop on the same line as Suizenji Kōen. It costs ¥2,500 per night. The hostel is closed December 30–January 2. No alcohol allowed.

The quiet decor of the **Higoji Guest House** (Tel. 096-352-7860, 9812) makes a nice change. It costs ¥3,100 a night without meals, ¥5,650 with meals. If you call from JR Kumamoto-eki they will come and fetch you.

The **Minshuku-Ryokan Kajita** (Tel. 096-353-1546) is a member of the Japanese Inn Group, and charges ¥4,000 for one person in a Japanese-style room without a private bath or meals. For two, the charge is ¥7,600. This small ryokan is well located for visiting the castle area. It is a two-minute walk from the Shinmachi *teiryūjo* (bus stop). They take American Express.

Escaping

Kumamoto is on a wide plain, and the cityscape seems to go

on forever. To escape north, take a train on the private line to Kita Kumamoto-eki. To get on the private rail line from downtown, walk to the Fujisaki Jingū-mae-eki, past the end of the Kamitori walking mall. (Fujisaki Jingū is the name of a shrine near the station.) Kita Kumamoto-eki is two stops north.

Highway 3 runs beside Kita Kumamoto-eki. Avoid doing this during rush hour. Early morning, around 7:00 A.M. (I usually hitch just past the McDonald's restaurant) is best. You can stay on Highway 3 all the way to Fukuoka. Or, if you want to get on the expressway, ask to be dropped off at the Ueki IC.

ASO

Instead of returning to Fukuoka directly from Kumamoto, you really should travel east and expand your itinerary to include Aso-zan, home of the largest active volcano in the world. It is this volcano that has earned central Kyushu the nickname, Hi no Kuni, the Land of Fire. The circumference of the outer caldera is over 100 km. According to the tourist board it is also "the only live volcano in the world that tourists can safely look down." How safely is debatable: In 1979 Aso-zan hiccuped and killed three people standing 2 km away. At times the ash from Aso-zan reaches all the way to Kumamoto. Several towns, ranches, train routes, and over 90,000 people are nestled inside the volcanic caldera, with room to spare. It is a green rolling landscape, with a sunken valley and a barren ash-gray volcano in the middle.

Note: The name Aso (or Aso-zan) refers to the entire region. Aso-machi is the main town, north of the volcanoes. The active volcano in the center is **Naka-dake**. There are four other volcanic peaks clustered in the caldera, but for sightseers Naka-dake is the most accessible. The official term for this concentration of volcanoes is Aso Go-gaku (Aso Five Peaks), but it is rarely used.

Getting There

Instead of hitching to Aso-zan, you may want to spend the money and take a train from JR Kumamoto-eki (station) to Aso-eki. It costs ¥930 and takes one hour and 22 minutes.

An authentic old-style steam locomotive, named Aso Boy, also makes the trip. Tickets cost ¥1,730 and the trip takes about two hours. The Aso Boy runs May 18–November 27. The days and times change every year, but usually it runs on weekends and holidays. You will need to make reservations well in advance.

To hitchhike to Aso, take a local train east from Kumamoto on the Hōhi Line to Musahizuka-eki, which will put you beside Highway 337 (formerly part of Highway 57 and still labeled as such in the atlas). Hitchhike east and this highway soon meets up with the "new" Highway 57. From there it is an hour's ride into the Aso region.

Where to Obtain Information

Highway 57 will take you to Aso-eki, where there is an information center. Make sure you stop to pick up maps and get your bearings.

There are two skyline roads that run south up Naka-dake; both have a ropeway at the top. If you remember that *nishi* means "west" and *higashi* means "east" you won't have any trouble keeping it straight.

- Across the highway from Aso-eki, the **Aso-tozan-dōro** scenic toll road begins. This road will take you up the side of Naka-dake. There is a steady stream of sightseers, so hitching up it and back down is not a problem. The driver you hitch a ride with may be stopping at the **Aso-zan-Nishi Ropeway**, which runs to the very top of Naka-dake for ¥820, round trip. If you don't want to pay, you can walk up in about half an hour. You may notice the many not-so-discreet concrete bunkers located around the area. These are provided so that you will have a place to cower in if the volcano erupts. Try not to think about it.

- The **Sensuikyō-dōro Skyline** leads to the Aso-zan-Higashi Ropeway. The train station nearest the start of this skyline is Miyaji-eki. The **Aso-zan-Higashi Ropeway** is much longer than the one up Naka-dake, and trying to hike up the steep mountainside isn't worth it. Take the ropeway. It costs ¥1,200 for a round trip. This ropeway is sometimes erroneously reported in guidebooks as being closed down, but I took it in 1993 and again in 1995.

At the top of the Aso-zan-Higashi Ropeway is a sign posted in Japanese that lists restrictions on things you are not allowed to bring with you. (Naturally, they post this sign at the top *after* you have already taken the ropeway up.) Among the prohibited items—alcohol, flammable materials, and matches—is a rather bizarre one. According to the regulations, you are not allowed to bring human corpses up the ropeway.

Although the road up the eastern side is nowhere as spectacular as along the western route, I like this view of Aso because it is quieter and has fewer tourists—which also means less traffic during the week. Try both routes and compare.

Komezuka, the "rice bowl," is a small, lush green, perfectly formed volcanic cone, just 50 meters high. You will pass it on the way up the western Aso-tozan-dōro. If you have the time, stop and spend an hour or two climbing Komezuka and exploring the area.

Aso Jinja: Walk north of Miyaji-eki for about half an hour to Aso Jinja. On September 25, this shrine hosts a harvest festival featuring sumo, traditional theater, and horseback archery. Aso Jinja is best visited on the way *out* of the Aso area, because to the east of the shrine, running north from Miyaji-eki, is Prefectural Highway 11, which turns into the Yamanami Highway.

Where to Stay

The **Aso-no-Fumoto Minshuku** (Tel. 0967-32-0264) is five minutes from Aso-eki. Call and they will pick you up. Rooms start at ¥5,000 per night with two meals.

As you approach Aso on Highway 57, ask your driver to turn south on Aso-tozan-dōro and you will come to the **Aso Youth Hostel** (Tel. 0967-34-0804), which is ideally located. The hostel is closed December 31–January 2. There is a campsite located nearby as well. If you come in by train, you can walk to the hostel from Aso-eki in about 20 minutes.

Near the Aso Youth Hostel, a five-minute drive farther up Aso-tozan-dōro, is the **Bōchū Camp-jō** (Tel. 0967-34-0351), which is is open from May to the end of August. It costs ¥300 per person and ¥300 for a space. Rent an eight-man tent for ¥2,000.

From Aso-eki drive one minute east (toward Ōita) and you will see a red cow statue. Turn right; a three-minute drive will take you to the **Aso Mina-no-mori Auto Camp-jō** (Tel. 0967-34-2151), which is open April 1–November 30. It costs ¥400 per person. No tent rentals. In Japanese, instructions from Aso-eki are: *Aso eki kara Ōita-hōmen ni ippun. Aka ushi o sugite usetsu shite sanpun no kyampu-jō.*

Escaping

Hitchhike north on Prefectural Highway 11 and you will come up out of the caldera, with a vast view of the magnificent, sunken landscape of Aso. At the top of the caldera wall, the highway officially becomes the Yamanami Highway continuing north through the rolling grasslands of the Senomoto Plateau. I would rank the Yamanami on a non-holiday weekend as one of the best hitchhiking routes in Japan. Be warned, however, that during peak holidays, the Yamanami can be one long, scenic traffic jam.

KUROKAWA

From Aso to Beppu, there are some worthwhile side trips which you should consider. Highly recommended is a side trip to the hot-spring town of Kurokawa. Once you get out of the caldera, leave the Yamanami and hitchhike west on Highway 442. Continue west 7 km and you will come to the mixed bathing hot-spring town of Kurokawa nestled along a stream—this is one of the best places in central Kyushu for a long soak.

Where to Stay

If you wanted to spend one night at an expensive, traditional Japanese ryokan this is the time to do it. The **Shinmeikan Ryokan** (Tel. 0967-44-0916) has several outdoor baths, a traditional decor, and even a steamy cave *onsen*. Prices start at ¥15,000 per person including two meals—it is well worth the splurge. If, instead of staying in a string of overpriced hotels, you have been camping along the way, you will have saved enough money to blow it on pure, decadent luxury.

Even if you decide to stay in the youth hostel, a visit to Kurokawa is worthwhile. Turn west when the Yamanami meets Highway 442. One kilometer down, you will pass the entrance to the **Senomoto-Kōgen Youth Hostel** (Tel. 0967-44-0157) on your right. The hostel costs ¥2,300 per night. It is closed June 20–29. This hostel fills up during holidays, so make sure you call ahead.

There are several campsites on the way to Kurokawa: Just south of Highway 442 is the **Fantaji no Mori** campsite (Tel. 0967-44-0912), which is open all year. You are required to call ahead and make a reservation. It costs ¥600 per person and ¥1,000 for a space. This is a convenient location for making a day-trip to Kurokawa. The campsite has its own hot-spring *rotenburo* as well.

Near the Senomoto Kōgen Youth Hostel and south of the

highway is the **Chaya-no-Hara Camp-jō** (Tel. 0967-44-0220), which also requires a reservation. It is open March 20–October 30 and costs ¥500 per person and ¥500 for a space. No tent rentals.

On the west side of the Yamanami, south of the intersection with Highway 442, is the **San-ai Kōgen Auto Camp-jō** (Tel. 0967-44-0013), which also requires reservations. It is open all year but occasionally closes due to bad weather between November and March. It costs ¥500 per person and ¥1,500 for a space. No tent rentals available.

KUJŪ-SAN

After your detour to Kurokawa, return to the Yamanami Highway. Continue north and you will soon pass Kujū-san on your right. At 1,787 meters, this is the highest peak on the Kyushu mainland. Fortunately, the Yamanami takes you most of the way up, and it is an easy climb to the summit. The stairs at the beginning are actually more tiring than the climb to the peak. The hike to the top of Kujū-san takes about two hours; only at the very end does the path suddenly sweep upward. Allot a full morning to climb Kujū-san.

From the summit, you will be rewarded with a breathtaking vista of the entire **Aso caldera,** a panorama said to rival the African plains. This vista is the best long-distance view of Aso there is, so don't hitchhike past Kujū-san without stopping.

Other than the hike and vista, the Kujū area's other attractions are its many horse ranches, but these are of limited interest to a Western visitor.

YUFUIN

The Yamanamai Highway will take you all the way into the quiet hot-spring craft town of Yufuin (population 12,200). The older, traditional area is farther over, around Kinrin-ko (pond) and the craft center. Here, Yufuin has the timeless, tranquil feel of old Japan.

Where to Obtain Information

The **Yufuin Visitors' Office** (Tel. 0977-84-2446) is at Yufuin-eki and is open 9:00 A.M.–7:00 P.M. daily. Unfortunately, the town has little in the way of English maps and materials.

The best way to see Yufuin is on bicycle, and these can be rented at the station, ¥300 for the first hour and ¥100 for each following hour. From April to November, horse-drawn cabs called *tsujibasha* make one-hour sightseeing circuits of the valley. Tickets cost ¥1,200 and can be arranged at the station information desk. You will need to reserve a space ahead of time.

What to See and Do

Kinrin-ko (pond) is fed by a natural underground hot spring, and in winter or chilly autumn mornings, steam and mist rise and roll; have your camera ready. At one end is a shrine whose torii gate stands in the water. To the left of the shrine, along the shore, is the **Yufuin Mingei Mura** (craft village). A nearby coffee shop looks out over the pond.

At the opposite end of the pond from the shrine is a **public bath** built into the water. Pay the ¥100 fee on the honor system—there is a pay slot at the entrance—disrobe and climb in. The bath looks out over the pond.

A rare, thatched-roof temple, **Bussan-ji,** is a five-minute stroll from the pond. Take the main road running away from the shrine. The area around Yufuin is known for its traditional thatched-grass roofs, called *kayabuki*. Bussan-ji is the most accessible and famous example of this style.

Yufu-dake (1,583 meters) can be climbed in two hours and offers a wide view of the Yufuin valley. It is a 25-minute bus ride from Yufuin-eki to the start of the hiking trail. Get off at the Yufu Tozan-guchi *teiryūjo*. Ask at the Yufuin-eki information desk for bus schedules.

For an odd but delicious experience, try the Spanish villa-restaurant **Ibiza** (Tel. 0977-85-2294), which is not far from the station and near the river. Ibiza is a replica of a Spanish farmhouse—the owner simply *loves* Spain. They bake their own delicious bread in a wood-burning oven. The place is hard to miss with its white Spanish chimney. You may still be allowed to sign your name with felt markers on the walls.

Yunohira: In the greater Yufuin area, there are several old towns and hidden spas. The cobblestone streets and old-style *onsen* of nearby Yunohira are definitely worth a trip. The roads out to these hidden mountain towns are confusing for hitchhikers. If you are planning to spend a few days exploring the outlying area around Yufuin, you should use buses or train. The information center in Yufuin-eki can provide times and routes.

Where to Stay

Yufuin is not a budget destination. There are many upscale, expensive traditional inns in Yufuin, but no hostel. The cheapest place to stay is the Yufuin Kokumin-shukusha, the **Sansō Guest House** (Tel. 0977-84-1205), which costs ¥5,900 with two meals. It is a three-minute walk from the train station.

Escaping

To escape Yufuin, take a train from Yufuin-eki one stop south to Minami Yufuin-eki. From there, hitch east on Prefectural Highway 11 and you will be in Beppu within the hour.

Note: Prefectural Highway 11 from Minami Yufuin-eki to Beppu is shown in green but not numbered in the atlas. It is part of the Yamanami Highway.

En Route

As you approach Beppu on Prefectural Highway 11, there is a campsite south from the highway near Shidakako (lake). The **Beppu Shidakako Camp-jō** (Tel. 0977-25-3601) is open all year and costs ¥400 per person. No tent rentals.

Note: Shidakako is shown but not named in the atlas. It is located southwest of the Rakutenchi Ropeway, and to the right of the secondary road shown in yellow.

It is best to stop at this campsite on your way into Beppu. If you want to get to the campsite from downtown Beppu, it is a 40-minute bus ride back out from Beppu-eki to the Tori-i *teiryūjo*. Or you could take the Rakutenchi Ropeway (¥1,500 round trip) and then hike uphill another hour to Shidakako. Be warned, it's a long hike.

BEPPU

Beppu (population 130,000) is a seedy hot-spring city often compared to Las Vegas, a slur on the good name and sophistication of Las Vegas. Beppu is jaded, steamy, mildewed, tawdry— it is definitely not glittery. Beppu is built in a low, coastal basin and the road drops dramatically as you enter the city.

Where to Obtain Information

The **Japanese Tourist Information Desk** in Beppu-eki can give you a map to the nearby English visitors' center, which is also called the SOS Information Center. The **SOS Tourist Information Center** (Tel. 0977-23-1119) is a few blocks south of Beppu-eki, on the third floor of the Kitahama Biru (building). If you're feeling travel-weary, pick up some information and then head to, the public bath on the first floor. From Beppu-eki, walk past the Kentucky Fried Chicken and down two blocks. The SOS Tourist Information Center will be on your left.

What to See and Do

A short walk from the station is the **Takegawara Onsen,** where you can pay good money to have ladies shovel hot sand on you. I would think that having hot sand shoveled on you is the kind of thing you would pay old ladies *not* to do. It costs ¥600 to enjoy this Japanese form of endurance, which is supposed to cure rheumatism, muscle aches, stress, and a number of other ailments. Bring your own towel and remember not to bake too long or you will feel exhausted.

In addition to its hot springs, mud baths, and sand baths, Beppu promotes touristy, tacky "hells" (*jigoku*), variously colored hot ponds, usually with caged animals as an added attraction. Every English pamphlet ever published about Beppu has a map and listing of all the various "hells." There are bus tours and package tickets to visit crocodiles, trapped hippos, and sad little penguins in concrete cells. I don't recommend these.

Also in the **Jigoku Hell area** is the overpriced Hinokan Sex Museum, just behind the Kamenoi Bus Terminal and across from the Ashiya Hotel. This museum has rooms stuffed to the rafters with phalluses and stone vulvas from all over the world, as well as several fertility shrines and an odd display of erotic mannequins, including Snow White in post-erotic stupor. At ¥1,500, the Sex Museum isn't really worth it.

Beppu Castle, ignored by most English guidebooks, is perched on a hill overlooking the city. The castle is impossible to miss, and it's an easy walk from the Jigoku Hell area. Inside, on the top floor of the castle, you will find an unusual wooden statue that combines the features of Jesus Christ and Shaka Buddha in one form, and which is referred to as "The Universal God." No word on how the Muslims feel about this.

The castle, built in 1956, is not so much a reconstruction as an eccentric folly. It is also known as **Matsunoki-jō,** the Pine Tree Castle, after the impressive pine-tree support beams inside that give the castle its unique construction. The building is fascinating even if it is not historically authentic.

Even more fascinating is the **White Snake Shrine** in front of the castle. Inside the shrine are two albino boa constrictors, one dead and preserved in formaldehyde, the other listless but alive. The live one is three meters long and is the offspring of the dead one. Both are venerated as incarnations of Benten, the Goddess of Art and Music. It is an odd sight to see men dressed in suits and ties, and prim women carrying Chanel bags, stopping to offer prayer in front of albino snakes.

For a view of Beppu, pay ¥1,500 round trip and take the **Rakutenchi Ropeway** to the top of the mountain. The area at the top has the usual tourist trappings and amusements. The view is good, but after Aso you may not be all that impressed.

Suginoi, a *huge* bathing complex, is the closest Beppu comes to Vegas. It is hard to describe—imagine Caesar's Palace, but with nude guests. Suginoi is everything that hot springs are *not* supposed to be: gaudy, big, and noisy. It will cost you ¥1,800 to step in, but for sheer spectacle it is almost worth it.

Where to Stay

The **Beppu Youth Hostel** (Tel. 0977-23-4116) has (surprise) its own hot spring. The hostel is far up the hill from the city, near the famous Suginoi Palace Hotel. The hostel costs ¥2,500 and doesn't offer meals. This is one of the few hostels in Kyushu that accepts VISA. It is closed May 25–June 10. Don't try to walk it— take a bus to Suginoi instead. If you want to go to the hostel first, on your way into Beppu, *don't* hitch all the way to downtown Beppu. You will pass near the hostel as you come in, so ask to be let off at the Suginoi Palace, which everyone knows.

The **Minshuku Kokage** (Tel. 0977-23-1753) is a member of the Japanese Inn Group, and has Japanese rooms with a private bath for ¥4,000 a night, meals not included. Doubles cost ¥6,000 without a private bath, and ¥7,000 for a Western or Japanese room with a bath. There is also a ¥150 spa charge for use of the hot spring. They accept American Express, Visa, and MasterCard. The *minshuku* is a two-minute walk from Beppu-eki; from the main exit, walk straight down the right side of the busy street that runs away from the station. After 100 meters, you will pass an optician's shop and a bakery on your right. The *minshuku* is behind the bakery, on a small side street.

There are many cheap business hotels near Beppu-eki, but if it is late in the day when you arrive, don't go all the way down to the station. Instead, get off in the Jigoku Hell area; ask to be dropped off near the Oniyama Jigoku and you will see a string of love hotels across the road. The **love hotels in the Jigoku Hell** area are all drive-in style; make sure you turn off the red light when you enter. Most of these love hotels are in the ¥7,000–¥8,000 range for an overnight stay, but they raise prices during the peak New Year's and Golden Week season. They are also very miserly and strict about going over the time limit. We called a minute *before* check-out time, but by the time the maid knocked on the door and we opened the secret compartment to pass the money through, it was three minutes *after* checkout time and we had to pay an additional ¥1,000.

Escaping

To complete your Northern Kyushu Loop, hitchhike back to Fukuoka along the newly completed Ōita Expressway (part of the larger Kyushu-Ōdan Expressway). You can get on at the Beppu IC. If you stayed at the Beppu Youth Hostel or in the Jigoku Hell love hotels, hitchhike up the highway you came in on. Now is a good time to use an "IC" sign. Don't write "Beppu IC," because drivers may not notice the "IC" and will think you are trying to get back into Beppu.

Take the Ōita Expressway to the Tosu Junction. At Tosu change onto the Kyushu Expressway north and you will soon be back in Fukuoka, completing the loop. Get off at the Dazaifu IC and take a train into the city. If haven't visited Dazaifu Shrine yet, this is your chance. From Beppu back to the Dazaifu IC on the expressways will only take three or four hours. You should be able to visit Dazaifu Shrine in the same day and beat it into Fukuoka in time to go on a pub crawl of the Nakasu area.

Timing: It will take 16–20 days to do the complete Northern Kyushu Loop. Count on two days to get from Fukuoka to Nagasaki, with a night in Karatsu. If you are interested in visiting the kilns of Imari and Arita add a day. Two days and two nights minimum in Nagasaki, and two more if you decide to travel across the Mount Unzen area. Two to three days in Amakusa. Minamata can be seen in a day and a night, and then on to Kumamoto. One day and one night in Kumamoto. Four days in the Aso-Kujū region, including a climb up Kujū-san and a visit to the Kurokawa Hot Springs. If you leave early, you can get from the Kurokawa area to Beppu in a day, including a stop in Yufuin. To do a limited Fukuoka-Nagasaki-Amakusa-Kumamoto loop without visiting Aso or Beppu would take a week. If you are short of time, skip Beppu.

Extending your trip from Beppu

If you want to extend your travels, there is no need to rush back to Fukuoka. Beppu is a major sea transportation hub; you can take ferries to Shikoku or across the Inland Sea to Osaka and then take a train inland to Kyoto. Or, if you want to see southern Kyushu, turn south at Beppu and follow the coast down to Miyazaki.

To Usuki: After a visit to the tawdry town of Beppu, Usuki, 45 km to the south, is a real antidote. You can take a train out of the city and then hitch south on Highway 10. By the time you clear the Beppu–Ōita urban clutter you will already be halfway to Usuki, so you might want to stay on the train all the way. The advantage of hitching into Usuki is that your driver will probably take you out to the Stone Buddhas and spare you the bus ride from the station.

In a hillside grove southwest of town are more than 60 sublime stone *sekibutsu* carvings which date back 1,000 years. They are labeled "Usuki Wall Relief Buddhist Image" in the atlas. You can try to hitching out, but it is just as easy to catch one of the many buses that run from Usuki-eki. The **Usuki-no-Sekibutsu** area costs ¥420 to enter and is open 8:30 A.M.–5:00 P.M.

Take time to explore some of Usuki's old wooden pagodas and quiet, traditional neighborhoods. An informative English booklet is available at the stone carvings area and at the station.

To Kyoto: A ferry runs from Beppu harbor to Osaka. (From Osaka take a train to Kyoto.) Overnight ferries from the Beppu-Kankō-kō to Osaka-minami-kō are ¥6,900 for the cheap seats. Overnight (14-hour) ferry rides are cost effective; you don't have to spend money on accommodations. The down side is that you pass through the islands of the Inland Sea at night, and unless it is a full moon and a clear night, you won't be able to enjoy the scenery.

Ferries also run from Beppu to Uwajima and Yawatahama in Shikoku, so you could combine a Kyushu journey with one through Shikoku. (See previous itinerary for full details on Shikoku-Kyushu ferries.)

THE SOUTHERN KYUSHU LOOP

You have seen only the northern half of Kyushu at this point. If you want to continue south to connect with the Southern Kyushu Loop described in the following section, I would advise taking a train to Usuki and then hitching down the coast to Miyazaki.

This varied loop is more off-beat than the one through northern Kyushu, and one of my favorite routes in all of Japan. The loop starts and ends in Kagoshima. However, if you are flying into Kagoshima-Kokusai-kūkō, you are already north of the city. You may want to take the shortcut listed later.

KAGOSHIMA

Called the Naples of Japan, Kagoshima (population 530,000) has its own Vesuvius across the bay: the very active volcano called Sakurajima. Its name in Japanese means Cherry Blossom Island, and it *was* once an island, but a violent eruption and massive lava flow in 1914 welded it to the eastern shore, turning it into a peninsula. A highway runs across this neck of land now, creating a unique shortcut for travelers.

The people of Kagoshima Prefecture are traditionally referred to as Satsuma-jin. They have earned a reputation as the Latins of Japan: hot-tempered, passionate, radical, and hard-drinking. In all my hitchhiking in Japan, no one came close to matching Kagoshima for its friendly, back-slapping welcome.

The great hero of Kagoshima—and a typical Satsuma-jin—is the burly, square-jawed samurai reformer Saigō Takamori. After helping to set in motion the Meiji Restoration that ended the shogun system and opened up Japan to the West, Saigō was horrified when things began to spin out of control. Among his grievances, the new constitutional government began allowing commoners into the armed forces, once an exclusively samurai-class preserve.

Saigō rebelled against the very revolution he helped create and led his troops in a doomed expedition that climaxed in the siege of Kumamoto Castle, which burned to the ground in 1877. Battered by the Meiji forces, he fell back to Kagoshima and—heroically in the eyes of the Japanese—committed suicide on Shiroyama Hill. His tomb is nearby, in Nanshū-bochi.

Where to Obtain Information

The **Tourist Information Center** outside of Nishi-Kagoshima-eki (Tel. 0992-53-2500) has English maps and brochures and is open 8:30 A.M.–6:00 P.M. daily. Kagoshima-eki is on the other side of downtown, nearer the ferry port to Sakurajima.

For a limited selection of English books, try the **Shunendō Shoten** bookstore (Tel. 0992-22-2131), open 10:00 A.M.–8:00 P.M. daily in the Tenmonkan Pira-mōru arcade walking mall. English books are on the third floor. They don't carry the atlas, but if you call at least three weeks before you arrive, they can order it and have it waiting when you arrive. I would advise trying to get the atlas before you arrive in Kagoshima.

What to See and Do

The **asa-ichi** (morning market) is held daily, except Sundays and New Year's, in front of Nishi-Kagoshima-eki. It peaks at around 7:00 A.M. and lasts until noon.

The mildly interesting—and for some, very disappointing—**Iso Tei-en** (garden) is south of the city near the beach. The garden was created in 1660 as a villa for a local feudal lord, and it uses the Japanese technique of "borrowed scenery," in this case the volcanic peak of Sakurajima in the background. Later, in the town of Chiran, you will see other fine examples of this technique.

Both the garden and the nearby beach have good views of Sakurajima, rumbling across the bay. A typhoon recently destroyed the ropeway to the top of the garden's central hill, but it should be operational soon. The garden costs ¥800 to enter, though with recent renovations, this price may be going up. It is open 8:30 A.M.–5:30 P.M. during the summer and until 5:00 P.M. during winter.

Dominating the local landscape is **Sakurajima,** a rumbling, angry volcano surrounded by rubble, scars, and hardened lava flows. A wide road, easily hitched, circles the volcano. The southern shore has more traffic, most of it consisting of sight-seers who will be stopping at the various lookout points along the way. Sakurajima continues to spew smoke and debris, and the air in Kagoshima is often heavy with gray volcanic ash. You may even see gardeners "dusting" their flowers.

On the northeastern corner of the volcano is the **Kurokami Buried Torii.** Once the gateway to a village shrine, an eruption buried everything save the top of the torii gate. The villagers returned and rebuilt their community, and the top of the buried torii gate now peers out of the earth from a small side street. Unfortunately, the torii is surrounded with concrete pillars which ruin the effect. The buried torii gate is just a bit off the path for most sightseers in Sakurajima. You will have to hitch-hike south around and past the land bridge. When explaining where you want to go, say *torii maibotsu-chi* (buried torii). Most drivers will make a detour for you. It is worth the effort to see; an entire village lies buried below your feet, underscoring the immense power of Sakurajima.

Getting There

To get to the volcanic island of Sakurajima, take a ferry from the Sakurajima Sanbashi ferry port. Ferries run often, take 13 minutes, and cost ¥150 one way, payable on the Sakurajima side. The last ferry leaves from Kagoshima to Sakurajima at 11:30 P.M., but if you were planning to stay at the Sakurajima hostel this will be too late—unless you have called ahead of time and managed to wheedle your way in.

Where to Stay

There are a couple of **drive-in love hotels** on the coastal road to Iso Tei-en, near the beach. Walk back along the bayside road toward downtown and you will pass one on your right in about ten minutes. The rooms begin at ¥6,000 for overnight.

A wider selection of love hotels are huddled together on

Shiroyama Kōen Hill, up from the large stone torii gate. Look for **Hotel France** with the Mickey and Minnie rooms, or the one with the **Statue of Liberty** out front. They are all in the ¥5,000–¥7,000 price range for an overnight stay. Love hotels are always entertaining and fairly luxurious, and Kagoshima seems to have a more creative selection than usual.

Beside Nishi-Kagoshima-eki is the **Oimatsu Ryokan** (Tel. 0992-54-7725), which costs ¥3,000 per night with no meals.

A three-minute walk from the station is the **Business Wakamatsu** (Tel. 0992-53-9796), which costs ¥4,000 per night.

A seven-minute walk from the station is the **Ryokan Hyūga Bekkan** (Tel. 0992-57-3509), which costs ¥4,000 per night.

Near Terukuni Jinja (shrine) is the **Hotel Mikasa** (Tel. 0992-25-5111), which has rooms for ¥5,000 without meals.

The **Nakazono Ryokan** (Tel. 0992-26-5125) is a member of the Japanese Inn Group and has Japanese rooms without a private bath for ¥4,000 for one, and ¥7,600 for two, meals not included. They accept American Express. This ryokan is near Kagoshima-eki, not far from the ferry port for Sakurajima. From the station, walk down the left side of the tram street that leads away from the station. You will pass a temple on your left. Turn left down the next side street and you will soon come to the ryokan on your left. If you reach wide Ōdōri Boulevard, you've gone too far.

The **Crystal Palace Capsule** (Tel. 0992-25-2500) is downtown, near the Hayashida Hotel and the Tenmonkan Densha tram stop. It is on the walking mall. It costs ¥4,500.

There is no longer a youth hostel in the city itself, but there is one across the bay at the foot of the volcano. The **Sakurajima Youth Hostel** (Tel. 0992-93-2150) is a seven-minute walk from the Sakurajima ferry terminal, near the site of old lava formations. No alcohol allowed. There were no bicycle rentals. The hostel costs just ¥1,850 per night—¥2,050 during July, August, and New Year's. This place gets my vote for the grubbiest hostel in Japan. Still, for all its seediness, this is an ideal location for visitors, and the morning view of Sakurajima almost makes up for it all.

EBINO

The full loop begins in Kagoshima, crosses Sakurajima, and then hitchhikes north to Ebino Kōgen. If you arrive at Kagoshima Kokusai-kūkō, you are already halfway to Ebino Kōgen, and you can save Kagoshima for your return. The airport is north of the city, just 40 km from the Ebino Kōgen (plateau). Hitch south from the airport until you get to Highway 223. Turn and hitchhike north. Once you are on Highway 223 pointed north, the hitching becomes easy.

Highway 223 will meet the Kirishima Skyline road. Continue north on the skyline and in 11 km you will arrive at Ebino Kōgen.

Note: You want to go to Ebino Kōgen, not Ebino city. Make this clear to your driver.

If you decide to go into Kagoshima *before* setting out for Ebino, combine your trip to Ebino Kōgen with a visit to Sakurajima. Take the ferry out to Sakurajima and then hitchhike along the southern shore of this volcanic island. This will take you past several scenic lookouts and finally connect you with the mainland on the other side.

Hitchhike north on Highway 220, along the northeastern shore of Kinkō-wan. There is not a lot of traffic along this route, but I have always found the hitching to be reliable. The people of Kagoshima are second to none in their kindness to hitchhikers. At Kokubu you will reach Highway 223, which runs inland. Take Highway 223 north to Ebino Kōgen.

KIRISHIMA NATIONAL PARK

Ebino Kōgen is inside Kirishima National Park, which straddles the Kagoshima and Miyazaki prefectural boundaries. The name Ebino comes from *ebi*, meaning "shrimp." In autumn the area's high-alkaline soil tints the pampas grass a pinkish-red color, reminiscent of shrimp. Near Ebino Kōgen, at the start of the mountain hike, is a lowland of sulfurous green rubble, with steam vents and thermal pockets.

What to See and Do

Ebino Kōgen is also the gateway to a dramatic five-volcano hike across the roof of Kyushu. The tourist center has simplified but adequate maps. This is the best mountain walk in Japan and is worth a day's outing. Bring a light pack with a good supply of water, a *bentō* lunch, rain gear, suntan lotion, and plasters for your feet in case of blisters. You need a good pair of walking shoes or lightweight hiking boots. High-top runners with good ankle support will do in a pinch, but the last run up Mount Takachiho-no-Mine can be tricky with lots of scree and steep slopes. Still, there are no ropes or grappling involved.

The five- to six-hour hike begins at Ebino and takes you up a busy footpath to the top of **Karakuni-dake** (1,700 meters). The name means "Korea-viewing mountaintop" and while this is an exaggeration, the view on a clear day is still impressive. You will be able to see distant Sakurajima, the Vesuvius of Kagoshima Bay.

Continue east along the path and you will go down into a valley and then up along a ridge and over **Shinmoe-dake** (1,420 meters). On your left you will see another volcanoe, Ya-take. The path is remarkably varied, running through tangled scrub, up narrow paths, and even skirting the rim of a vile-looking volcanic lake. You will see deer grazing right at the edge of steaming vents. Eventually you will come out at the parking lot near the base of Takachiho-no-Mine. For most of the way, the trail runs along the prefectural boundary between Kagoshima and Miyazaki, so you can see it marked on the atlas.

No matter how tempting it may be, don't skip the last and

toughest mountain, **Takachiho-no-Mine** (1,574 meters). Its summit marks the point where the gods first descended to rule Japan, and climbing it is a climb toward Heaven—or Hell, depending on your physical condition.

It is a one-and-a-half-hour climb up Takachiho-no-Mine and another hour down. A well-marked path takes you first through forest, then up a tiring and seemingly endless series of stairs, until—finally—you come to the dramatic slope of Takachiho-no-Mine. Now the hike becomes exciting. Halfway up, you will come to the edge of the magnificent Takachiho crater, with its steep inner slopes.

Push on, up the last slope, over rough scree to the peak. An old man sells cold beer for ¥600 a can, though he could probably get much more for it if he wanted to. The top is wind-swept and breathtaking and well worth the inevitable aches and groans you will experience the next day.

I advise breaking the hike up. Do the cross-volcano walk the first day, and then climb Mount Takachiho-no-Mine the next. Trying to do both in one go will be exhausting. From the Mount Takachiho-no-Mine area you can return to Ebino Kōgen by hitchhiking west along the Kirishima Skyline road.

Note: The Kirishima Skyline is actually Prefectural Highway 1. It is shown in green but not labeled in the atlas. This same highway runs through the Ebino Kōgen area and all the way to the Kobayashi IC, making it the key to hitchhiking in this area. When hitching back to Ebino Kōgen from the base of Takachiho-no-Mine, make sure that your drivers understand you are going back to Ebino Kōgen. One driver tried to take me down into Kirishima town.

Mi-ike lakes (three lakes) around Ebino Kōgen have a well-marked forest-walk which involves little climbing. If it is overcast or drizzly you may have to settle for a lake stroll. Don't miss the sulfurous pits and rubble at the base of Mount **Karakuni-dake**. The green, steaming landscape is straight from a Star Trek set.

Where to Stay

Hotels in Ebino Kōgen are fairly expensive. The usual souvenir shops and tourist-oriented restaurants abound as well. A bowl of *niku udon* (noodles) is about the most filling inexpensive meal offered.

The **Kokumin-shukusha Ebino Kōgen** (Tel. 0984-33-0161) costs ¥7,000 with two meals.

The **Ebino Kōgen Camp-jō** campsite (Tel. 0984-33-0800) is ¥150 per person and ¥500 for a space. This campsite becomes an entire self-sustaining mini-city during the weekend. You need to reserve ahead of time.

A ten-minute walk (or two-minute hitch) down the road—past the lakes—will take you to the quiet lodge and outdoor hot springs of **Ebino Kōgen Rotenburo** which I *highly* recommend. You can call the city office 9:00 A.M.–5:00 P.M. (Tel. 0984-35-1111) to make reservations. But if you are coming during the week or on the off-season, just show up. There are usually spaces available except in the peak Golden Week and mid-August season. Most people visit the outdoor hot springs without spending the night at the cabins. Lights are out at 9:00 P.M. so make sure you have candles or a flashlight. Space in the lodge costs ¥970. Separate five-man cabins cost ¥1,230. You can also rent a blanket for ¥200. There are no eating facilities nearby, so make sure you bring food and drink with you from Ebino Kōgen. The lodge has coin-operated propane stoves.

The outdoor hot springs are just a few steps from the front door of the cabins. If you are not spending the night, you may pay ¥200 to soak in the hot springs. The baths are beautiful—one has a bamboo spout to massage your shoulders. Most of them are mixed, but one is reserved for women only.

If your plane arrives in the late afternoon, or if you don't think you can make it to Ebino Kōgen before nightfall, you may want to camp along the way. On Highway 223, about 8 km past Makizono town is the **Kirishima Kōgen Kokumin Kyūyōchi Camp-jō**

(Tel. 0995-78-2004), which requires a reservation, even if it's just a day ahead. The campsite is open all year. It costs ¥200 per person and ¥1,500 for a space. Tent rentals are available. This campsite is far from the heart of things, however, and unless it's late in the day, I really recommend that you push on and stay at the *rotenburo* cabins at Ebino instead.

Escaping

Prefectural Highway 1, also called the Kirishima Skyline, runs past Ebino Kōgen and the Ebino Rotenburo Cabins. This is an easy road to hitch. It will take you all the way to the Kobayashi IC, and from there you can take the expressway into Miyazaki.

You can also hitchhike in on the highways which will almost be as fast as taking the expressway. When you get to Kobayashi, instead of going to the IC, ask to be dropped off east of town on Highway 268. (If you want to see the two-headed snake shrine described below, hitchhike southeast on Highway 221 instead. See following section for more details.)

There is enough traffic between Kobayashi and Miyazaki that hitching isn't a problem, and the drive through the mountains is beautiful. Halfway to Miyazaki, Highway 268 turns into Highway 10 without any change of direction; Highway 10 runs right into downtown Miyazaki .

En Route

As I was hitching from Ebino and I asked my standard question: "What is the most unusual or interesting thing in this area?" The woman thought a moment and then said, "Well, there is the two-headed snake shrine. Do you think you'd find that interesting?" There are actually two snake shrines, located in the same area: **Takama-ga-hara Jinja** (Tel. 0984-42-4540; your driver may want to call to get exact directions) is home to an unusual deity, a two-meter-long, golden python from India.

Although a Shinto shrine, Takama-ga-hara has an unusual

connection with Buddhist folklore. Legend has it that a golden snake appeared at the birth of Siddhartha, the Indian prince who became known as the Buddha. The current snake is said to be the direct ancestor of the original one present at the birth of Buddha, more than 2,600 years ago.

The shrine is open daily 9:00 A.M.–5:00 P.M. How the defender of Buddhism came to be enshrined in a remote Shinto shrine half a world away is something of a mystery.

Kasumi Jinja, in the same area, has an even rarer deity enshrined in the form of a living, two-headed snake. It protects against misfortune and disaster, and when an earthquake destroyed large parts of Kobe in 1995 and left thousands dead and many more homeless, the caretakers of Kasumi Jinja sent their two-headed snake to Kobe on a mission of mercy.

Getting There

These two remarkable snake shrines are located near the Takaharu IC. From the IC, take Prefectural Highway 29 north toward Nojiri. (This highway is marked in green but not numbered in the atlas.) You will soon come to a large intersection with traffic lights. Left (west) will take you to the Hasutarō Onsen (hot springs). Right (east) will take you to Kasumi Jinja. To get to Takama-ga-hara Jinja, stay on the road. The road splits into two; it doesn't matter which route you take. Takama-ga-hara Jinja is farther up, between the two branches of road. If you are coming in on the expressway, you will have to get off at the Takaharu IC, and then circle around underneath the expressway. If you want to hitch in on national highways (which is how I did it), take Highway 221 south from Kobayashi toward the Takaharu IC.

MIYAZAKI

Miyazaki (population 287,000) has a sense of faded grandeur about it. It was once the honeymoon capital of Japan, but the romance and allure have passed. Palm trees line the main streets, but the paint is peeling on the hotels and pachinko is the sport of choice. The good news is that, because the boom has passed, Miyazaki has lots of half-empty hotels, making it one of the most affordable places to find cheap accommodations. In fact, Miyazaki has the lowest cost of living and accommodations in all of Japan.

This side of Kyushu is much warmer and more pleasant than the rest, even in winter. The Black Current from Okinawa washes along its shores, keeping the waters here at semitropical temperatures most of the year.

The **Miyazaki hostel** is downtown, not far from the Kenchō (prefectural office). The Kenchō is easier to find than the hostel, so if you want to check into the hostel when you arrive, ask to be dropped off at the Kenchō. If your driver drops you off at Miyazaki-eki, it is a 15-minute walk from the station to the Kenchō. Anyone should be able to show you the way. During office hours you can get English maps and materials at the **Kankō Visitors' Center** inside the Kenchō.

Where to Obtain Information

There is a **Tourist Information Center** (Tel. 0985-22-6469) inside Miyazaki-eki open 9:00 A.M.–5:15 P.M. daily; they carry a selection of English maps and pamphlets.

What to See and Do

Miyazaki is noted for its clay figurines, called *haniwa*, which date back to the Kofun Period (300–700) and can be found in ancient Japanese burial tombs. The burial tombs, like the larger key-shaped tumulus in Nara, are of Korean origin, a fact hotly denied by Japanese nationalists. In Kyonju, Korea, you can see tombs in almost the exact same style.

Some *haniwa* themselves are cartoon-like in appearance and some are downright amusing. If you are interested in *haniwa*, the

Miyazaki Heiwa-dai Kōen has replicas on display in Haniwa Garden, and of course you can buy souvenir *haniwa* to carry in your pack and worry about breaking for the rest of your trip. The Haniwa Garden is behind the wooded Grand Shrine, Miyazaki Jingū, west of Miyazaki-jinja-eki.

You may also want to make a side trip to the Saitobaru Kofun-gun burial mounds, where you can view excavations of tumuli that contained *haniwa*. You can even enter a couple of the tombs. The burial mounds are 30 km to the north of Miyazaki, in Saito. They are marked in the atlas as "Saitobaru Old Mound Group."

Miyazaki has a small but lively night-life district, not far from the Kenchō. Ask for directions to the Washington Hotel, which is on the southern edge of the night-life district. Look for Meiji-ya, a Japanese-style diner inside an old steam locomotive engine. It's hard to miss, and though you'll be cramped inside, the food is cheap and refreshingly unhealthy. Lots of unsaturated fats, cold beer, and noisy customers. It's on the street running north, to the left of the Washington Hotel. From Meiji-ya, continue north and you will be in the heart of the entertainment area.

The local specialty of Miyazaki is *chikin namban*, deep-fried chicken with a mayonnaise sauce said to have been introduced by foreign missionaries.

Where to Stay

In Miyazaki, some business hotels are almost as inexpensive as youth hostels—and no curfew. Try the Asahi Hotel (Tel. 0985-26-1251) near the Kenchō. Prices start at ¥4,200 for a single. This hotel is slightly difficult to find; ask for directions at the police headquarters at the prefectural office.

Turn left on the main road that runs past Miyazaki-eki (parallel to the tracks) and you will soon come to the Miyazaki Oriental Hotel (Tel. 0985-27-3111) on your right. It has singles for ¥5,900 and doubles for ¥9,500.

Across the street and one block east of the Kenchō, is the **Fujin Kaikan Youth Hostel** (Tel. 0985-24-5785), which costs ¥2,300. Closed December 30–January 3. Some English is spoken, and bicycle rentals are available. This small hostel has only 26 beds, so make sure you call before leaving the Ebino Kōgen area.

Escaping

Miyazaki is spread out; hitchhiking out of the city is frustrating. Highway 10 north is one long clutter of pachinko parlors and traffic lights, and it isn't much better going south.

The good news is that you can combine a visit to the **island shrine of Aoshima** with a southern escape from Miyazaki. Take a train south to Aoshima-eki beside Highway 220; trains run from Miyazaki-eki 16 times a day, cost ¥310, and take 20 to 30 minutes.

AOSHIMA

For some reason, guidebooks inevitably dismiss Aoshima as a tourist trap, yet it is no more over-developed than the shrines of Kyoto or Nikko. In fact, Aoshima is the brilliant beginning of one of Japan's finest hitchhiking routes. Aoshima is a small tuft of green that clings to the Devil's Washboard, a geological formation of ridged, rocky coastline that extends for more than 50 km to the south, from Aoshima to Cape Toi.

Before you start hitchhiking, walk out to the small garden-like shrine of **Aoshima Jinja**. The shrine is built on a tiny jungle island near the point where the Black Current touches Kyushu, making these the warmest waters north of Okinawa. A footbridge leads to the island, and a path encircles it. Here you can see some of the geologic wonder of the Devil's Washboard up close.

Where to Stay

If you want to see Aoshima at night, or watch the sun rise, the

Aoshima Youth Hostel (Tel. 0985-65-1657) is a five-minute walk from Kodomo-no-kuni-eki. It costs ¥2,200 per night. No alcohol allowed. This hostel is a favorite spot for school excursions, so go out early enough that you can change your mind and catch a train back into the city if the place is filled with noisy students.

Note: Kodomo-no-kuni-eki is shown but not labeled in the atlas. It is the first station north from Aoshima.

Escaping

Highway 220 along the **Nichinan Kaigan of Miyazaki (coast)** is one of the best hitchhiking routes in Japan—provided you don't arrive in the tourist season. This road has it all: beautiful scenery, historic shrines set in dramatic locations, distant wind-swept capes, wild monkeys, free-roaming horses, and—best of all—steady traffic. The Japanese you share the road with will be sightseers like yourself, so they will be open to detours and stops at scenic lookouts.

Oni-no-Sentaku, the Devil's Washboard, gives the entire coast a striking appearance best seen at low tide. Though it is in open countryside, the entire Nichinan coast is one big traffic jam during Golden Week and just after New Year's, when people flock to **Udo Jingū** for their first shrine visit.

Udo Jingū is just off Highway 220, built in a striking location overlooking the ocean. Udo Jingū is dedicated to the father of Japan's legendary first emperor, who descended from the gods—well, from Korea, actually, but why split hairs? Udo Jingū ranks with Dazaifu as the most important shrine in Kyushu.

The usual carnival atmosphere surrounds the entrance to Udo. The entrance to the cave is along a boardwalk overlooking the ocean. At the shrine, you can buy small clay balls to toss at a rope circle laid out on top of Tortoise Rock. Men are supposed to use their left hand as more of a challenge, but women can use either. If you get a pebble inside the rope ring, you will be blessed with good fortune, prosperity, fertility, longevity, and all the usual stuff.

To reach Udo Jingū, hitchhike south on 220.

Escaping

Hitchhike south from Udo Jingū on Highway 220. Be careful; the highway that runs near the shrine exit is wide and busy. An older highway runs nearer to the shrine entrance. Do *not* hitchhike on this older highway; traffic is almost nonexistent. These two parallel sections of highway are shown in the atlas. Make sure you get onto the one farther west. At Nangō, the highway splits. Don't stay on 220; continue south on Highway 448.

KŌJIMA

South of Nangō, along the coast on Highway 448, you will pass near **Kōjima,** the Monkey Island. A boat will take you across in a few minutes and drop you off on a shore jumbled with boulders. Scramble across the boulders and you will come to a small sandy cove where the monkeys congregate, enticed by scattered seeds in the sand.

Although small, these are wild, bad-tempered monkeys. Do not stare into their eyes or they may lunge at you, and whatever you do, do not bring any food with you, even in your packs. Leave it in the boat or on shore.

There are monkeys on the smaller island of **Tori-shima** as well; the monkeys occasionally swim between the two islands— really. The word for monkey is *saru* and island is *shima* so if you need directions just say *saru no shima* and everyone will understand.

If you visit Aoshima in the morning, you should have no problem hitchhiking to Toi-misaki (cape) that same day, with a visit to Udo Jingū and Monkey Island thrown in. But I advise breaking it up and taking a more leisurely pace. You can stop near Nangō *before* you reach Monkey Island and see the monkeys and make it to Toi-misaki the following day.

Where to Stay

The beach across from Kōjima is peaceful at night. I once camped out under the stars on this beach, although it is not an officially designated campsite.

Just north of Nangō, and with a splendid coastal view, is the **Nichinan-Kaigan Youth Hostel** (Tel. 0987-27-0133), which costs ¥2,300 per night. This hostel is on the coast of the small peninsula that juts out just above Ōdotsu-eki. Ask to be dropped off at the Youth Hostel-mae *teiryūjo*, remembering to pronounce it *yū-su ho-su-te-ru*. The hostel is a seven-minute walk east from the bus stop. Drop a hint and you will be driven right to the front door.

About 2 km south of Nangō-eki on Highway 448 is the **Sakae-matsu Camp-jō,** located on the Sakae-matsu Kaisui-yokujō beach. For more information call the **Kankō visitors' section** at the town office (Tel. 0987-64-1111). During July and August the campsite charges ¥800 for a space. Rent a five-man tent for ¥1,500. For the rest of the year the campsite is free, but services are limited. There is no drinking water or showers during the off-season.

TOI-MISAKI

After Monkey Island you can easily hitchhike all the way to the grassy fields and palm trees of Toi-misaki, usually with a single ride, because most of the traffic will be heading there anyway. Prefectural Highway 37 runs from Highway 448 down to the cape. This highway is marked in green but not numbered in the atlas. Aside from the rolling hills, lighthouses, and ocean views, the main attraction at Toi-misaki are the **"wild" horses**. It should be noted that in this case, "wild" means "free-ranging." Spend a few minutes to wander away from the tourist zones to thoroughly enjoy the beauty of the cape.

Where to Stay

The **Min-ei Kokumin-shukusha Shimizu Ryokan** (Tel. 0987-76-1000) at Toi-misaki costs ¥6,100 per night with two meals included.

The **Toi-Misaki Youth Hostel** (Tel. 0987-76-1397) is near the south lighthouse (*minami tōdai*). It costs ¥2,000 (¥3,250 with two meals). If you do spend the night at Toi-misaki, get up early and watch the sunrise from one of the scenic lookouts. At 6:00 A.M. there are no tour groups, and dawn at Toi-misaki is sublime. At least that was what I was told by my travel companion—I slept right through it.

Escaping

From Toi-misaki, it is an easy hitch on Highway 448 to Kushima. At Kushima, Highway 448 meets Highway 220. If your ride is only going as far as Kushima, ask to be dropped off on the coast on Highway 220. In Japanese, the question would be *Kaigan-zoi no ni-ni-zero gō-sen made ii desu ka*? You can hitchhike along Highway 220 all the way to Kanoya.

En Route

If it is late in the day, you can stay at **Daguri-zaki,** on the coast of Shibushi-wan. Close to the tourist zone complete with Ferris wheel, roller coaster, and waterslide is the **Kokumin-shukusha Dagurisō** (Tel. 0994-72-1478), which costs ¥6,500 per night with two meals.

Nine kilometers south of Ōsaki on Highway 448, and near the mouth of the Kimotsuki-gawa, is the **Kashiwabara Kaigan Camp-jō** (Tel. 0994-63-8818), which is open only July 21–August 31. No tent rentals, and no swimming—there are dangerous undertows. This campsite is free, but it is not in a very convenient location if you are heading into Kanoya. Still, the price is right and you should be able to catch rides with other campers both down and back.

Kanoya (population 78,000) is the largest city in the area; all traffic seems to flow into it. There is really no need to linger in Kanoya.

Kanoya was once a departure point for kamikaze pilots, and the city has a museum and memorial for them, but you will pass through Chiran later, which also has a kamikaze museum and is a more attractive town.

Kanoya is not a crowded city, but it is spread out over a wide area. I was dropped off in downtown Kanoya before I knew what was happening, and I was completely disoriented. When you hitchhike into Kanoya, ask your driver to drop you off west of town on Highway 269, hopefully on the coast. The request, similar to the one used earlier for Kushima, is *Kaigan-zoi no ni-roku-kyū gō-sen made ii desu ka*? If you tell them that you are headed for Sata-misaki, they will understand where you need to be.

Enroute

On Highway 269, above Ōnejime and near the mouth of the Kaminokawa (river) is the **Kamikawa Camp-jō** (Tel. 09942-2-1446). If there is no answer, call the **town office** (Tel. 09942-2-0511) instead. This campsite is open July 1–August 31, and costs ¥100 per person and ¥500 for a space. Rent a five-man tent for ¥1,000. As is usually the case, you should be able to camp during the off-season if you are discreet.

SATA-MISAKI

Highway 269 will take you south along the coast all the way to Sata-chō (town). Sata-misaki, farther down along a scenic toll road, is the southernmost tip of mainland Japan. The road leading to Sata twists its way down in a series of hairpin curves, and the view from the cape is striking: rocky islands jut out of the water, waves crash far below, and out at the end of it all is the oldest lighthouse in Japan, built in 1871. On a clear day you can reportedly see Tane-ga-shima and Yaku-shima (islands). Both were invisible in haze when I visited Sata, and indeed one Japanese lady I rode with told me that she had lived near Sata for three years and had never seen either island, so count yourself lucky if you do. Admission to Sata-misaki is controlled by a tunnel entrance that closes at 6:00 P.M. (4:30 P.M. October–March).

Where to Stay

At the entrance of the Sata-misaki Road Parkway (the toll road that leads to the cape) is a second road that runs south, to the **Kokumin-shukusha Sata-misaki-sō** (Tel. 09942-7-3121) which costs around ¥7,000 with two meals included. Pricey, but convenient for exploring the cape.

Near the Kokumin-shukusha is the **Ōdomari Camp-jō**. Call the **town office** (Tel. 09942-6-0511) for more information. This campsite is officially open only July 20–August 31. There is no charge and tent rentals are not available. Coming in from the north, you don't have to take the toll road.

Escaping

North of Sata-misaki on Highway 269 is the small town of Nejime; from here, catch a ferry to Yamagawa. The **Nejime ferries** run six times a day, across the bay from Nejime to Yamagawa. From March 1 to November 30, the last ferry is at 6:20 P.M. During the winter, the last ferry is at 4:40 P.M. The ferry takes 40 minutes and costs ¥400. If you miss the ferry, hitch north on Highway 269 to the Kamikawa Camp-jō listed earlier.

YAMAGAWA

Yamagawa is an attractive port town south of Ibusuki across the bay from Sata-misaki. From Yamagawa-kō (port) it is an easy hitch north to Ibusuki. (You can pick up English maps and information on the entire Ibusuki area at the Information Office in Ibusuki-eki.)

What to See and Do

Yamagawa is near the picture-perfect mountain, Kaimon-dake. Visit **Kaimon-dake** first and then head to Ibusuki.

Near Yamagawa are two less-visited attractions: One is quiet **Unagi-ike** (pond), north of Highway 226 and east of Ikedako (lake); it's famous for its delicious eels. The other site is the sand-bath beach and hot springs of **Fushime Onsen**. Sand baths are open until 7:00 P.M. (until 5:00 P.M. during the rest of the year) July–September. Fushime Onsen is just ten minutes from Yamagawa port by car. Hitchhike south from the port, checking with passersby to make sure you are on the right road. Throughout Ibusuki, many of the signs are posted in English, which makes it easy to get your bearings.

IBUSUKI

For a resort town, Ibusuki (population 32,000) is still very rural. The surrounding area has a subdued beauty that contrasts nicely with the wilder, more rugged scenery across the bay at Sata. The entire landscape seems to change when you take the ferry across to the Ibusuki peninsula.

Where to Obtain Information

The **Ibusuki Tourist Office** (Tel. 09932-2-4114) is not a member of the TIC network, but they have English maps and materials and are very helpful. The office is inside Ibusuki-eki, and is open 9:00 A.M.–7:30 P.M. daily.

What to See and Do

The big attraction in Ibusuki is the natural, hot-sand baths (*suna-mushi-buro*) on the beach in front of the Ginshō Hotel. Try the sand baths but don't feel you have to endure more than you can handle. For around ¥600, women will bury you to your neck in scalding sand. Leap out any time you have had enough, which for most Westerners is about two minutes. A short shower follows, and you should feel on top of the world. The sand baths are meant to be a remedy for a number of ailments including rheumatism and various digestive disorders.

South along the beach from the hot sands, you will come to the Kankō Hotel, which has an entire complex of hot baths surrounded by jungle-like growths and named, appropriately, the **Jungle Onsen**. It's about double the price of the beach baths, but this includes admission to the hotel's own indoor hot-sand baths. If the outdoor sand baths are closed due to bad weather, try the more expensive ones at the Kankō Hotel.

Where to Stay

Unlike Miyazaki, Ibusuki is still a thriving resort town, so the hotels are expensive and usually full. Fortunately, there are three youth hostels in Ibusuki, but you should call ahead for reservations, especially in or around peak seasons.

The **Tamaya Youth Hostel** (Tel. 0993-22-3553) is in the best location, a mere "70 paces" from the hot-sand-bath beach. This Japanese-style hostel has its own hot spring and costs ¥2,000 per night. No bicycle rentals.

A four-block, ten-minute walk north from Ibusuki-eki brings you to the more dreary *and* more expensive **Ibusuki Youth Hostel** (Tel. 0993-22-2785, 2271). It costs ¥2,600 per night and has its own hot spring. This is the only hostel that rents bicycles.

You can usually rent a bicycle here, even if you are staying elsewhere.

One half-block farther north and around the corner is the new **Yunosato Youth Hostel** (Tel. 0993-22-2580), which costs ¥2,800 per night.

The **New Yunohama-sō** (Tel. 0993-23-3088) is a member of the Japanese Inn Group and has Japanese rooms for ¥3,000 per person without a private bath and ¥4,000 for rooms with a bath. It has its own hot spring as well, and is located beside the famous sand-bath area, not far from the Tamaya Hostel. The "Yunohama-sō" part of the sign is written in Japanese, but the "New" part is written in English, so you should be able to spot it without too much trouble. They accept American Express and VISA.

KAIMON-DAKE AND IKEDAKO

Forget Mount Fuji—**Kaimon Dake** is the real reason to come to the Ibusuki area. Mount Fuji looks great from afar, but up close it's a pile of litter, scree, and tourists, and is cluttered with factories at the bottom. In contrast, verdant Kaimon-dake, "the Kyushu Fuji," is a perfectly shaped volcanic cone, lush green and—at just 922 meters—an easy, two-hour climb.

North of Kaimon-dake is **Ikedako** (lake), with a mirror-like view of the Kaimon-dake. The mountain and the lake are perfect opposites, one as deep as the other is high, or so the story goes. The two allegedly represent the Feminine and Masculine for reasons poetic and obvious.

Recently, Ikedako has become famous for sightings of a Loch Ness-type creature, dubbed "Isshi," by the quick-thinking people at the Kagoshima Tourist Office. Sightings began in 1973 and peaked with the formation of the Isshi Investigation Team, which—amid plenty of hoopla and PR—set out to fish for Isshi using a 1.5-meter hook. They didn't locate anything but they did "discover" Isshi's gender. Observers noticed that their rafts began to veer wildly whenever a woman was on board, and— using impeccable male logic—concluded that Isshi must be female, "prone to fits of jealousy."

Where to Stay

Make an effort to reserve a space at **Nagasakibana Camp-jō** (Tel. 0993-35-0111), nestled along the southernmost cape along the peninsula. It is well worth the required effort to reserve a spot at this site, because it is perfectly situated. The hours of operation are convoluted: It is closed April 27 –May 8. From May 9 to July 20 it is open Sundays and National Holidays only. From July 20 to August 31 it is open every day except Monday. In September it is open only on Saturdays, Sundays, and National Holidays. (Can you tell this is a government-run campsite?) One night costs ¥300 per person and ¥400 for a space. No tent rentals.

Escaping

From Ikedako, continue around to Highway 226, which runs straight up the inside of Kinkō-wan (bay) to Kagoshima. It changes into Highway 225 halfway up, but this doesn't concern you. Just stick to the coast.

As always, it is easy to hitchhike *into* a major city. Once you get on the coast above Ibusuki it should only take one ride to get you all the way to Kagoshima, so this may be a good time to hold up a sign reading "Kagoshima" to save yourself the trouble of making short hops. Most people who stop assume you want to go all the way to Kagoshima anyway. Tell your driver you are going to Kagoshima-shi.

Alternatively, you can bypass Kagoshima city if you are headed straight for the airport. From Ikedako, a secondary highway runs north across the mountaintops and turns into the Ibusuki Skyline road, which offers impressive mountaintop views of

Kinkō-wan. (The highway is marked in green in the atlas.) The Ibusuki Skyline turns into the Kyushu Expressway, the most direct route to the airport in the area. Take the skyline until you reach the Kagoshima IC; from there take the expressway north to the Mizobe-Kagoshima-kūkō IC, which puts you right beside the airport. Thus, you can hitchhike directly from Ikedako to the airport without having to change directions.

En Route

If you are hitching directly from Ibusuki to Kagoshima along Highway 226, you will pass through the port town of Kiire, which has a **campsite** on the Nukumi Kaisui-yokujō beach. The campsite is open from the first Sunday of July to August 31. For more information, call the Kankō Kyōkai tourist office (Tel. 0993-43-0028).

CHIRAN

Instead of rushing back to Kagoshima or the airport, I recommend a side trip to the mountain town of Chiran (population 14,500). Chiran is a tea-growing center; throughout the area you will see carefully trimmed, hedged rows of tea.

Getting There

You can get to Chiran easily from Ibusuki if you hitchhike along the Ibusuki Skyline. Get off the skyline at the Chiran intersection and hitchhike south and west on Prefectural Highway 23 into Chiran.

Note: Prefectural Highway 23 is shown in green but not numbered in the atlas.

What to See and Do

Samurai Gardens: The gardens and old houses of Chiran, called *buke-yashiki*, run parallel to the town's peaceful main street. People still live in most of the houses and are surprisingly cheerful about strangers peering in at their front yards.

As you enter the neighborhood and pay your ¥310 admission to the seven gardens, you will receive a pamphlet in English. The gardens are open daily 9:00 A.M.–5:00 P.M. Look for the use of "borrowed scenery," such as distant mountains, which add depth to garden composition.

In the **Kamikaze Memorial Museum** the irony is acute. The same samurai spirit that pervades the quiet gardens also led to the suicidal sacrifice of young kamikaze pilots in World War II. In the dying, desperate days of the war, the Japanese military was convinced that the attack of suicide pilots would be the next kamikaze (wind of the gods).

The tone of the Memorial Museum is unsettling. The tragic young men who flew kamikaze missions are presented as stalwart Japanese heroes fighting for "peace." Note the heroic stance of the kamikaze immortalized in bronze outside the museum and the statue of the Tome Torihama, the "Mother of the Kamikaze"; she took care of the young boys in the days before their deaths.

You may see Japanese women weeping as they read the journals the boys left behind. It is said that most died in flames crying out for their mothers, not yelling "Long Live the Emperor." Unfortunately, the displays at the museum are only in Japanese.

The correct term for kamikaze is *tokkōtai*, or Special Attack Force. The museum is known in doublespeak as the Chiran Tokkō Heiwa Kaikan, or the Special Forces Peace Museum. It is open 9:00 A.M.–5:00 P.M. daily and costs ¥310.

Where to Stay

Chiran can be seen in an afternoon; if you start from Ibusuki early in the morning, you should be able to visit Chiran and still get back to Kagoshima before dark. However if you would like to spend a night in this quiet town, try the **Tomiya Ryokan** (Tel.

0993-83-4313) on the main street, across from the Chiran *teiryūjo* (bus stop). From Tomiya, it is only a short walk, over the bridge and to the right, to get to the samurai street. Costs range from ¥8,000 to ¥10,000 per night, with two meals included. The name "Tomi-ya" refers in part to the Tomiya Ryokan, which Tome Torihama, "the Mother of the Kamikaze," operated.

Escaping

Prefectural Highway 23 is the main street of Chiran (the one with the carp moat alongside it) and runs parallel to the samurai street. If you want to go into Kagoshima , hitchhike east on Highway 23, *past* the skyline, and down to Highway 226. Highway 226 follows the coast north to Kagoshima, and most traffic will be going to Kagoshima. If, however, you want to hitchhike directly from Chiran to the Kagoshima-kūkō (airport), turn north on the Ibusuki Skyline. The Ibusuki Skyline turns into the Kyushu Expressway which leads to the Mizobe-Kagoshima-kūkō IC.

If you are already in Kagoshima and need to get to the Kagoshima-kūkō, a bus leaves Nishi-Kagoshima-eki every ten minutes 6:10 A.M.–6:20 P.M. The bus takes one hour and costs ¥1,100. The schedule changes at times to connect with flight alterations.

Timing: A complete Southern Kyushu Loop will take 10–14 days. Count on at least three days in the Ebino Kōgen area and another day in Miyazaki. Two days down the Nichinan coast to Cape Toi, a day to get from Toi down to Sata, another day from Sata to Ibusuki. Spend two days in the Ibusuki area, and add one full day to get from Ibusuki to Kagoshima, with a stop in Chiran.

Notes on Kyoto and Nara

The itineraries detailed in this guidebook are aimed at exploring the far reaches and back roads of Japan. Japan's two great historical cities, Kyoto and Nara, are at the heart of the standard tourist beat and are not really hitchhiker's destinations. This doesn't mean they should be skipped. Kyoto and Nara should be on the itinerary of every traveler to Japan. Fortunately, they can be incorporated into a hitchhiking journey through Kyushu, Shikoku, or Tohoku. Hokkaido is too far away to include a trip to Kyoto. Tohoku is a stretch, but you can do it.

The specific details, ferry times, and expressway connections are given in each of the itineraries.

- **From Kyushu,** ferries run to Osaka, which is a short train ride from Kyoto.
- **From Matsuyama** in Shikoku you can take a ferry across the Inland Sea to Hiroshima and then hitchhike to Kyoto on the expressways, or you can simply take a ferry directly to Osaka.
- **From Tohoku,** make sure you come in "from the back door," down the Japan Sea Coast and then in along Biwako (lake).

If it is your first trip to Japan, you must visit Kyoto and Nara. Though tourist meccas, they are national treasuries of Japanese culture, steeped in history. Both cities are full of beautiful temples, pagodas, Zen gardens, and Buddhist statuary.

Kyoto and Nara are near each other and are easily visited by local train. There are entire guidebooks written just on these two cities, and English information abounds. Like Hiroshima, these cities are geared for Western visitors and you will be able to find all the maps and materials you need. The main **TIC information center** across the street from the JR Kyoto-eki is the best stocked in Japan. Stock up on information for both cities in Kyoto, because English services and information are not as readily available in Nara.

I have only three pieces of advice to add to the mountain of commentary already available:

1. Be aware that Kyoto is a busy, modern city. It has hundreds of impressive temples and some of the finest Buddhist art in northeast Asia, but it is not a particularly attractive city. First-time visitors are often disappointed, but don't worry. The old Kyoto *is* there, amid the trappings of modern Japan. Don't let the initial impressions deceive you. Plan on spending *at least* three days in Kyoto, just to skim the surface. Give Kyoto a week of your life and she will reward you grandly.

2. Even more importantly, don't skimp on Nara! Many travelers, following well-intentioned but flawed advice from JNTO, focus their attention on Kyoto and leave Nara to the end and see it as a quick day-trip. Big mistake. When it comes to allotting your time in Kyoto and Nara, ignore Japanese advice. The Japanese have different tastes than Western tourists, and the fact that so many absolutely famous places are crowded into Kyoto and its suburbs is central to their recommendations. Western travelers, however, want to get lost in the atmosphere of a place. In Japanese culture, travel is very much an assignment, a field

trip to see as much as humanly possible in the quickest amount of time. Most Japanese look for efficiency in their travels plans. The spacious parks and slower pace of Nara are more attuned to the tastes of independent travelers not on a rigid schedule. Spend time exploring Nara and I think you may—as I do—actually prefer it to Kyoto. Divide your time between the two: The best would be three days in overwhelming Kyoto and then another three days in older, more staid Nara.

3. Realize that you can't see every famous place. Limit yourself and choose carefully. Reserve a couple of afternoons—or even an entire day—for just wandering aimlessly around some of the older areas. Kyoto can be exhausting. Don't run yourself ragged. A good example of this is the magnificent temple of **Kiyomizu-dera,** with its grand scaffolding and highly entertaining Shinto "love" shrine inside its premises. Many tourists rush in, admire the temple, and then rush off across town to their next Famous Site. Yet right beside Kiyōmizu-dera (to the right as you leave) is a narrow lane filled with teahouses and craft shops that will lead you down into the labyrinth that is Old Kyoto.

Oh yes, one last note. Make sure you carry a small flashlight for when you visit the older wooden temples with their darkened halls of statuary. Have fun "unwrapping" these two magnificent, historical cities.

APPENDIX I

Essential Vocabulary

bijinesu hoteru	business hotel
byōin	hospital
chūsha-jō	parking lot
dōkutsu, -dō	cave
de-guchi	exit
eki	station
ferī pōto	ferry port
gensei kaen (also *gensei kōen*)	natural flower park
hama	beach
hantō	peninsula
hashi, -bashi	bridge
hon-ya, shoten	bookstore
ike, -chi	pond
intāchenji (written as "IC")	interchange
iri-guchi	entrance

jidō-hanbaiki	vending machine
jinja, jingū, -gū	shrine
jankushon (written "JCT")	junction
kado	corner
kaigan, -ura	coast
kaihin kōen	marine park
kaku-eki teisha	local train
kankō annaisho	visitors' center
kapuseru hoteru	capsule hotel
kazan	volcano
kawa, -gawa	river
keisatsusho	police station
ken	prefecture
ken-dō	prefectural highway
kōban	police box
kōen	park
koku-dō	national highway
kōsaten	intersection, crossing
kōsoku dōro	expressway
kokumin-shukusha	public lodging house
kokuritsu kōen	national park
kūkō	airport
kusuri-ya, yakkyoku	pharmacy, drugstore
kyampu-jō, ōto kyampu-jō	campsite
kyampu-yōhin-ten	camping equipment store
kyōkoku, -kyō	gorge or canyon
kyūkō	express train
machi, -machi, -chō	town
minato, -kō	port
mine, -dake	peak
minshuku	family-run inn/bed and breakfast
misaki, -saki, -zaki	cape
mizu-umi, -ko	lake
mura, -son	village
niwa	garden

noriba	track/train platform
numa	small pond or marshland
ōfuku	round-trip ticket
onsen	hot spring or spa
rabu hoteru	love hotel
rindō	forestry road
rotenburo	outdoor hot spring
rōpu-uei	cable car
ryokan	Japanese-style inn
sābisu eria	service area
saka, -zaka	slope
shinkansen	Bullet Train
shi, -shi	city
shima, -jima, -tō	island
shingō	traffic lights
shiro, -jō	castle
shiyakusho	city office
shokudō	restaurant
shokuryōhin-ten	food store
sukai-rain rōdo	skyline road
taki, -no-taki	waterfall
teiryūjo, basu-tei	bus stop
tenbōdai	observation point, lookout
tera, -ji,	temple
tokubetsu kyūkō, tokkyū	limited (slower) express train
umi, -kai	sea
wan, ura	bay
yakuba	town office
yama, -dake, -san, -zan,	mountain
yūbin-kyoku	post office
yūsu hosuteru	youth hostel

Important Phone Numbers and Addresses

When calling from a pay phone, you do not need any money to dial 110 (**Police**) or 119 (**Fire/Ambulance**). Just press the red button on the phone and then dial.

The **Japan Helpline Card** has a handy list of emergency phrases as well. See Chapter 6 for information on how to obtain the card.

To make a toll-free (0120-) call in Japan, insert a ¥10 coin and dial. The dial tone comes on after the coin has been inserted. The coin will be returned after the call. Use a green phone only.

The Japan Helpline (emergencies only) . .   0120-461-997
Tokyo English Life Line   03-3968-4099

The JNTO operates a nationwide toll-free English assistance telephone service for travelers, 9:00 A.M.–5:00 P.M. daily:

Eastern Japan   0088-22-2800
Western Japan   0088-22-4800
Tokyo   3503-4400
Kyoto   371-5649

The **Japan National Tourist Organization** (JNTO) operates offices abroad and within Japan. The overseas offices listed below have maps and information in English:

North America

Rockefeller Plaza
630 Fifth Ave., Suite 2101
New York NY 10111
Tel. 212-757-5640

401 N. Michigan Ave., Suite 770
Chicago, IL 60611
Tel. 312-222-0874

2121 San Jacinto St., Suite 980
Dallas TX 75201
Tel. 214-754-1820

360 Post Street, Suite 601
San Francisco, CA 94108
Tel. 415-989-7140

624 S. Grand Ave, Suite 1611
Los Angeles, CA 90017
Tel. 213-623-1952

165 University Avenue
Toronto, Ont. M5H 3B8
Tel. 416-366-7140

Australia

Level 33, The Chifley Tower
2 Chifley Square
Sydney, N.S.W. 2000
Tel. 02-232-4522

United Kingdom

167 Regent Street
London W1
Tel. 0171-734-9638

Asia

Two Exchange Square
Suite 3606
8 Connaught Place
Central Hong Kong
Tel. 2522-7913

Wall Street Tower Building
33/61, Suriwong Road
Bangkok, Thailand 10500
Tel. 02-233-5108

10 Da-Dong
Chung-ku, Seoul, Korea
Tel. 02-752-7968

JNTO's Tourist Information Center in Tokyo and Kyoto are open 9:00 A.M.–5:00 P.M. Monday–Friday and until noon on Saturdays.

JNTO Tokyo Tourist Information Center

Tokyo Kokusai Forum B1
3-5-1 Marunouchi
Chiyoda-ku, Tokyo 100
Tel. 03-3201-3331

The Kyoto office is across the street from the JR Kyoto station:
JNTO Kyoto Tourist Information Center
1st Floor, Kyoto Tower Bldg.
Higashi-Shiokojicho
Shimogyo-ku, Kyoto 600
Tel. 075-371-5649

The JNTO operates **82 regional Tourist Information Centers** across Japan. These offices can provide English information and provide travel assistance. They try to keep English speakers on staff, but this is not always possible. These offices are usually designated by a "i" information symbol.

Aizu-Wakamatsu	0242-32-0688
Aizu-Wakamatsu (Tsurugajo castle)	0242-29-1151
Aomori	0177-34-2500
Arita	0955-43-3942
Atami	0557-81-6002
Beppu	0977-24-2838
Chiba	043-224-3939
Fujiyoshida	0555-22-7000
Fukuoka (city)	092-431-3003
Fukuoka (Prefecture) Bus Center	092-473-6696
Fukuoka International Assoc.	092-733-2220
Fukuyama	0849-22-2869
Hakodate	0138-23-5440
Hikone	0749-22-2954
Himeji	0792-85-3792
Hiroshima (Peace Park)	082-247-6738
Imari	0955-22-6820
Ito	0557-37-6105
Ito Station	0557-37-3291
Kagoshima (city)	0992-53-2500
Kagoshima (Prefecture)	0992-23-5771
Kanazawa (Ishikawa Prefecture)	0762-31-6311
Kawaguchiko (Fuji Visitors' Center)	0555-72-0259
Kawaguchiko	0555-72-2460
Kobe	078-322-0220
Kōchi	0888-82-7777
Kumamoto	096-352-3743
Kumamoto Airport (Mashiki)	096-232-2810

Kurashiki	086-422-0542
Kurashiki Station	086-426-8681
Matsue	0852-21-4034
Matsumoto	0263-32-2814
Matsuyama (Ehime Prefecture)	0899-43-6688
Matsuyama	0899-31-3914
Miyazaki	0985-22-6469
Morioka	0196-25-2090
Nagasaki	0958-23-3631
Nagasaki (Prefecture)	0958-26-9407
Nagoya (Chunichi Bldg.)	052-262-2918
Nagoya (Kanayama)	052-323-0161
Nagoya Station	052-541-4301
Nagoya International Center	052-581-0100
Nagoya Port	052-654-7000
Naha Airport (Okinawa Prefecture)	098-857-6884
Nara	0742-22-3900
Nara (Kintetsu Nara Station)	0742-24-4858
Nara (Sarusawa)	0742-26-1991
Narita	0476-24-3198
Narita (tourist pavilion)	0476-24-3232
Niigata	025-241-7914
Nikko	0288-53-3795
Nikko (Tobu Nikko Station)	0288-53-4511
Okayama	086-222-2912
Okayama Prefectural Int. Exchange	086-222-0457
Onomichi (Shin-Onomichi Station)	0848-22-6900
Osaka (Shin-Osaka Station)	06-305-3311
Osaka (JR Osaka Station)	06-345-2189
Osaka	06-941-9200
Osaka World Travel Plaza	06-625-2189
Otsu	0775-22-3830
Sapporo (Tourism Office)	011-211-2377
Sapporo (Int. Communication Plaza)	011-211-3678
Sapporo (Odori Subway Station)	011-232-7712
Sendai (International Center)	022-265-2471
Sendai	022-222-4069
Shirahama	0739-42-2900
Takamatsu	0878-51-2009
Takayama (Hida Tourist Information)	0577-32-5328
Takeo	0954-22-2542

Index